W9-ATF-917

Bloody Engagements

ᘓᙡᙓ

Bloody Engagements

John R. Kelso's Civil War

John R. Kelso

Edited by Christopher Grasso

Yale

UNIVERSITY PRESS

NEW HAVEN AND LONDON

Copyright © 2017 by Christopher Grasso.
All rights reserved.
This book may not be reproduced, in whole or in part, including illustrations, in any form (beyond that copying
permitted by Sections 107 and 108 of the U.S. Copyright Law and except by reviewers for the public press), without
written permission from the publishers.

Yale University Press books may be purchased in quantity for educational, business, or promotional use.
For information, please e-mail sales.press@yale.edu (U.S. office) or sales@yaleup.co.uk (U.K. office).

Set in Fournier type by IDS Infotech Ltd., Chandigarh, India.
Printed in the United States of America.

ISBN 978-0-300-21096-5 (hardcover : alk. paper)

Library of Congress Control Number: 2016952139

A catalogue record for this book is available from the British Library.

This paper meets the requirements of ANSI/NISO Z39.48–1992 (Permanence of Paper).

10 9 8 7 6 5 4 3 2 1

For Karin

Contents

Acknowledgments

I am grateful for advice on research in Missouri from Joseph Beilein, William Foley, Gary R. Kremer, Christopher Phillips, William Piston, and Bruce Nichols. I am indebted to many archivists, especially: Jill D'Andrea, National Archives; Anne E. Cox, Laura R. Jolley, and Dennis Northcut, all at the State Historical Society of Missouri; Olga Tsapina, Norris Foundation Curator of American Historical Manuscripts, Huntington Library; and Steve Welden, Jasper County Archivist.

Special thanks to John F. Bradbury, Jr., Assistant Director Emeritus, State Historical Society of Missouri (Rolla), for generously sharing his research files on Kelso. Items that I first saw in those files I have listed as "Bradbury Collection" in the notes.

Thanks to John Demos for supporting the project in the early stages; to Roy Ritchie, Karen Halttunen, and Deborah Harkness for enabling research time at the Huntington Library; and to Becky Wrenn for the great maps. I appreciate the good work of Chris Rogers, Erica Hanson, Margaret Hogan, Clare Jones, Margaret Otzel, and the anonymous readers at Yale University Press.

My deepest thanks to Karin Wulf, for everything.

Introduction

John Russell Kelso (1831–91), who fought for the Union Army in Missouri, experienced the Civil War in several different ways: as an infantry private marching with his regiment to fight in large battles, as a spy traveling in disguise through enemy territory and gathering intelligence, as a cavalry officer leading his company against Confederate guerrillas and outlaws, and as a lone gunman emerging like a ghost from the dark woods to take revenge on the secessionists who had wronged him. He was also a soldier away from his family, worried that his wife would come to love him less in his absence and suffering at the news of his child's death.

Kelso saw both aspects of the conflict that tore apart Missouri: the conventional battles of uniformed armies facing each other on battlefields and the brutal guerrilla warfare in which neighbors burned down each other's homes and gunned one another down on their doorsteps. The importance of conventional warfare in Civil War Missouri has long been slighted by historians captivated by the larger scale of battles east of the Mississippi (Union and Confederate commanders fought with hundreds or thousands of men in the West and with tens of thousands in the East). But soldiers had the same chance of dying or being maimed in western battles. Moreover, their victories and defeats in Missouri had important strategic significance, with control of the lower Mississippi Valley and the Missouri River's western corridor hanging in the balance. As a foot soldier, cavalry officer, and spy, Kelso worked to keep Missouri in Union hands and in doing so disrupt the Confederacy's larger defensive strategy.[1]

---

1. The argument for the overlooked significance of conventional warfare in Missouri is made in Louis S. Gerteis, *The Civil War in Missouri: A Military History* (Columbia: University of Missouri Press, 2012), 1–7. See also Marvin R. Cain and John F. Bradbury, Jr., "Union Troops and the Civil War in Southwestern Missouri and Northwestern Arkansas," *Missouri Historical Review* (hereafter *MHR*) 88 (Oct. 1993): 29–47.

Even when Union armies pushed the Confederacy's conventional forces out of the state, however, smaller squads of southern partisans, sometimes collaborating with local guerrillas, continued to strike at targets throughout the Missouri countryside, especially in the counties bordering Kansas and Arkansas. Some of this vicious fighting was an outgrowth of the Border War of the late 1850s between Kansas Free Soilers and proslavery Missourians. Some was the result of a descent into lawlessness as the norms of civilized behavior broke down. As Kelso hunted guerrillas and bandits throughout the Ozarks, the rules of war were bent, twisted, and sometimes broken completely.[2]

The extant wartime chapters of Kelso's handwritten "Auto-Biography" and two of his political speeches from 1864 and 1865, all published here for the first time, present a fascinating account of this extraordinary ordinary man's battlefield experiences as well as his evolving interpretation of what the Civil War meant. Kelso's experience of the Civil War is revealing but hardly typical, and his narrative is much more than a conventional soldier's memoir of battles and skirmishes. Kelso began writing his autobiography in the early 1880s. A bookseller—perhaps one of the few people to have seen the manuscript—later wrote that Kelso was "a remarkable man . . . the history of whose life reads more like romance than reality." The historian Wiley Britton, however, could have verified that Kelso's war stories were not colorful fictions. Like Kelso, Britton had fought for the Union Army in Missouri during the Civil War. Britton published his own *Memoirs of the Rebellion on the Border, 1863* and a two-volume history, *The Civil War on the Border*, among other books. The latter work was based in part on several thousand postwar interviews Britton conducted in Missouri as he investigated pension and property compensation claims for the War Department. Stories of Kelso's "fearless operations against Southern bandits were familiar to nearly every family in Southwest Missouri," Britton wrote, and he heard from "the many witnesses examined who had reminiscences to relate of [Kelso's] daring acts in the war." But Britton also had a brother and

2. On guerrilla warfare in Missouri during the Civil War, see esp. Michael Fellman, *Inside War: The Guerilla Conflict in Missouri during the Civil War* (New York: Oxford University Press, 1989); Mark W. Geiger, *Financial Fraud and Guerilla Violence in Missouri's Civil War, 1861–1865* (New Haven, Conn.: Yale University Press, 2010); and Bruce Nichols's encyclopedic *Guerilla Warfare in Civil War Missouri*, 4 vols. (Jefferson, N.C.: MacFarland, 2004–14). See also Daniel E. Sutherland, *A Savage Conflict: The Decisive Role of Guerrillas in the American Civil War* (Chapel Hill: University of North Carolina Press, 2009).

brother-in-law who had served with Kelso, and the historian had corresponded with the man himself. While those who sympathized with the Confederacy hated Kelso and even called him a monster, Britton thought of him as a hero who "was without fear and a genius in many respects and like a tiger in his warlike activities."[3]

Britton had heard that Kelso had written "an account of his life and adventures in the war" but "was never able to locate the manuscript."[4] Indeed, the manuscript of Kelso's "Auto-Biography" seems to have disappeared sometime after his death in 1891. A partial version carrying his life story up to early 1863, which Kelso in the early 1880s had copied into a folio ledger book containing some of his other written works, also vanished from public view for a century. Although a forgotten figure by the early 1900s, Kelso—the preacher and schoolteacher turned Civil War guerrilla fighter who subsequently became a congressman calling for the impeachment of President Andrew Johnson, then later a public agnostic, a spiritualist lecturer, and eventually an anarchist—lived a remarkable and controversial life.

Before the War

John R. Kelso was born on March 23, 1831. With his father, mother, and five siblings, Kelso spent most of his first decade in a small log cabin on a new farm they tried to carve out of the "wilderness" of central Ohio. In the fall of 1840, the family moved to Daviess County, Missouri. The autobiography's early chapters portray a boy growing up in a rough backwoods cabin and becoming ashamed of his patched trousers and dirty bare feet. Kelso describes his traumatic religious conversion in his fourteenth year, an experience mingled with his overwhelming desire for a local minister's pretty daughter. He educated himself by the light of the fireplace, became a schoolteacher and

---

3. John R. Kelso, "Auto-Biography," in "John R. Kelso's Complete Works in Manuscript," Huntington Library, San Marino, Cal., 668–800; "Radical Literature," *Lucifer the Light-Bearer*, June 15, 1901, 176 ("a remarkable man"); Wiley Britton, *The Union Indian Brigade in the Civil War* (Kansas City: Franklin Hudson, 1922), 225 ("fearless operations," "was without fear"); Britton, *The Aftermath of the Civil War: Based on Investigations of War Claims* (Kansas City: Smith-Grieves, 1924), 232 ("the many witnesses"); Britton, *Memoirs of the Rebellion on the Border, 1863* (Chicago: Cushing, Thomas, 1882); Britton, *The Civil War on the Border*, 2 vols. (New York: G. P. Putnam's Sons, 1899, 1904).

4. Britton, *Aftermath of the Civil War*, 222–23.

Methodist preacher, and married seventeen-year-old Mary Adelia Moore in the fall of 1851.[5]

Kelso felt successful in everything but wedded life. The couple had two children—Florella in 1854 and Florellus in 1856—but Kelso's young, unhappy wife seemed forever on the verge of a mental breakdown. She finally confessed to being in love with another man. When Kelso announced the end of his marriage from his pulpit, his congregation turned against him. Kelso then left the church in a spectacular fashion, intending, as he put it, "to burst a bomb in the camp of the Lord and to leave all in consternation." His private studies had led him to doubt some of the central tenets of Methodism, and of Christianity itself. But being rejected by his congregation had pushed him over the edge. So at the annual conference of Methodist ministers he stood up and renounced the faith. Opponents—including his father-in-law— tried to silence his heresies by blaming him for destroying his marriage. Kelso nearly responded with a pistol. By the end of 1856, he wrote, he found himself "a wifeless, homeless, churchless, and almost friendless and money- less wanderer upon the earth. I was free, however, and the world was before me." He considered the possibility of becoming a mercenary in Central America: "I thought of my two little children, however, who would need me, and my desire to rise above my enemies, finally induced me to take what I suppose was a wiser course."[6]

By the spring of 1861, Kelso had rebuilt his life. He had earned a degree at Pleasant Ridge College and established a successful school in Buffalo, Missouri, the Dallas County seat. He had married one of his students, Susie Barnes, and they lived with the two children from his first marriage and a child (Iantha) the couple had together on a "beautiful little farm" about a mile and a half from town. But circumstances would again prompt him to stand up alone and declare heretical principles before a hostile community, throwing another bomb into another congregation as he asserted his independence. The attack on Fort Sumter and the rallying of secessionist

5. Kelso, "Auto-Biography," 668–92, 674 ("wilderness"); 1840 U.S. Census, Bennington Township, Delaware County, Ohio; 1850 U.S. Census, District 27, Daviess County, family no. 181, www.ancestry. com; *Missouri Marriage Records, 1805–2002* (online database; Provo, Utah: Ancestry.com, 2007): John R. Kelso and Mary (Adelia) Moore, married Aug. 28, 1851.
6. Kelso, "Auto-Biography," 702 ("to burst a bomb"), 703 ("a wifeless," "I thought"). The names Florella and Florellus are variants for the Latin word for flower (*flora*); Florellus is a character in the verse dialogue "Pastoral III. Night," in Robert Fergusson, *The Poetical Works of Robert Fergusson* (Parsley, Scotland: R. Smith, 1799), 12–16.

sympathizers in Missouri prompted the schoolteacher to take a stand—and caused his life to take a dramatic turn.[7]

Missouri had a population of more than 1,180,000, including nearly 115,000 slaves. Most of the state's enslaved people worked in households or in small groups on farms, not large plantations: a quarter of the state's 24,000 slaveholders had only one slave and nearly three-quarters held less than five. Yet the dominant political culture was clearly pro-southern and proslavery: 85 percent of the men elected to office in the 1850s were slaveholders. In the presidential election of 1860, Missourians split 117,000 votes between the two candidates who continued to try to compromise on the slavery question: Northern Democrat Stephen A. Douglas and John Bell of the Constitutional Union Party. Missouri voters gave the proslavery and pro-secessionist Southern Democrat John C. Breckinridge 31,300 votes and Republican Abraham Lincoln, who opposed slavery in the territories but promised not to interfere with it in the states, slightly more than 17,000 votes. Democrat Claiborne Fox Jackson, who endorsed Douglas but was actually a man of strong pro-southern sentiments, won the governor's race.[8]

In Dallas County, too, about 70 percent of the voters chose either Douglas or Bell, though Breckinridge ran stronger and Lincoln weaker. Kelso's town of Buffalo had more of a pro-southern tilt than either the county or the state. Benton Township, which included Buffalo, was on average wealthier than the other five townships in the county. Over 18 percent of Benton households listed occupations other than farming, as opposed to fewer than 4 percent for the rest of the county. The county had 5,892 residents (1,024 families) in 1860; 40 were slaveholders, who held 114 slaves. Thirteen of those slaveholders, holding 37 slaves, lived in Benton. So in Dallas County as a whole, slightly less than 4 percent of households had slaves; in Benton, 8 percent did. The number of household heads born in

7. Kelso, "Auto-Biography," 707 ("beautiful little farm"); 1860 U.S. Census, Benton Township, Dallas County, Missouri, roll M653_617, p. 191, J B [R] Kelso; *Missouri Marriage Records:* John R. Kelso and Martha S. (Susie) Barnes, married Sept. 23, 1858. The name Iantha is a variant of the Greek word for a violet (*ianthe*); Percy Bysshe Shelley ponders Ianthe sleeping at the beginning of *Queen Mab: A Philosophical Poem* (London: P. B. Shelley, 1813).
8. William E. Parrish, *A History of Missouri*, vol. 3, *1860–1875* (Columbia: University of Missouri Press, 1973), 6–8; Geiger, *Financial Fraud*, 12. Slaves were especially concentrated in seven "Little Dixie" counties in the center of the state; see R. Douglas Hurt, "Planters and Slavery in Little Dixie," *MHR* 88 (July 1994): 397–415, and Robert W. Frizzell, "Southern Identity in Nineteenth-Century Missouri: Little Dixie's Slave-Majority Areas and the Transition to Midwestern Farming," *MHR* 99 (April 2005): 238–60.

slaveholding states, however, was somewhat higher in the county at large than in Benton: 84 as compared to 76 percent. A majority in the county came from the upper South, especially Tennessee. Slavery for many of the hard-scrabble white farmers and Ozark Mountain folk who favored it was valued less as a vital economic system than as a guarantor of white supremacy.[9]

Kelso himself, though he came from an ardently proslavery family, hated the institution and resented haughty slaveholders, but before the spring of 1861 he had kept his opinions to himself. Events made that no longer possible. Seven southern states, beginning with South Carolina on December 20, 1860, seceded from the Union. In his January inaugural address, Governor Jackson insisted that Missouri would stand with its sister slaveholding states. In St. Louis, site of a large federal arsenal, paramilitary organizations on both sides started organizing and drilling. Temporarily dashing the private hopes of Jackson and a powerful group of pro-southern legislators, the state constitutional convention, which met in March, rejected secession. Then, on April 12, 1861, the South Carolina militia attacked the U.S. garrison at Fort Sumter in the Charleston harbor.[10]

Kelso's Civil War

Jackson quickly rejected Lincoln's call on April 15 for 75,000 volunteers to put down the rebellion: "Your requisition, in my judgment, is illegal, unconstitutional, and revolutionary in its object, inhuman and diabolical, and cannot be complied with. Not one man will the State of Missouri furnish to carry on any such unholy crusade." On April 22, the governor called for a special session of the legislature to reorganize the militia, and on May 3 he called for the militia to assemble. Claiming in public to be assuming a defensive posture of "armed neutrality" in the conflict between North and South, behind the scenes the governor was trying to maneuver Missouri out of the Union, and he wrote to

9. On politics in Dallas County and Buffalo, see chap. 1, note 7, below; on slaveholding and wealth in Dallas and Benton, see chap. 1, note 13, below. Kelso discusses proslavery attitudes among non-slaveholding whites in chap. 3. On the state's smaller slaveholders, see esp. Diane Mutti Burke, *Missouri's Small-Slaveholding Households, 1815–1865* (Athens: University of Georgia Press, 2010). For the culture of poorer whites in the region, see also T. J. Stiles, *Jesse James: Last Rebel of the Civil War* (New York: Knopf, 2002), and Jeremy Neely, *The Border between Them: Violence and Reconciliation on the Kansas-Missouri Line* (Columbia: University of Missouri Press, 2007).
10. Kelso, "Auto-Biography," 697; William E. Parrish, *Turbulent Partnership: Missouri and the Union, 1861–1865* (Columbia: University of Missouri Press, 1963), 1–17; Louis S. Gerteis, *Civil War St. Louis* (Lawrence: University Press of Kansas, 2001), 67–96.

Confederate president Jefferson Davis requesting artillery. By May 6, nearly nine hundred militiamen had established "Camp Jackson" on the eastern edge of St. Louis, threatening, the Unionists thought, the federal arsenal there.[11]

The fearful excitement that Kelso so vividly describes electrified citizens in all the states, North and South, but was especially intense in border states like Missouri where sentiment was divided. Secessionists and Unionists began arming and mobilizing across the state, the balance of power between them shifting from county to county. Sometimes the words and actions of a few people could help tip that balance one way or another. In Buffalo, Kelso mounted the courthouse steps and in front of a strongly pro-southern citizenry denounced Claiborne Jackson and his secessionist supporters as traitors. In Hickory County, the pro-southern forces took the initiative, organizing around the rhetoric of a few local orators and the military leadership of a former sheriff. In Newton County, secessionist speakers held a rally and passed resolutions in favor of Jackson and the Confederacy. When they tried to do the same thing in Dallas County, Kelso and his allies disrupted the meeting and rallied support for the Union. Kelso's description of that volatile scene and his account of his impassioned argument in favor of the Union (see chapter 1) resemble the experience of Robert Pinckney Matthews, a young pro-Union orator at a heated debate in Springfield. There, however, political sentiment was more evenly divided and voicing opposition to secession was, for the moment, less dangerous. As in other counties, in Kelso's Dallas, the Unionists organized Home Guard militia regiments to counter the mobilization of Jackson's State Guard.[12]

On May 10, Capt. Nathaniel Lyon, commander of the St. Louis Arsenal, surrounded Camp Jackson with about eight thousand troops and forced the militiamen to surrender even before they had a chance to unpack the four Confederate artillery guns they had smuggled into camp. As Lyon's men marched the militia under guard through the streets of St. Louis to the arsenal, enraged civilians began pelting the Federals with rocks and debris. The raw troops, many of whom had enlisted only a few weeks before, fired

11. Gov. C. F. Jackson to Secretary of War Simon Cameron, April 17, 1861, *The War of the Rebellion: A Compilation of the Official Records of the Union and Confederate Armies* (hereafter *OR*), ser. 3, vol. 1 (Washington, D.C.: Government Printing Office, 1899), 82–83. See also Christopher Phillips, *Missouri's Confederate: Claiborne Fox Jackson and the Creation of Southern Identity in the Border West* (Columbia: University of Missouri Press, 2000), 247–48.
12. On Hickory County, see chap. 1, note 22; on Newton County, see chap. 1, note 11; and on Matthews and Springfield, see chap. 1, note 17, all below.

into the crowd and soon twenty-eight people were dead—a bloodletting that struck southern sympathizers and even some moderates as a sure sign of federal tyranny.[13]

Lyon, promoted to brigadier general while being called a murderer in the pro-southern press, met with Governor Jackson on June 11. Lyon was a stubborn Republican abolitionist from Connecticut, and he refused to compromise with what he considered to be treason. "This means war," he said, abruptly ending the meeting and walking out of the room. The next day Jackson called for 50,000 state volunteers to enlist in the State Guard and resist federal despotism. The day after that, Lyon led a force of about 2,500 from St. Louis to the state capital in Jefferson City, but by the time he got there, Jackson and his State Guard force had already evacuated to the southwest.[14]

In July, Lyon's army, growing with new recruits, was moving toward Springfield in the southwest and toward an engagement with the State Guard, which was also growing and would be joined by Confederate forces coming up from Arkansas. Not far from Springfield, Kelso's Dallas County Home Guard regiment was hunting rebels and planning to support Lyon. Kelso met Lyon at Springfield in early August, just days before the Battle of Wilson's Creek. At that battle on August 10, the second major one of the Civil War (the Union had lost at Bull Run in Virginia on July 21), State Guard and Confederate forces of about 12,000 men defeated Lyon's army of 5,400. General Lyon was killed and became the first general to be mourned and celebrated as a martyr in the northern press. As Union troops retreated to the northeast, Kelso's Home Guard regiment broke up. Although he had been a major in the Home Guard, he enlisted in the 24th Infantry Regiment as a private to make a point about putting patriotism before self-interest. But even as a private his special talents were quickly recognized: by late August he was heading back alone to enemy-occupied Springfield on a spy mission.[15]

13. Christopher Phillips, *Damned Yankee: The Life of General Nathaniel Lyon* (Columbia: University of Missouri Press, 1990), 185–99; Gerteis, *Civil War St. Louis,* 100–115.

14. Phillips, *Damned Yankee,* 211–22, 214 (quotation); Gerteis, *Civil War in Missouri,* 32–40. Lyon's remarks, however, come only from Thomas Snead, Price's aide-de-camp, writing a quarter century later in *The Fight for Missouri: From the Election of Lincoln to the Death of Lyon* (New York: Charles Scribner's Sons, 1886), 200. Lyon's army skirmished with the State Guard at Boonville on June 17 before the latter retreated to the southwest; see Paul Rorvig, "The Significant Skirmish: The Battle of Boonville, June 17, 1861," *MHR* 86 (Jan. 1992): 127–48.

15. On the battle, see William Garrett Piston and Richard H. Hatcher III, *Wilson's Creek: The Second Battle of the Civil War and the Men Who Fought It* (Chapel Hill: University of North Carolina Press, 2000).

The commander of Union forces in Missouri was now Gen. John C. Frémont, famous from the antebellum period as the so-called Pathfinder of the West and a presidential candidate in 1856. But Frémont insulated himself behind a bloated staff and seemed more interested in elaborate uniforms and expensive fortifications than in taking decisive action in the field. He quickly alienated his main political supporters in Missouri. His martial law decree of August 30 angered Abraham Lincoln by announcing that anyone found with arms within Union lines would be shot and by declaring that all rebels' slaves would be freed. The first provision would have prompted the enemy to retaliate in kind. The emancipation provision moved much more quickly on the slavery issue than Lincoln, desperate to keep the border states in the Union, was willing to go. The president rescinded both provisions. And on November 2 Frémont, who by that time had moved a large army very slowly back down to Springfield, was removed from command.[16]

As winter came to southwest Missouri in late 1861, the Union Army again retreated, leaving loyal Missourians at the mercy of local southerners. Jackson and his pro-southern legislature had reconvened in Neosho, in the southwest corner of the state, and had passed an ordinance of secession on October 28. The Unionist state convention in St. Louis had appointed a new provisional state government back in July. Lincoln and the United States recognized the provisional government; Jefferson Davis and the Confederacy recognized Jackson and his portion of the old state legislature, and welcomed Missouri into the Confederacy. To citizens in southwest Missouri, what mattered most was which military power was in charge. And when the Union retreated a second time, secessionists turned on their Unionist neighbors. A petition from the southwest to the new Union commander pleaded for help and claimed that Confederate troops and local vigilantes had robbed three to five thousand people of their money, food, clothing, and shoes, and then forced them from their homes into the cold to starve. Kelso, evacuating loyal citizens from Buffalo, saw this happen to his own and other families, and he swore that he would get revenge.[17]

16. On John C. Frémont (1813–90) in Missouri, see Allan Nevins, *Frémont: Pathmarker of the West* (New York: D. Appleton-Century, 1939), 473–549. See also Parrish, *Turbulent Partnership*, 48–76; Andrew Rolle, *John Charles Frémont: Character as Destiny* (Norman: University of Oklahoma Press, 1991), 190–213; Donald B. Connelly, *John M. Schofield and the Politics of Generalship* (Chapel Hill: University of North Carolina Press, 2006), 23–40; and Dennis K. Boman, *Lincoln and Citizen's Rights in Civil War Missouri: Balancing Freedom and Security* (Baton Rouge: Louisiana State University Press, 2011), 36–62.
17. Parrish, *Turbulent Partnership*, 77–100. On the petition, see chap. 4, note 9, below.

The next Union effort to push the Confederates out of southwest Missouri was led by Gen. Samuel R. Curtis. After going on some spy missions for Curtis, including one where he was captured and sentenced to death but escaped, Kelso rejoined his regiment and marched south with Curtis in February 1862, chasing an army led by Gen. Sterling Price. The Battle of Pea Ridge, Arkansas, on March 6–8 was a decisive victory for the Union. Confederates would never again occupy a significant amount of Missouri territory.[18]

In early April, Kelso began his career in the Missouri State Militia Cavalry as a lieutenant. Although large Confederate armies no longer held territory in Missouri, smaller groups constantly raided from Arkansas, and local guerrilla bands as well as outlaw gangs with southern sympathies continually harassed the countryside. Kelso's regiment's first major encounter with the enemy was a stinging defeat on May 30 at Neosho—a disaster he blamed on the incompetence (at best) of his commanding officer, Col. John M. Richardson. Not every expedition after that was honorable and heroic. On one scout in particular, under the command of Maj. John C. Wilbur, Kelso saw how plundering Union officers could be nearly as bad as the rebel bandits they were supposed to be thwarting. But by the summer of 1862 Kelso and his friend Capt. Milton Burch began to establish their reputations as guerrilla fighters. In August they defeated Col. Robert Lawther's Confederate raiders twice. In September Kelso led a daring attack on the Medlock brothers' outlaw hideout. In another raid, Kelso again disguised himself as a Confederate to capture rebels and attack a saltpeter mine (for making gunpowder).

Kelso's manuscript autobiography ends with his account of the Battle of Springfield and its aftermath in January 1863. Confederate general John S. Marmaduke had moved his brigade quickly up from Arkansas and intended to take arms and provisions at the undermanned post at Springfield. After a day of intense fighting, the defenders, including soldiers pulled from their hospital beds, held the town. Kelso fought on the battlefield all day and then crept into the rebel camp to spy at night. "You and your troops are heroes," General Curtis telegrammed the post commander from St. Louis. When the battle was over, southern sympathizers, assuming Marmaduke had won, drove wagons

---

18. On Curtis, see esp. Terry Lee Beckenbaugh, "The War of Politics: Samuel Ryan Curtis, Race, and the Political/Military Establishment" (Ph.D. diss., University of Arkansas, 2001). On the battle, see William L. Shea and Earl J. Hess, *Pea Ridge: Civil War Campaign in the West* (Chapel Hill: University of North Carolina Press, 1992).

into town for their share of the booty and to make deals with the conquerors. One man, trying to sell some horses, mistook Kelso for a Confederate officer. Kelso, as he had done many times before, used the case of mistaken identity to his advantage and pounced. He took the man's horses and forced him into Union service at the point of a bayonet: "Now you shall help us or die. You do not deserve the treatment of a prisoner of war, and you will not receive it. We are Federals; I am Kelso; now you know what to expect."[19]

People in war-torn Missouri increasingly came to know what to expect from Kelso. Large Confederate forces made other strikes from the south: Marmaduke again in April 1863; Col. Jo Shelby in October 1863; Gen. Sterling Price in September 1864. Week to week in southwestern Missouri, however, the threat was from raids by smaller groups of Confederates, local guerrilla bands, and gangs of bandits. Kelso and the 8th Missouri State Militia Calvary spent most of the war battling these groups. It was against them that Kelso made a name for himself.

Kelso's ascent was only briefly interrupted by a court martial on March 11, 1863. He had been accused of "conduct to the prejudice of good order and military discipline." His commanding officer, Capt. Samuel A. Flagg, charged that back in January, in camp at Ozark, Kelso had refused an order to march to Forsyth, considering it a "wild goose chase." Kelso admitted that he had asked to see Flagg's written orders before marching but explained that there had been problems with officers (including, he strongly implied, Flagg) issuing orders while drunk. Kelso was acquitted and immediately returned to duty. A month later, during Marmaduke's second raid into Missouri (April 18–May 1, 1863), Kelso dressed in civilian clothes to trick rebel cattle thieves into thinking that he was Marmaduke's dispatch bearer. The ruse led to four dead cattle rustlers and the recovery of forty head of cattle.[20]

19. Gen. Samuel R. Curtis to Gen. Egbert Benson Brown, Jan. 8, 1863, 9:00 p.m., *OR*, ser. 1, vol. 22, part 1, 179; Kelso, "Auto-Biography," 798 (quotation). On the Battle of Springfield, see [Return Ira Holcombe], *History of Greene County, Missouri* (St. Louis: Western Historical Company, 1883), 424–56; Paul M. Robinett, "Marmaduke's Expedition into Missouri: The Battles of Springfield and Hartville, January, 1863," *MHR* 58 (Jan. 1964), 151–73; Elmo Ingenthron, *Borderland Rebellion: A History of the Civil War on the Missouri-Arkansas Border* (Branson, Mo.: Ozarks Mountaineer, 1980), chap. 25; Frederick W. Goman, *Up from Arkansas: Marmaduke's First Missouri Raid, Including the Battles of Springfield and Hartville* (Springfield, Mo.: N.p., 1999); and Larry Wood, *Civil War Springfield* (Charleston: History Press, 2011), chaps. 10–11.
20. John R. Kelso Court Martial Case File, Springfield, Mo., Jan. 21, 1863, NN-2499, Record Group 153, Records of the Office of the Judge Advocate General (Army), National Archives and Records Administration, Washington, D.C.; *OR*, ser. 1, vol. 22, part 1, 314.

Kelso became known for riding his claybank horse, Hawkeye, and for carrying a large shotgun rather than a rifle. "Hawkeye seemed to possess, like Kelso, a charmed life," according to later recollections. "The horse was never touched in battle, though often the most conspicuous target for Confederate bullets." As for Kelso's favorite weapon, a reporter later wrote that "Kelso killed his first Confederate with a shotgun and he would never exchange the weapon for any of the improved army rifles." Yet when his luck finally evaporated in the late summer and early fall of 1863, it was a shotgun blast and an accident with Hawkeye that gave him injuries that would trouble him for the rest of his life.[21]

While battling guerrillas in Carthage on August 7, 1863, he received the contents of a double-barrel shotgun in the chest and left hand. A doctor was able to pick out the thirteen buckshot that did not penetrate deeper than the skin on his chest but had to leave one, which remained lodged painfully beneath his sternum. Some buckshot remained embedded in his left hand too, permanently limiting the use of two fingers. A month later, on September 7, he was riding with Burch and his men after bushwhackers who had captured some sutler's wagons in Laurence County. Hawkeye, getting tangled in a hitch rope in the pursuit, turned a somersault and landed on Kelso. Both of the lieutenant's hips were injured (the right one was dislocated). For the rest of his life, Kelso complained of a hernia and kidney problems that he attributed to this accident. Whether from getting crushed by Hawkeye or from some other incident, Kelso also injured his left shoulder, leaving it permanently higher than the right one. In later years, he would be reminded of his injuries whenever he tried to get in or out of a chair, put on an overcoat, or touch the buckshot still lodged in his hand and chest.[22]

His injuries, however, did not keep him from the field for long. The records show him attacking rebels in Jasper County in November 1863. In the spring of 1864, after being promoted to captain, he rode against the 2nd Cherokee Indian Regiment in Spavinaw, Arkansas; insurgents at Mill Creek and Honey Creek, Missouri; and a guerilla band near Neosho. Burch reported that on an expedition to Cowskin Creek on August 13, 1864, Kelso engaged

21. "The Scout of the Ozarks: John R. Kelso's Mysterious and Bloody Career in Southwest Missouri," *St. Louis Republic*, June 18, 1893.
22. Kelso's injuries are detailed in over a dozen affidavits in John R. Kelso, Pension File, National Archives. "Bushwhacker" was a term applied to irregular combatants (not officially connected to any recognized military unit); sutlers were people following the army and selling provisions to the soldiers.

and killed "Lieutenant Baxter, a noted bushwhacker." In early October, Kelso was providing intelligence on the advance of Confederate General Price's army before the Battle of Westport. A month later, Kelso's Unionist admirers elected him to Congress.[23]

Hero or Monster

Kelso's exploits made Union Army veteran and historian Wiley Britton think of Ulysses and Diomed in the Tenth Book of the Iliad, Greek warriors who entered a Trojan camp at night, slaughtered enemy soldiers, and triumphantly returned with trophies. "But this grandest of scenes in the description of individual heroism in war scarcely surpasses some of the daring acts of Kelso, the student, teacher, and soldier."[24]

Kelso was remembered as a polite and scholarly man, always pacing about camp with a book in his hands, but especially as a fighter with remarkable courage. Britton commented repeatedly about Kelso's reputation for fearlessness. Describing one skirmish, Britton wrote that Kelso "displayed his usual tact, daring, and coolness. In fact, it was asserted by those who had served with him from the beginning of the war that he never became disconcerted under the most trying situations." Kelso "frequently exposed himself in the most perilous situations without any outward signs of fear or excitement. He was always equal to an emergency. When in a fight or dangerous situation, no interposing obstacle disconcerted him at the critical moment." Britton recorded several stories to illustrate the point that "as far as outward signs were concerned, [Kelso] seems to have been absolutely without fear." On one occasion, Kelso was scouting in southern Taney County with a small detachment of his men when he learned that several southern families were sheltering pro-Confederate bandits:

> Early the next morning he surrounded one of the houses in which some of the bandits were known to have spent the night, taking himself the most dangerous position. Coming up in front of the house, he saw three bandits within, and keeping his eyes on them and his hands on his shotgun in the position of "ready," crossed the fence and started for the door. In a moment after crossing the fence,

23. For Kelso's military activities after Jan. 1863, see *OR*, ser. 1, vol. 32, part 1, 314, 761–63; vol. 22, part 2, 330; vol. 34, part 2, 384–85; vol. 34, part 1, 921–22, 957–58, 966–67; vol. 34, part 4, 344; vol. 41, part 1, 194–98, 737–38; vol. 41, part 4, 411–12; vol. 48, part 1, 1127.
24. Britton, *Civil War on the Border*, 2:204.

a big dog came snarling and growling at him and seized him by the calf of the leg. Not in the least disconcerted by this unexpected attack of the dog, he stopped, and keeping his eyes on the bandits took with his right hand his revolver from the scabbard, and feeling for the dog's neck shot the beast dead. He proceeded as if nothing had happened, and entering the door, found that the bandits had escaped through the opposite door. His daring amazed them so that they fled without firing a single shot at him.[25]

Kelso's "name was connected with so many acts of daring adventure in Southern and Southwest Missouri during the war," and he "was so much talked about by the Unionists and secessionists" in that region, Britton wrote, "on account of the numerous victims upon whom his avenging hands had fallen." Of course, "he was popular with and liked by the Unionists and sincerely hated by the Southern people." R. I. Holcombe, a less sympathetic local historian writing in the early 1880s, called Kelso "a desperate man" who was "fanatical in his Unionism" and who believed that all Confederates were traitors deserving death: "It is said of him that he killed many a man without a cause. Stories are told of him that make him appear . . . fit only to be denominated a monster, and entitled only to execration. Doubtless some of these stories are exaggerations, but the fact remains that Kelso was a 'bad man,' and held human life in very cheap estimation."[26]

In 1893, the *St. Louis Republic* published an article of over 5,300 words that conveyed something of both sides. "The Scout of the Ozarks: John R. Kelso's Mysterious and Bloody Career in Southwest Missouri" was based on interviews with people who knew him and knew of him, including three men who had fought at his side. Kelso's name, the reporter wrote, was still "spoken with a shudder by many people along the Missouri and Arkansas border, though nearly 30 years of peace have helped to sustain or palliate the deeds of this fanatical partisan of the Union cause." Some of the stories about the man might "sound like the nursery tales of mythical desperadoes," but, the journalist assured his readers, they were "well authenticated by witnesses still living." The article described Kelso as "brave to the point of recklessness" and marveled at his preternatural composure under fire: "Kelso was a

---

25. Britton, *Civil War on the Border*, 2:201 ("displayed his usual"), 202–3 ("frequently exposed"), 206 ("as far as"), 203 ("Early the next morning").

26. Britton, *Civil War on the Border*, 2:204; Holcombe, *History of Greene County*, 477.

man of phenomenal self-control. He never lost his cool, methodical judgment in the most perilous situations. He could not be scared by any unexpected assault. He loved to fight, but the intoxication of hand-to-hand encounter only steadied the man's nerves and sharpened his perceptions." But the reporter also described him as a remorseless, ferocious, inhuman "rebel-killer" who "butchered his victims" with an "unforgiving heart."[27]

Even in Britton's appreciative account Kelso's darker side can be seen. In the episode with the dog, for example, after Kelso entered through the front door, "he shot the man of the house and severely wounded his son, holding that those who gave aid and comfort to the bandits were as deserving of punishment as the bandits themselves." The author of "The Scout of the Ozarks," who heard the same story from an eyewitness, added details that painted an even more brutal picture:

> An old man was found in the cabin, whose wife and son, a young man hardly grown, completed the family. Kelso shot down the aged husband and father as soon as the fleeing soldiers dodged his aim. The boy ran out of the house and was climbing over the fence around a little "truck patch" when the Captain fired the other barrel of his shot-gun at him. The lad fell down among some pea vines and Kelso thought he was killed. The wounded youth crawled under the matted vines and escaped to tell in after years his sad story. Kelso went back into the house and searched for more soldiers and left the helpless old woman alone with her dead husband and, as she thought, murdered boy.[28]

Friend and foe alike marveled at "the fearless and energetic manner in which Kelso had hunted down the bandits, frequently penetrating their most secret hiding places and engaging them in hand-to-hand conflicts." Both his admirers and detractors remembered a story about a trophy quilt. The reporter for the *St. Louis Republic* heard it from a Mart Hancock, who had served in Kelso's cavalry regiment. Britton told the tale this way:

> While stationed at Ozark, in Christian County, he made a scout with his company into the White River Mountains of Taney County, near the Arkansas line, and encamped for the night in the vicinity where a small party of bandits had their retreat. After supper he started out

27. "The Scout of the Ozarks."
28. Britton, *Civil War on the Border*, 2:203; "The Scout of the Ozarks."

afoot to reconnoiter for information as to whether there really were any Southern bandits in the neighborhood. He returned to his camp about dark, and told his men that he had found where the marauders were camped, and that he intended to visit them that night. He offered to let any of his men accompany him who desired to do so, but the night was dark, and they knew that some desperate plot was in his mind, and no one volunteered. He started out alone, prepared for bloody work, and returned the next morning with six horses, saddled and bridled. His account of his night's adventure, as he related it to his men on his return, was thrilling in the extreme. It is not necessary to follow him over each devious step after he left camp, for the adventure itself shows him moving along cautiously over the dim path through the darkness to the immediate vicinity of the camp of the bandits, carefully scanning every object in front, with revolver in hand and ears alert to the slightest sound in any direction. After he gets up near to the marauders' camp, who can follow him through his careful reconnoitering of it on up to the commencement of his terrible slaughter, without his heart beating audibly? He finds three bandits sleeping under their crude shelter, and as he has already found six horses saddled near at hand. Where are the comrades of the sleeping bandits? He ascertains that the sleeping bandits are covered with a beautiful quilt, which he desires to take unstained with blood as a trophy, and carefully draws it off them, and in another moment like a tiger springs on his victims and shoots them to death before they are conscious of danger. In the short and desperate struggle the comrades of the victims do not come to their rescue, and Kelso mounts one of the horses standing saddled and rides it into camp, leading the other five as trophies of his bloody adventure.

Greek heroes Ulysses and Diomed, too, had slain sleeping Trojan soldiers before making off with their horses and chariot. Britton was quick to explain that despite Kelso's interest in trophies, "he was never charged with committing acts of plunder, or of turning captured property into channels of private gain," but Britton admitted that Kelso's "acts were of course characterized as cruel by those who sympathized with the South."[29]

---

29. "The Scout of the Ozarks" references "Mart Hancock." Martin Hancock was a private in Co. F, 8th and 14th Regt., Missouri State Militia (MSM) Cavalry (National Park Service, "Civil War Soldiers and Sailors System," http://www.nps.gov/civilwar/soldiers-and-sailors-database.htm [hereafter NPS Soldiers' Database]); Britton, *Civil War on the Border*, 2:230 ("the fearless and energetic"), 202 ("While stationed at Ozark"), 71 ("he was never charged," "acts were of course").

Britton admired Kelso's intellect as well as his courage: "He was a great student of languages, philosophy, and mathematics," Britton wrote. "He had an insatiable thirst for knowledge—knowledge, too, of the profoundest depths." Holcombe, the Missouri historian writing in the early 1880s, called Kelso a "transcendentalist" who was "well versed in all the dogmas of the schools of modern thought. It is said that he always carried a book of some sort in his saddle pockets, and frequently engaged in the study of mental philosophy and the subtleties of metaphysics while lying in the brush by the roadside waiting to 'get the drop' on a rebel!" The *Republic*'s reporter wondered how "this strange man could return from a bloody scout and take up his studies with as much earnestness as though he had been at college preparing for commencement." Britton commended Kelso's "characteristic earnestness." Holcombe concluded that "much learning made him mad." Britton noted Kelso's self-discipline: "He was strictly temperate in his habits of life, and he prided himself in asserting that he had never taken a chew of tobacco, nor used the weed in any form; nor touched a drop of intoxicants of any kind. No language ever escaped his lips that was not fit for the most refined and cultured ears." Holcombe recorded that Kelso "believed in diet and plenty of exercise as brain-producing elements" and dismissed him as a "crank."[30]

Britton did not dismiss Kelso, but he struggled to explain what drove the man to pursue his foes with such relentless determination. Britton speculated that as a spy who had entered the enemy's camps, Kelso had seen firsthand how Confederates mistreated Union prisoners and heard how rebels, conspicuous before the war "for their domineering conduct towards political opponents," now boasted of killing Union men for trifling causes. According to Britton, Kelso refused to be promoted any higher than a captain of a company because he did not want to miss "the opportunity of participating in the personal conflicts with the enemy, which appears to have been almost a burning desire with him."[31]

The War Continued as Politics

Kelso reported that friends and admirers started mentioning his name for Congress even before the fall election in 1862. He was able to set aside his reservations about splitting the Republican vote for the 1864 contest and ran

30. Britton, *Aftermath of the Civil War*, 222 ("He was a great student"); Britton, *Civil War on the Border*, 2:205 ("He had an insatiable thirst"), 207 ("characteristic earnestness"), 204–5 ("He was strictly temperate"); Holcombe, *History of Greene County*, 477; "The Scout of the Ozarks."
31. Britton, *Civil War on the Border*, 2:207 ("for their domineering"), 208 ("the opportunity of participating").

as an Independent Republican against the sitting congressman and Republican Party nominee Col. Sempronius H. Boyd, previously Kelso's commanding officer in the 24th Regiment, Infantry Volunteers. Granted a short leave from his regiment, Kelso rode throughout his district campaigning and carrying, it was said, his oversized shotgun. The vote was very close, with about 100 to 300 votes separating the candidates out of more than 8,200 cast. Kelso was declared the winner, but Boyd challenged the election, charging that several hundred votes for Kelso were illegal—cast by nonresidents, minors, and voters who had not first taken the prescribed oath. After a subcommittee investigation, which produced over 170 printed pages of evidence, Kelso retained his seat.[32]

Through the election, Kelso became known in widely circulated press accounts as the guerrilla fighter who had vowed "that he would not cut his hair and beard until he had killed twenty-five bushwhackers with his own hand. He recently passed through St. Louis for Washington, close-cropped, and boasts that his vow is fulfilled." A description of Congressman Kelso first published in the *New-York Daily Tribune* multiplied the body count:

> In another part of the House stands a little, small person, barely beyond boyhood, with eyes and hair of midnight black, yet looking and moving like a tiger. This is John R. Kelso of extreme Southern Missouri, who is said to have killed more than 60 Rebels with his own hand. He is scarred and shot from sole to crown, and in the border episodes of the war holds a strange wild prominence, where in the bitterness of the fight he retorted upon individual Rebels the violence they inaugurated, and hunted them, alone and persistently, like one in a *vendetta*. Here he is quiet, amiable, grave; but this studded roof, with its soft emblematic medallions, are in odd consonance with the dark and bloody vistas he has haunted.

The account was wrong on at least two points: Kelso was neither small nor young. He was six feet tall, two hundred pounds, and in 1866 he was thirty-five years old. But even the Missouri press, which liked to laugh when eastern tenderfoots romanticized and exaggerated the daring deeds of

32. On Kelso campaigning with his shotgun, see "Hon. J. R. Kelso," St. Joseph, Mo., *Herald and Tribune*, Dec. 13, 1864, and Britton, *Aftermath of the Civil War*, 222. On the election see appendix 1, note 14, below.

Missouri heroes, helped build the legend of John R. Kelso. The Springfield *Patriot* snorted derisively at an article on "Wild Bill" Hickok in *Harper's Monthly*, which claimed that Bill had personally dispatched not a few dozen but several hundred rebels with his own hands. "We dare say that Captain Kelso, our present member of Congress, did double the execution 'with his own hands' on the Johnnies, during the war, that Bill did." (Kelso's military record claimed that he had personally killed twenty-six enemy combatants.)[33]

The term of the 39th U.S. Congress ran from March 4, 1865, to March 3, 1867. Gen. Robert E. Lee did not surrender at Appomattox Court House until April 9, 1865, and even after he did, there were still over ninety thousand Confederate soldiers in the field. The assassination of President Abraham Lincoln, the attempted assassination of Secretary of State William H. Seward, and the planned assassination of Vice President Andrew Johnson on April 14 convinced many in the Union that the war was continuing in a new form. In May, some Confederates west of the Mississippi still persisted in thinking that they could keep fighting. Despite President Johnson's proclamation on May 10 that the armed insurrection had virtually ended, Union soldiers continued to fight guerrillas in Missouri through the end of May and skirmishes went on in Texas.[34]

Even as violence threatened a final achievement of peace and security, political resistance threatened to overturn what had been won on the battlefield. The war had simply assumed "the form of political contest," Kelso said in a speech given at Walnut Grove, Missouri, on September 19, 1865: "Armies are no longer hurled upon armies . . . yet the *real struggle, the irrepressible conflict* of antagonistic principles, is still going on. *Slavery*, though dead in name, still exists in *reality*. The *rebellion*, though overthrown in *arms*, is by no

33. Harrisburg, Pa., *Weekly Patriot and Union*, Nov. 30, 1865; *New-York Daily Tribune*, June 20, 1866; "Springfield, Mo., versus Harpers' Monthly. 'Wild Bill, Harpers' Monthly and 'Colonel' G. W. Nichols," Springfield *Missouri Weekly Patriot*, Jan. 29, 1867, reprinted in Atchison, Kans., *Weekly Champion and Press*, Feb. 14, 1867; John R. Kelso, Individual Muster-Out Roll, Compiled Military Service Record, National Archives.

34. The first session of the 39th Congress ran from Dec. 4, 1865, to July 28, 1866; the second session was Dec. 3, 1866, to March 3, 1867. On how the continuation of violence past Appomattox affected the 39th Congress, see Richard L. Aynes, "The 39th Congress (1865–1867) and the 14th Amendment: Some Preliminary Perspectives," *Akron Law Review* 42 (2009): 1019–49, esp. 1028–35. On the 39th Congress generally, see William H. Barnes, *History of the Thirty-Ninth Congress on the United States* (New York: Harper and Brothers, 1868). On Reconstruction, see esp. Eric Foner, *Reconstruction: America's Unfinished Revolution, 1863–1877* (New York: Harper and Row, 1988); see also Douglas R. Egerton, *The Wars of Reconstruction: The Brief, Violent History of America's Most Progressive Era* (New York: Bloomsbury Press, 2014).

means subdued in *spirit;* nor has treason yet been made odious. Unpunished traitors, emboldened by the lenity of our government, are still plotting its destruction." Kelso, the sole Independent Republican in the House, aligned himself with the Radical wing of the large Republican majority. Radicals insisted that the rights of citizens, including black ones, must be protected. Like the leading Radical in the House, Thaddeus Stevens, Kelso believed that the seceding states had given up their rights as states and could now be treated as conquered territories; like leading Senate Radical Charles Sumner, Kelso held that the Declaration of Independence was as foundational as anything in the Constitution and that it demanded equality before the law.[35]

Andrew Johnson did everything he could to block the Radical Republican Reconstruction agenda. Johnson, previously a slaveholding Democrat, began courting southern leaders in June 1865, and through the rest of the year welcomed provisional governments in the South that empowered former secessionists and restricted black civil rights. In 1866, Johnson vetoed the bill to enlarge the powers of the Freedmen's Bureau and then the Civil Rights Act, though the latter veto was overridden and passed. In 1867, he vetoed the law giving the vote to African Americans in the District of Columbia and then the First Reconstruction Act (both vetoes were overridden and passed). On January 7, 1867, on behalf of the Radical caucus, Kelso followed his Missouri colleague Benjamin F. Loan and offered resolutions to impeach the president. Loan's and Kelso's attempts were defeated by procedural maneuvers, but a third attempt, by James M. Ashley of Ohio, was put to a vote and passed, 107–39. By the time Johnson was tried in the Senate (March 30–May 16, 1868) and acquitted, after the vote was one short of the two-thirds necessary to convict, Kelso had returned to private life as a schoolteacher in Missouri.[36]

35. John R. Kelso, "Speech Delivered at Walnut Grove Mo. Sept. 19th 1865," in "John R. Kelso's Complete Works," 10–27, 12 (quotations). Party divisions of the winning candidates on Election Day: 136 Republicans, 38 Democrats, 13 Unconditional Unionists, 5 Unionists, and Kelso, the Independent Republican; see U.S. House of Representatives, "Congress Profiles," 39th Congress, http://history. house.gov/Congressional-Overview/Profiles/39th/. On Congressional Radical Republicans, see esp. Foner, *Reconstruction*, 228–39.
36. *Congressional Globe*, 39th Cong., 2nd sess., Jan. 7, 1867, 37, part 1, 319–21. See Milton Lomask, *Andrew Johnson: President on Trial* (New York: Farrar, Straus, 1960), 222–23, and Hans L. Trefousse, *Impeachment of a President: Andrew Johnson, the Blacks, and Reconstruction*, 2nd ed. (New York: Fordham University Press, 1999), 54–62; see also David O. Stewart, *Impeached: The Trial of President Andrew Johnson and the Fight for Lincoln's Legacy* (New York: Simon and Schuster, 2009).

He tried to regain his seat in the fall of 1868. Republican Sempronius Boyd was again his opponent, and Capt. Charles B. McAfee also ran for the Democrats. Boyd won easily with over 8,900 votes; McAfee received nearly 5,000, and Kelso, running on a "negro equality" and "anti-bondholder" platform, tallied only 1,304. In his home county (Greene), Kelso polled merely 74 of 1,969 votes cast. Writing a quarter century later, the author of "The Scout of the Ozarks" in the *St. Louis Republic* thought that Kelso's rejection at the ballot box was a sign of a sobered electorate that had been rapidly distancing itself from the "fanaticism" that had provoked the war and produced such horrific bloodshed. Another commentator remembering Kelso in the 1890s wrote that "things have changed very much" since the days when Missouri voters would send a man like Kelso to Washington, and "it would be hard to find a man who actually voted for him to acknowledge it in public." Kelso, however, may have become politically unpalatable less for his reputation for violence than for his progressive politics. After all, other violent Missourians, like the gambling gunslinger Wild Bill Hickok and the sociopathic criminal Jesse James, would be turned into folk heroes in the postwar period. But as white southerners embraced the myth of the Confederacy's noble Lost Cause and white northerners retreated from the egalitarian promises of Reconstruction, a champion for "negro equality" and against the entrenched power of wealth cut against the grain of a hardening white conservatism. The *Republic* article noted that in later years, Kelso "became a fiery champion of the causes of the 'wage slave.' He attacked the greed of corporations and capitalists with as much bitterness as he ever denounced 'rebels' on the Missouri border in the eventful days of the '60s." For the author, however, this was merely a new channel for Kelso's fanaticism, a new fad for a restless mind.[37]

37. Liberty, Mo., *Weekly Tribune*, Oct. 2, 1868; "Election Returns," Liberty, Mo., *Weekly Tribune*, Jan. 8, 1869; Holcombe, *History of Greene County*, 513; "The Scout of the Ozarks"; Beverly A. Barrett to unknown, Feb. 22, 1897, typescript, John F. Bradbury, Jr., Private Collection (hereafter Bradbury Collection). On racial politics after the war, see David Blight, *Race and Reunion: The Civil War in American Memory* (Cambridge, Mass.: Harvard University Press, 2001). On postbellum politics in Missouri, see William E. Parrish, *Missouri under Radical Rule, 1865–1870* (Columbia: University of Missouri Press, 1965). On Hickok, see Joseph G. Rosa, *They Called Him Wild Bill: The Life and Adventures of James Butler Hickok*, rev. ed. (Norman: University of Oklahoma Press, 1974). On James, see Stiles, *Jesse James*.

In the War's Wake

After his career in Congress ended, Kelso opened a school in Springfield, but his life's path turned sharply again, this time because of the death of one son, the tragic suicide of another, and the failure of his second marriage. Devastated, Kelso began divorce proceedings and in 1872 moved to California, living for a time with his daughter and son-in-law. He became involved in the civic life of Modesto, a railroad boom town that sprang up in 1870 and grew on the wealth of the surrounding wheat fields. Modesto was controlled by the men who ran its many saloons, brothels, and gambling houses—except on the dramatic occasions when 250 other citizens, perhaps including Kelso, armed themselves, covered their faces, and rode at night as vigilantes to try to clean up the town. In the 1870s, too, Kelso would continue to pursue the studies that led him from Christianity to atheism, delivering the lectures that would constitute the five books he published in the next decade, including *The Real Blasphemers* (1883) and *Deity Analyzed* (1890). He also became an outspoken critic of conventional attitudes about sex and marriage and a promoter of spiritualism.[38]

In 1873, he began to fill the eight hundred pages of a large ledger book with copies of his congressional speeches, poetry, and public lectures. The title page described the volume as "The Works of John R. Kelso," dedicated to his surviving son and posterity. On June 6, 1882, in his fifty-second year, on page 668 of this ledger book, he began his "Auto-Biography," dedicated to his three children. "Knowing that the sun of my life is now nearing its setting, and believing that a brief account of my eventful career will be of interest, and probably of some benefit to yourselves and your posterity, I have concluded to give you such an account," he wrote. "While I wish you to be indulgent critics, I do not wish you to be blind to my many errors. I wish you to see, to forgive and to avoid those errors. If you do all these things, even my errors will not have been utterly in vain. The world will be at least a little better off for my having lived in it, and the great desire of my heart will be realized."[39]

---

38. Their final divorce decree was rendered on Jan. 30, 1874 ("Abstract of Divorce Records, 1837–1899," Greene County, Missouri Circuit Court, http://thelibrary.springfield.missouri.org/lochist/records/d1873.htm). Kelso's main published works are *The Real Blasphemers* (New York: Truth Seeker, 1883); *The Bible Analyzed in Twenty Lectures* (New York: Truth Seeker, 1884); *Spiritualism Sustained in Five Lectures* (New York: Truth Seeker, 1886); *The Universe Analyzed* (New York: Truth Seeker, 1887); *Deity Analyzed in Six Lectures* (New York: Truth Seeker, 1890); and *Government Analyzed* (Longmont, Col.: Privately printed, 1892).
39. Kelso, "Auto-Biography," 1, 668 (quotation).

Kelso then filled the remaining pages of the ledger with a vivid account of what he called his "checkered career." The story breaks off, on the bottom of the ledger's final page, in late January 1863, with the main character buying a house in Springfield for his family and being ordered to Neosho to battle bushwhackers, while the writer looks back bitterly from his perspective two decades later, knowing what would happen next.[40]

In Kelso's final years, his political radicalism intensified. In 1885, he moved to Longmont, Colorado. He declared himself to be an anarchist at a Colorado rally in 1889, and tried to explain what he meant in his final book, *Government Analyzed*, a work his third wife, Etta Dunbar Kelso, completed after his death and published in 1892. In that book he also reflected on what at the end of his life he considered to be the misguided patriotic blindness that had caused him to kill his fellow men in the war, realizing that he had merely substituted a sacralized Nation for the God that he had left behind when he abandoned Christianity: "Believing that I was thereby fulfilling a sacred duty, and proving myself a good, brave and patriotic man, I cheerfully bore, for more than three years, every conceivable hardship and privation; took part in nearly a hundred bloody engagements; with my own hands, slew a goodly number of brave men, and after the fearful tragedy had been successfully enacted . . . I looked back with exultation upon the part I had enacted. . . . How blind I was, and yet how honest. How blindly, how piously, how patriotically inhuman even the best of us are capable of being made by superstition." Nearly done writing his chapter on "War," at the end of a discussion of the American Civil War and slavery and in the middle of a sentence, John R. Kelso in early January 1891, suffering from typhoid fever, put down his pen. He died on January 26. His wife blamed not the fever but a gastric inflammation caused by that last rebel bullet, which had been festering painfully beneath his sternum for nearly three decades.[41]

The Meanings of the Civil War

Kelso's writings offer different interpretations of the larger meaning of the Civil War. When he first stood before his pro-southern neighbors in Buffalo in the spring of 1861, he voiced a commitment to the Union that was

40. Kelso, "Auto-Biography," 675.
41. Kelso, *Government Analyzed*, 48–49; Etta D. Kelso, "Widow's Declaration for Pension" (July 3, 1891), John R. Kelso, Pension File, National Archives.

nothing less than a sacred cause. The struggle, as he explained it, was between traitors who would ruin the peaceful and prosperous country they could no longer rule and those who would preserve the republican government that had been created by the revolutionary forefathers and had stood as a beacon of freedom to the world. But after the Confederate victories and Union retreat from southwest Missouri in the fall of 1861, Kelso had other reasons to fight. When pro-southern neighbors stole his property, burned down his house, and drove his family and the families of other loyal friends into the bitter cold to suffer (and some of them to die), Kelso became motivated by personal revenge. He acknowledged, too, that he had an ambition to lead men into battle and make a name for himself.

By 1863, the Emancipation Proclamation had added the abolition of slavery to preserving the Union as a war aim, and Kelso too came to see slavery as the center of the contest—slavery as the utter denial of the ideal of political equality expressed in the Declaration of Independence and as a manifestation of the tyrannical behavior of a small group of aristocrats over the common American people, white and black. Kelso rode the Radical Republican wave to Congress, joining those who believed that the South and America at large had to be thoroughly reconstructed both politically and socially to live up to the nation's highest ideals.

Thirty years after he had stood on the Buffalo courthouse steps and pledged his life to save the Union, and twenty-five years after he had stood in Congress demanding that African Americans be given the right to vote if their freedom from slavery was to have meaning, John R. Kelso had come to see the patriotism that had prompted him to fight as a delusion and the outcome of the Civil War as a cruel joke. Seeing an America by the last decade of the nineteenth century riddled with corruption and ruled by an oligarchy of large corporations, Kelso bitterly regretted his wartime exploits. What he had once thought of as patriotic heroism he now considered a misguided righteousness of the most dangerous kind, a blindness that led to state-sanctioned destruction and slaughter.

The reporter in the *St. Louis Republic,* puzzling over Kelso's character two years after his death, could only conclude that "John R. Kelso was one of the enigmas of the war." He was a "mysterious" combination "of courage, cunning, hate, earnestness, [and] fanaticism," and yet he undoubtedly possessed "the tastes and aspirations of an idealist." The Kelso that emerges in the pages of his "Auto-Biography" is a coldly efficient killer in the midst of a soldier's bloody engagements but also a man with tender sentiments and powerful passions that he found almost too much to bear. He fought bravely for his country but also thought deeply about the causes of the war and the moral character of the struggle. John R. Kelso's Civil War, like the man himself, was no simple thing.[42]

42. "The Scout of the Ozarks." For a full account of Kelso's life, see Christopher Grasso, *Teacher, Preacher, Soldier, Spy: The Civil Wars of John R. Kelso* (New Haven, Conn.: Yale University Press, forthcoming).

Bloody Engagements

Figure 1. John R. Kelso, c. 1861–65. John R. Kelso, carte de visite, folder 25, Charles Lanham Collection, State Historical Society of Missouri, Columbia. Photograph courtesy of the State Historical Society of Missouri.

1. Secession and War

April to July 1861

And thus, as described in the last chapter, my affairs stood in the spring of 1861, when I was 31 years of age.[1] My school for that term would have closed about the first of June. I closed it, however, a few weeks earlier. This I did in consequence of the intense excitement that followed the firing upon Fort Sumpter by the secessionists of South Carolina.[2] Like the most fearful earthquake ever known to man, that first mad act of treasonable warfare aroused a commotion which threatened to shatter our own country—our beloved "Union" into a thousand fragments, and which caused all the nations of the world to stand in awe and to tremble. War of the most terrible nature was now bound to sweep, like the besom of destruction, over our beautiful and once-happy land. From end to end and from side to side of our country, a great cry arose;—a cry for war and for blood. Throughout the South, this cry was for a war that should destroy the "accursed Union" and cause the

Source: Kelso, "Auto-Biography," chap. 9, 708–15. Spelling, punctuation, capitalization, paragraph breaks, and chapter divisions are Kelso's. His interlineations have been rendered in line. His underlines appear here as italics and his double underlines as bold print. The editor has supplied the chapter titles.
1. Kelso had separated from his wife Adelia in the fall of 1856. Their divorce was finalized two years later, immediately after which he married Martha S. ("Susie") Barnes. He graduated from Pleasant Ridge College in Weston, Platte County, Mo., in June 1859. He, Susie, and his two children from his first marriage, Florella (b. 1854) and Florellus (b. 1856), moved to Buffalo, Dallas County, Missouri. He and his wife purchased a 120-acre farm a mile and a half from town, and Kelso opened his "Academy," beginning with seven students (his sister Ella was an assistant teacher). See Kelso, "Auto-Biography," 702–7, and *Missouri Marriage Records*.

2. The Confederates began their bombardment of Fort Sumter in Charleston Harbor, S.C., occupied by the U.S. Army, at 4:30 a.m., April 12, 1861.

rivers to run red with the blood of the "_____ Yankees" and others who had dared to oppose the extension of the "divine institution of slavery." Throughout the North, it was for a war that should preserve the "glorious Union," cause the rivers to run red with the blood of "traitors" and forever "to wipe out the inhuman and damnable institution of slavery." One who never witnessed any thing of the kind can not well conceive of the fearful excitement that prevailed at that time. Fearful every where, this excitement was more fearful in the border states which were bound to be the theater of the greatest carnage ever known upon earth, and in which the people were more divided in sentiment than they were any where else.[3] Human nature among the people, seemed all at once to become perverted. Mild men became fierce, and fierce men became almost fiendish. Women would gladly have changed their sex and rushed into the conflict; and even the children would gladly have changed their play-grounds for the battle-field, their toys for the instruments of death. Farmers, mechanics, teachers,—all classes of the people, forsaking their several employments, in vast, surging, burning masses, crowded the public squares and blockaded the streets of our cities and towns. At every corner, fiery orators, with burning words and wild gesticulations, heightened still the already morbidly inflamed passions of the multitude. Religion, that greatest of all fomenters of discord and of blood-shed, rushed, like a hungry vulture, into the conflict, and added increased blackness to the awful storm-cloud that was just bursting upon us. On every hand was heard the deafening clang, clang, clang of the cruel iron tongue of the church bell, calling for blood. From every pulpit was heard the equally heartless clang of the priest's voice, yelling to his god, in blasphemous prayers, to help them dye the rivers with the blood, and to enrich the soil with the unburied bodies of their brethren—his children. While the secession priest was informing his god, with these frantic and blasphemous yells, that slavery was a divine institution, founded and fostered by this god himself, the Union priest, often not far away, was informing this same god, with equally

---

3. The border states (slave states that remained in the Union) were Delaware, Maryland, Kentucky, and Missouri. In the 1860 presidential election, Missouri cast 58,801 votes for Stephen A. Douglas (National [Northern] Democratic Party, which supported "popular sovereignty" in the states on the slavery question); 58,372 for John Bell (Constitutional Union Party, which wanted to compromise and preserve "the Union as it is"); 31,317 for John C. Breckinridge (Constitutional [Southern] Democratic Party, proslavery and supporting the right of secession); and 17,028 for Abraham Lincoln (Republican, promising not to interfere with slavery in the states but opposing it in the territories). Parrish, *History of Missouri*, 3.

frantic and blasphemous yells, that slavery was an institution of hell—an abomination in the sight of this god. While the former priest was distinctly informing his god that he (the god) certainly should and certainly would destroy the Union and utterly overwhelm the abolition hordes of the North, the latter was just as distinctly informing him that he certainly should and certainly would preserve the Union and utterly overwhelm the proslavery rebel hosts of the South.[4] What this god would have done had the two parties been equal in strength I do not know. As it was, he evidently helped the stronger party.

As yet, I had kept silent in regard to the all absorbing question of the time. Outside of my own family, my political sentiments were not known in this community.[5] For a time, I determined to remain silent until the close of my school. My school-room, however, opening as it did right upon the public square, was exposed to all the uproar of the excited crowds that daily filled the square. Whenever any news arrived favorable to the South, there was loud cheering right at our door. Under these circumstances, my pupils, good and obedient as they were, began to partake of the prevailing excitement and to become unable to concentrate their thoughts upon their studies. This was especially the case with the larger boys and the young men. I, too, began to feel myself carried away by the general excitement. I determined, therefore,

---

4. On religion and the Civil War, see esp. James H. Moorhead, *American Apocalypse: Yankee Protestants and the Civil War, 1860–1869* (New Haven, Conn.: Yale University Press, 1978); James M. McPherson, *For Cause and Comrades: Why Men Fought in the Civil War* (New York: Oxford University Press, 1997); Randall M. Miller, Harry S. Stout, and Charles Reagan Wilson, eds., *Religion and the American Civil War* (New York: Oxford University Press, 1998); Steven E. Woodworth, *While God Is Marching On: The Religious World of Civil War Soldiers* (Lawrence: University Press of Kansas, 2001); Mark A. Noll, *America's God: From Jonathan Edwards to Abraham Lincoln* (New York: Oxford University Press, 2002), part 5; John Patrick Daly, *When Slavery Was Called Freedom: Evangelicalism, Proslavery, and the Causes of the Civil War* (Lexington: University of Kentucky Press, 2002); Harry S. Stout, *Upon the Altar of the Nation: A Moral History of the Civil War* (New York: Viking, 2006); Mark A. Noll, *The Civil War as a Theological Crisis* (Chapel Hill: University of North Carolina Press, 2006); Robert J. Miller, *Both Prayed to the Same God: Religion and Faith in the American Civil War* (Lanham, Md.: Lexington Books, 2007); David Rolfs, *No Peace for the Wicked: Northern Protestant Soldiers and the American Civil War* (Knoxville: University of Tennessee Press, 2009); and George C. Rable, *God's Almost Chosen Peoples: A Religious History of the American Civil War* (Chapel Hill: University of North Carolina Press, 2010).

5. Early in the "Auto-Biography," Kelso discussed his opinions in 1855: "Kansas was just across the river and there actual war was going on to determine whether slavery should or should not exist in that territory when it became a state. Every body on our side of the river was suspected and ostracized who was not wont to loudly hurrah for slavery, and to just as loudly curse the abolitionists and the 'Black Republicans.' Although I was a minister in the M. E. Church South, I had fully studied the subject of slavery, and had, in my own mind, fully condemned that divine institution. I was silent in regard to the matter but, in those days, such silence was very suspicious" (697).

to close my school at once. I did this, explaining to my pupils, in a kind little speech, my reasons for so doing. I told them also which side I intended to espouse. I told them that I should stand by the Union. I told them that I could not do otherwise and be true to my own conscience and my own manhood. Most of them seemed grieved when they heard this, and yet they all parted with me kindly. A few of the boys declared that they would stand with me for the Union.

Having closed my school and cut myself off from the sympathy of nearly all my pupils and other friends, who were nearly all secessionists, I felt that I was again standing alone and about to take the most critical step of my life. I had already made known to my parents and other near relatives the course I intended to take, and they had expressed their indignation and had ceased to correspond with me at all. If there were any Union men in the community where I then was, they were keeping extremely quiet. Not knowing my own sentiments, they had kept aloof from me. I did not know any one that I could certainly depend upon; and to stand alone for the Union was as much as my life was worth. That day there was an unusually large crowd upon the public square, and the excitement was intense. The news had just reached us of the seceding of several more states.[6] The speakers were jubilant, and represented the United States as virtually destroyed, the Confederate States as virtually established. The Union seemed to have no friends present.[7]

6. The seven states of the lower South (South Carolina, Mississippi, Florida, Alabama, Georgia, Louisiana, and Texas) seceded between Dec. 20, 1860, and Feb. 1, 1861 (the Texas referendum was Feb. 23). Virginia followed on April 17 (referendum on May 23), Arkansas and Tennessee on May 6 (Tennessee referendum on June 8), and North Carolina on May 20. Kelso was probably describing the events of May 6 or 7. Similar excitement occurred on May 7 during "Secession Day" in Rolla, Missouri. See the *Rolla Express*, May 13, 1861, cited in John F. Bradbury, Jr., *The Old Phelps County Courthouse and the Civil War* (Rolla, Mo.: Old Courthouse Preservation Committee and the Phelps County Historical Society, 1999), 4.
7. In Dallas County, as in the state at large, about 70% of the electorate in the 1860 presidential election voted for either Douglas or Bell, the compromise candidates, though in Missouri as a whole Douglas barely edged Bell by a few hundred votes, while in Dallas Douglas received 31% and Bell 41% of the vote. In the county, Breckinridge, the southern candidate, received somewhat more support than in the whole state (24% to 19%) and Lincoln significantly less (less than 3% to over 10%). The southern tilt of Buffalo can be seen in the 1860 governor's race. Sample Orr of the Constitutional Union Party got 42% of the vote in Missouri, 55% in Dallas County, and only 12% in Buffalo. Claiborne F. Jackson, a Democrat with what were thought to be moderate southern sympathies, won in Missouri with 47%, received 43% in Dallas, and 70% in Buffalo. Hancock Lee Jackson, the Breckinridge Southern Democrat, got 7% in Missouri, 6% in Dallas, and 18% in Buffalo (Parrish, *History of Missouri*, 2; "Missouri Returns," St. Louis *Daily Missouri Republican*, Nov. 14, 1860; "Election Results, 1860," Western Historical Manuscripts Collection–Columbia, University of Missouri, Columbia, Missouri Digital Heritage, www.sos.mo.gov/mdh/ [hereafter MDH]).

When the last speaker closed his hot secession harangue, I ascended the steps of the court house, and, calling the attention of the crowd, proceeded to read a series of Union resolutions which I had already prepared. When I closed, there was not an immediate outburst of fury against me as I expected there would be. My act had taken the crowd utterly by surprise, and they seemed thunder-struck by my audacity. For a time there was a general but indistinct murmur of low voices. Presently, I could hear certain voices louder than the others denouncing me as a "traitor to the South," and declaring that I "ought to be shot down like a wolf or a sheep-killing dog."

Among my resolutions were the following: "Resolved that the treasonable act of secession, though committed by the Governor, the Legislature and a majority of the citizens of our state, can not and does not in any respect absolve the balance of the citizens from the allegiance which they owe to the United States; and, therefore, Resolved that we, the loyal portion of the citizens of Missouri, will be true to our allegiance to the United States, that we will resist rebel force with force, and that, if necessary, we will whiten with our unburied bones the fair plains of Missouri which we fought to save." Our traitor Governor, Claiborne F. Jackson, had just issued a proclamation according to which these resolutions constituted treason against the state of Missouri and a capital offense. I called the attention of the crowd to this fact, and declared that Claiborne F. Jackson and I could not both live.[8]

After I had read my resolutions and finished my remarks upon them, I stepped down among the crowd and waited to see what they were going to do about it. When the storm of indignation against me began to assume a dangerous form, I felt the fingers of a child clutching one of my hands. Looking down, I saw the anxious face of one of my pupils, a bright little boy of eight years. Seeing that he wished to lead me away, I permitted him to do

8. Gov. Claiborne Fox Jackson (1806–62) had been publicly advocating "armed neutrality" for Missouri and privately working for secession and the state's admission to the Confederacy. On May 3, 1861, he called out the Missouri Volunteer Militia (his speech must be what Kelso refers to here). His later proclamation calling for all loyal Missourians to rise up and drive out the federal invaders was published in the *Boonville Times* on June 12, 1861. On Jackson, see Phillips, *Missouri's Confederate*. For his May 3 speech, see "Governor's Message," St. Louis *Daily Missouri Republican*, May 4, 1861, and Jackson, "Special Session Message," May 3, 1861, in Buel Leopard and Floyd C. Shoemaker, eds., *The Messages and Proclamations of the Governors of the State of Missouri*, vol. 3 (Columbia: State Historical Society of Missouri, 1922), 343–48. For the text of his June proclamation, see Silvana R. Siddali, ed., *Missouri's War: The Civil War in Documents* (Athens: University of Ohio Press, 2009), 69–71.

so. Indeed, I was glad of an excuse to leave the crowd just then, so that I should not seem to leave through fear. The little boy led me around behind some store buildings and into an old ware-house, the doors and windows of which were all closed. There, in the darkness, I found four men who said that they had managed thus to get me away before I was torn to pieces by the infuriated crowd. They said that they endorsed every word I had uttered, but that, by thus publicly proclaiming my principles, I was simply throwing my life away without doing any good. They begged me to let them conceal me for a few days until the excitement died away. To this, I dissented. I told them I would rather die than not to prove myself a man on that occasion. I asked one of them, the owner of the store and the ware-house, to loan me his revolver. He replied that he did not have it with him, and that he would not dare to loan it to me any way. I asked him where it was. He replied that it was under his pillow in his bed room. "Very good," said I, "when you look for it, it will not be there." Having added this revolver to the arms I already carried, I was prepared to sell my life at a dear rate, if I was compelled to sell it at all. I left the ware-house and crossed the public square on my way home. The crowd had mostly dispersed, by this time, and no one attempted to interrupt me. These four men, my first Union friends, were W. B. Edwards, Dr. E. Hovey, A. Lindsay, and A. Vanderford.[9]

About a week later, another grand meeting was called in our town. This meeting was to be addressed by Peter Wilkes and other able speakers from Springfield.[10] A fine Confederate flag was to be flung to the breeze from the dome of our court-house, guns were to be fired, secession songs were to be sung, Dixie and other appropriate airs were to be played by the band, and a

9. William B. Edwards (b. 1810 in Tenn.), D. A. Lindsey (b. 1830 in Tenn.), and Asa. R. Vandiford (b. 1818 in Ohio) were prosperous farmers in Dallas County (1860 U.S. Census, Benton Township, Dallas County, Missouri, family nos. 154 [Edwards] and 96 [Vandiford]); Dr. Eleazar Hovey (b. 1816 in N.Y.) was a dentist and physician (1860 U.S. Census, Benton Township, Dallas County, Missouri, family no. 241; "Eleazer Hovey," in Burton Lee Thorpe, *Biographies of the Founders, Prominent Early Members and Ex-Presidents of the Missouri State Dental Association* [St. Louis: Ev. E. Carreras, 1909], 33).
10. Peter S. Wilkes (b. 1826 in Tenn.) was an attorney, but one source also describes him as a minister. He served in the Missouri legislature and was a leader of the pro-southern party in Springfield in 1861. He would become a member of Capt. Dick Campbell's Company of the Missouri State Guard, organized near Springfield in May 1861, and serve in the Confederate Congress in the last year of the war (George S. Escott, *History and Directory of Springfield and North Springfield* [Springfield, Mo.: Patriot-Advertiser, 1878], 101; Holcombe, *History of Greene County*, 404; Obituary, *San Francisco Call*, Jan. 1900).

great boom generally was to be given to the rising rebellion.[11] The day arrived. A vast concourse of people assembled. A procession with music met the speakers and the flag, and, for a time, everything was lovely. Mr. Wilkes delivered a really eloquent oration urging the people to stand as a unit for secession. He said that the seven states which had then seceded were typified by the seven stars, the seven churches, the seven candlesticks, the seven years of plenty, the seven angels, and other sevens of the scriptures, all of a glorious, a heaven-approved character.[12] Many of his remarks were loudly applauded. I saw among the crowd, however, many men with pale earnest faces who did not join in the applause. I knew that some of these were Union men, and I supposed that they all were. Indeed, during the last week, I had learned that there was quite a strong Union element in the county,[13] and that, after my bold public declaration of my principles, I was coming to be regarded as the leader of that element. I had declared my intention to reply to Mr. Wilkes on this occasion. My friends did their best to dissuade me from carrying out this intention. They said that to attempt such a reply would be, on my part, an act of madness, and they could not agree to sustain me in so hazardous an attempt. My mind was made up, however, and no amount of dissuasion could deter me from carrying out my intentions. Perceiving that they could not dissuade me, some half dozen of my friends, under the leadership of a young merchant by the name of John

11. A similar rally was held in Newtonia, Newton County, Mo., on April 24, 1861: "Peter S. Wilkes of Springfield Mo. made an Eloquent and stirring speech on behalf of Southern Rights." Judge M. H. Ritchey also spoke. Then a committee passed resolutions in support of Governor Jackson and the southern cause ("Resolutions of a Public Meeting Pledging the Participants Support on the South and Gov. Jackson," April 24, 1861, Missouri Digital Heritage, Missouri Union Provost Marshal Papers [hereafter, MDH Provost Marshal Papers], reel F1611, file 9049, http://www.sos.mo.gov/archives/provost/provostPDF@t1).

12. Rev. 1:20: seven stars, golden candlesticks, angels, and churches; Gen. 41:29: seven years of plenty.

13. An analysis of the 1860 census reveals some socioeconomic differences between "greater Buffalo" and the rest of Dallas County, Missouri. Benton Township, which included Buffalo, was on average wealthier than the other five townships in the county ($2,076/household as compared to $1,582/household). Benton had the three richest households in the county and eight of the top twenty. The ten wealthiest households in Benton were 10% richer than the ten wealthiest in the rest of the county. Over 18% of Benton households listed occupations other than farming, as opposed to fewer than 4% for the rest of the county. The county had 5,892 residents (1,024 families) in 1860; 40 were slaveholders, who held 114 slaves. Thirteen of those slaveholders, holding thirty-seven slaves, lived in Benton. So in Dallas County as a whole, slightly less than 4% of households had slaves; in Benton, 8% did. The number of household heads born in slaveholding states, however, was somewhat higher in the county at large than in Benton: 84% as compared to 76%. A majority in the county came from the upper South, especially Tennessee.

McConnell,[14] banded themselves together and armed themselves to the teeth for the purpose of defending me to the death if any attempt should be made upon my life. Still hoping that I would yet give up my rash intention, they did not, however, let me know that they proposed thus to defend me. In the meeting, they took their places, as if by chance, near me, close to the speaker's stand. On the other side of the stand, were about thirty men who seemed to be banded together for some purpose. They were hunters from the Neongo [Niangua][15] hills—a rough looking set of customers. Many of them were dressed in buckskin, all carried long rifles, and all had their belts loaded with revolvers and bowie knives. What they meant, no one but themselves seemed to know. They had come from a distance of from 20 to 30 miles and from a locality in which the Union sentiment strongly prevailed. Afterwards, they told me that they had come on my account—that they had heard I was to be killed on that occasion if I attempted to speak, and that they had come to see who killed me and how the killing was done.

During the applause that followed Mr. Wilkes' speech, and before the next speaker could be introduced, I leaped upon the front of the stand and waved my hand for attention. Instantly a dead silence prevailed. No one in the audience seemed even to breathe. The very audacity of my act seemed to hold them all fixed with a kind of fascination. My whole soul aglow with a kind of inspiration, I seemed to see in great letters of flame the very words I should speak. I forgot myself and my danger. I thought only of the cause I was defending and of victory. I showed that the seven seceded states were typified by the seven lean kine, the seven years of famine, the seven plagues, the seven vials of wrath, the seven heads of the dragon, the seven devils, and many other sevens of the scriptures, all of a damnable, a heaven-abominated character. I showed that, as Satan had drawn away one third of the hosts of heaven, so the arch fiend of secession had drawn away one third of the hosts of our Union—our heaven of [sic; on] earth.[16] I recalled the struggles of our

14. John Newton McConnell (1837–1905) had come to Missouri from Tennessee after 1856. In 1860, he was a merchant living with his wife, Sarah, and his father-in-law in Benton Township, Dallas County, Mo. (1860 U.S. Census, Benton Township, Dallas County, Missouri, family no. 230).
15. Kelso gives the phonetic spelling; see Eva Murrell Hemphill, *Early Days in Dallas County* (N.p.: N.p., 1954), 7.
16. Gen. 41:3: seven lean kine; Rev. 15:5 and 21:9: angels bearing seven vials of the seven last plagues; Rev. 12:3: seven heads of the dragon. Rev. 12:4, describing a great red dragon who with "his tail drew a third part of the stars of heaven, and did cast them to the earth," is sometimes read as referring to fallen angels, formerly a third of the heavenly host.

forefathers, and repeated the inimitable words of our immortal Washington's Farewell Address. I depicted the unutterable horrors of the internecine war that they were blindly bringing upon us;—the blood, the carnage, the desolated homes;—the widows, the orphans, the childless parents;—the broken honor, the wasted virtue, the black despair, the gloating of vultures, the lost souls, the exulting howlings of the demons of hell. But few of my hearers had ever heard or read a word on my side of this great question. Tears—loyal tears rolled down the rough cheeks of many a brave and honest man who came there that day believing himself to be a secessionist. The real secessionists grew pale. The speaker whose place I was usurping trembled as if in an ague. A change was wrought in that great assembly. A tidal wave was rising that could not now be turned back, or resisted. When I closed, the pent up feelings of hundreds found vent in loud and hearty hurrahs for the Union and our brave old flag.[17]

The moment I closed, W. B. Edwards, of whom I have already spoken, an old wounded soldier of the War of 1812, hobbled with his crutches into my place.[18] Though a slave owner, he was as true as steel to the Union, and now, for a few moments, he poured forth a torrent of patriotic eloquence that I never heard surpassed. Under the inspiration of that eloquence, the loyal fire that I had kindled burst into a flame. When he closed, I called upon him to walk out upon one side of the square and represent Washington, the Union, and the Star-spangled Banner, and upon Mr. Wilkes to walk out upon the other side and represent Benedict Arnold, treason, and the Confederate flag, and see how the

17. Robert Pinckney Matthews (1837–91), an eighteen-year-old Union supporter in Springfield, Mo., remembered a similar experience (although there the Unionists and secessionists were more evenly divided) in May 1861: "Meetings were being held night and day to discuss the state of the country. Men in both parties were meeting in secret conclave night after night." At a debate in front of a large crowd, "excitement was at a white heat and a small spark was liable to make a mighty flame at a moments notice." The secessionist speaker raised his supporters "to the highest pitch of enthusiasm." Matthews rose to speak for the Union, and "a feeling came over me I cannot define. The whole subject and the consequences of disunion and disruption seemed to open before me and burn like fire on my brain. A sensation of exaltation was over me. What I said I know not, but when I was done, men were crowding around me shouting 'Union once and forever.' I realized the field was won and immediately formed a [Union] League of over 50 men who swore with uplifted hand to defend the 'Stars and Stripes' with every drop of blood in their veins" (Matthews, *Souvenir of the Holland Company Home Guards and "Phelps" Regiment, Missouri Volunteer Infantry*, c. 1890, C 1160, typescript, 7, State Historical Society of Missouri, Columbia).

18. The pension record for William B. Edwards, filed by his widow, Sarah, in 1890, lists his previous military experience as "Indian War," not the War of 1812 (*U.S. Civil War Pension Index: General Index to Pension Files, 1861–1934*, National Archives [online database, Provo, Utah: Ancestry.com, 2000], T288). In 1860, Edwards owned eight slaves, ages two to fifty-five (1860 U.S. Census, Benton Township, Dallas County, Missouri, Slave Schedules, family no. 24).

crowd would divide. As the old hero hobbled to his place, several hundred men waved their hats, hurrahed for the Union, and formed in a long line by his side. Mr. Wilkes did not walk out at all, and his party did not form in line. Indeed, they seemed thunder-struck and alarmed at this totally unexpected outcome of their great secession boom. They conferred together a few moments, then the speakers and the rebel flag were hurried away in wagons amid the cheers of the enthusiastic Union men. We had won a great, though a bloodless victory.

Knowing that the time to strike was "while the iron was hot," we proceeded at once to form ourselves into military companies called Home Guards.[19] I had the honor to be the first man to volunteer into this service. The second man was Milton Burch, a merchant of our town. He was lame from a wound received while a soldier in Mexico, but he made one of the foremost warriors of the army of the frontier. I shall often speak of him here-after.[20] I was elected Captain of one of the first companies formed. A week

19. In St. Louis, the state's largest city and, because of the federal armory, the flashpoint as sectional crisis turned to war, militia groups had been organizing since January. By late February, Capt. (later Brig. Gen.) Nathaniel Lyon (1818–61), U.S. Army, stationed at the arsenal, was drilling with some of these Union Guard companies. After the attack on Fort Sumter on April 15, Abraham Lincoln called for 75,000 troops; on April 17, Missouri governor C. F. Jackson denounced the call as illegal, unconstitu-tional, and diabolical, but 1,500 German Union guards volunteered for federal service and the War Department authorized sending 5,000 stands of arms to St. Louis. On April 22, Jackson under the Militia Act of 1858 called out the state militia for a week of drilling and called the assembly into session to consider a bill that would vastly expand his militia powers. Nearly 900 men camped on the eastern edge of St. Louis, flying secessionist flags. Lyon's forces surrounded the camp and captured most of them on May 10. In other parts of the state, Unionist Home Guard and pro-southern State Guard militia compa-nies organized. By June 1, Lyon had a force of 10,730 regulars and Home Guards, although the latter were still being paid from private funds. On June 12, the day after negotiations collapsed, Jackson issued a call for 50,000 troops to defend Missouri against federal invaders. On June 11, 1861, Lyon was author-ized by the secretary of war to enlist loyal Missourians to defend themselves, the state, and the United States; they would receive federal pay when called into active service. Many Unionist citizen militia units that had already been organized (in Springfield, for example) were officially recognized as Home Guards. The U.S. government quickly sent 10,000 stands of arms. Home Guard units existed for one to six months. The Dallas County companies were mustered in on June 24 and were intended to serve until Sept. 24, 1861, but were disbanded Aug. 10–11. See Holcombe, *History of Greene County*, 280–90; Britton, *Civil War on the Border*, 1:1–31; U.S. Pension and Record Office (War Department), *Organization and Status of Missouri Troops (Union and Confederate) in Service during the Civil War* (Washington, D.C.: Government Printing Office, 1902), 146–64; Phillips, *Damned Yankee*, 129–217; Phillips, *Missouri's Confederate*, 233–61; Gerteis, *Civil War St. Louis*, 78–131; and Gerteis, *Civil War in Missouri*, 8–40.

20. Milton Burch was a thirty-nine-year-old Buffalo merchant with a wife (Mary) and two small children (1860 U.S. Census, Benton Township, Dallas County, Missouri, family no. 244). The family had moved to Missouri from Illinois in the mid-1850s. Burch's pension record, which he filed as an "invalid" in 1886 twelve years before his death, listed him as a captain in Co. H, 1st Illinois Volunteers (Mexican War) (*U.S. Civil War Pension Index*). He is listed as a private in that company in Isaac H. Elliott, *Record of the Services of Illinois Soldiers in the Black Hawk War, 1831–32, and in the Mexican War, 1846–8* (Springfield, Ill.: H. W. Rokker, 1882), 204.

later, I was elected major. I was nominated for Colonel, but declined and insisted upon the election of my brave old soldier friend, W. B. Edwards. His election was unanimous. For Lt. Colonel, we elected Dr. E. Hovey, a popular physician of our town. After my promotion, Burch took my place as Captain.[21]

We now had a regiment of 800 men, about half of whom were armed with the old-fashioned long-barreled rifles used by the hunters of that time. A few had good shot-guns, and many had revolvers. In order to arm the balance of our men, we made raids upon various parts of the county, and seized the arms of disloyal men. We took possession of the court-house, established a system of signals, and, under the drill of a few old soldiers, soon came to know something of military discipline. Being thus the first to organize and to arm, we so forestalled the enemy that we were enabled to hold our own county without much trouble. Most of the rebels soon disappeared from the county. In an adjoining county, however, the rebels had been the first to act, and they, under the command of an able officer, Major Maybry, held that county as we held our own. That was Hickory County, and the Union men of that county seemed almost frightened out of their wits. They had all fled to the brush for hiding, and many of them, when they escaped and reached us, had blood-curdling tales to tell of the doings of Maybry and his band of rebels.[22] On one occasion, a small party of them came rushing

---

21. Col. William B. Edwards, Lt. Col. Eleazer Hovey, Maj. John R. Kelso, First Lt. Milton Burch, Dallas County Home Guards, June 24, 1861–Aug. 11, 1861, when the regiment was disbanded ("Soldiers' Records: War of 1812–World War I," Missouri Digital Heritage, www.sos.mo.gov/archives/soldiers [hereafter, "Soldiers' Records," MDH]; see also Gary Swift, Dallas County Home Guards, Reconstructed Roster, http://mogenweb.org/dallas/home_guard_roster.html).

22. Capt. John Mabary, Mabary's Missouri Company, CSA ("Soldiers' Records," MDH). See also F. Marion Wilson, *Wilson's History of Hickory County* (Hermitage, Mo.: Wilson Brothers, [1909]): "By 1861, the town [Preston, in Hickory County] had grown to be an important business point, but at the commencement of the Civil War nearly all of its inhabitants sympathized with the Confederacy and went South. . . . Early in 1861, the people of the town and that section of the country became greatly excited about the issues of the Civil War. John Mabary, an Ex-Sheriff and Collector, and a highly respected citizen, with the assistance of others, enlisted a Company of State Guards, at the instance of Claiborne F. Jackson, then, Governor of the State" (65–66). "In the spring of 1861, when [the Civil War] come on there was probably not more than 700 able bodied men between the ages of 18 and 45 years of age in [Hickory] county, and these were divided between the Union and Confederate armies. . . . It is, probably, not out of place, and justice to say, that Dr. Richard I. Robertson, Dr. J. F. Powers, a Vermont Yankee, who owned a cripple negro, Silas C. Howard, and Benj. F. Staten, were the principal and earnest advocates of secession in and about Preston, and were the cause of the organization of the Mabary company, with John Mabary, as Capt. because he had the nerve and courage while Robertson, Powers et al were purely noise makers and agitators" (78–79). "Captain Mabary died in 1863. Some of his men went South and were in General Sterling Price's army; some of them quit the service after a short time, and came home, or went elsewhere; some, even, went into the Federal army later" (66).

into our camps, their hats gone and their horses covered with dust and foam, and reported that Maybry was only a few miles away, rapidly advancing upon our position, burning every Union house that fell in his way, and *hanging* every Union man that fell into his hands. This report appearing to be reliable, threw our camps into a wonderful excitement. We were soon ready for battle, however, at first dreading to see the terrible Maybry approach, but, finally, growing bolder from impatience, we began to wish he would come and give us a taste of real war. Presently another party of fugitives arrived and informed us that the alarm was all a hoax gotten up by certain mischievous parties of rebel proclivities for what they were pleased to call "*fun*."

As soon as we learned that Maybry was not coming, we at once perceived that we could easily have "whipped h-ll out of him if he had come." Many of us, who had just been speaking of him in whispers, now boldly blasphemed his name out aloud. In some way, we all made known to one another the important fact that we were invincible heroes. Indeed, so ferociously brave did we become that we determined to send an expedition against Maybry to administer to him a severe chastisement. I was sent in command of this expedition. My force consisted of the available men of two companies, the one commanded by Capt. Burch, the other by Capt. McPheters.[23] We were fairly well mounted, but we were in citizens' dress, and were badly armed for any other than bush fighting. At Louisburg, eight miles north of Buffalo, we encountered a small party of rebels. These we captured without firing a gun, and sent them back to Buffalo. We then moved westward some 20 miles or more, over a beautiful but rather rough country, and camped for the night within eight miles of Black Oak Point. This is the county town of Hickory County, and was then regarded as the stronghold of the redoubtable Major Maybry. Hearing of our approach, the Union men came out of their hiding and joined us.[24] The rebels fled in great consternation. We soon bore as fearful a name as Maybry had borne when he was supposed to be on his way back to attack our strong hold.

23. Capt. Claiborne McPheters, Osage County Regiment, Home Guards ("Soldiers' Records," MDH).

24. Wilson, *Wilson's History of Hickory County*, 66: "In a very short time [after Mabary organized his State Guard company] Union men became so stirred up that . . . [they] raised Company 'D' Osage Regiment Missouri Home Guards, under an order of General Nathaniel Lyon, who was then in command of the Federal troops in the state."

That night, we had a violent thunder storm accompanied by heavy rain. Fearing that the enemy might try to surprise my inexperienced men, I volunteered to act as officer of the guard myself. I did not close my eyes in sleep. The next morning was fair and we were in motion early. As a reconnoitering party, I sent forward 25 well mounted men under command of Captain Burch. With the main body, I hastened on as fast as I could. I expected that the enemy would make a stand at Black Oak Point, and that Burch would have to fall back. In this expectation, however, I was deceived. When I arrived, I found that the terrible Maybry had fled during the night, and that Burch had captured about 51 armed rebel citizens and four rebel soldiers and had them shut up in a church. I immediately proclaimed martial law, and sent out parties to seize arms, cut off stragglers, &c. while I, as a high court from whose decision there was no appeal, proceeded to try the treasonable culprits that Burch had already captured. Most of these, except the four soldiers, I released upon their taking the oath of allegiance to the United States. The utter folly of administering this oath soon became apparent. Few if any of those who took it under such circumstances ever held it binding.

Having completed the trial of my prisoners, I moved out about four miles east, on the route taken by Maybry, and went into camp for the night. My camp was protected on the north and on the west by high rail fences. On the east and on the south extended an open prairie. But few of us having picket ropes, most of our horses were turned loose to graze in a fine large pasture that lay just west of our camp. I had my men lie down to sleep in two lines about 20 feet from the fence on the outside. I informed them, however, that, in the event of an attack by the enemy, we would retire to the other side of the fence. Knowing that Maybry was only a few miles away, and knowing that he was very likely to attack my camp that night, I again declined to sleep. When all were still and the lights extinguished, I went out alone and on foot a long way in the direction of Maybry's camp. I had learned that he occupied so strong a position that, to attack him in it would be an act of madness on my part. If we fought, he would be the attacking party.

When I was some three miles from my own camp, and within that distance of the camp of the enemy, I found the whole country, which was thickly settled, all in commotion. By the clear moonlight, I could see many small parties of horsemen hurrying toward Maybry's camp. Being on foot and alone, I could see these parties while I was invisible to them. When any of them were approaching, I would conceal myself in the high grass near the road, and there, with my gun cocked and bearing up on them as they drew near, I would wait and listen to what they were saying as they passed. I soon learned that they were rebel citizens who were coming in armed to help Maybry in the attack which he did propose to make upon my camp that night. Having learned this important fact, I hurried back to my own camp. On my way back, I had to hide from several small parties that came meeting me. I could easily have shot some of them, and I would have done so, had I not feared that I would thereby disarrange my plans for something better. I wished Maybry to attack my camps under the belief that he was taking us by surprise. Then, by a counter-surprise, we would punish him severely.

Just outside of my line of guards on that side, was a high point in the road from which my whole camp was distinctly visible. I was satisfied that the enemy would reconnoiter my camp before attacking it, and suspected that the reconnoitering would be done from this very point. I therefore concealed myself near this point and waited further developments. In a few minutes, two men rode up, sure enough, and stopped within twenty feet of the muzzle of my gun. They sat so in range between me and the moonlit sky that I could easily have sent a bullet through them both; and, had I known how the affair was to turn out, I should certainly have done so. I think one of them was Maybry himself. They seemed to think that they were going to surprise us completely, and utterly destroy us as they had recently surprised and destroyed a body of Union men at a place called Cole Camp.[25]

When they had departed, I entered my camp and made known to my officers all that I had learned. I ordered them to wake the men quietly and have them retire to the other side of the fence. The hats, saddles, and blankets were to be left so arranged as to look like men still asleep there on the ground. The guards on that side were called in. The way was now open for the enemy to swoop down upon our camp and fire into our blankets; while we, sky-lighting them from our low position behind the fence, each with a good rest for his gun, should pour in our deadly volleys. I still believe my plan was a good one. When a dozen or more men at the head of the line had been awakened and instructed, however, and when they were silently climbing over the

25. Cole Camp was in Benton County in west-central Missouri. Secessionists on June 18, 1861, surprised a newly formed Home Guard regiment that was temporarily quartered in barns, killing thirty-six and wounding fifty-one. Brig. Gen. Nathaniel Lyon described it as a "massacre" (Lyon to Col. Chester Harding, Jr., June 21, 1861, *OR*, ser. 1, vol. 3, 385; and see Britton, *Civil War on the Border*, chap. 5, "Action at Cole Camp, Missouri," 1:40–50).

fence into the field, a voice from among the refugees was suddenly heard crying aloud: "They're getting their horses to leave! They're getting their horses to leave!" Instantly, the whole body of refugees, some 50 or more, who were camped together on our right, rose up and rushed with great noise into the pasture to get their horses. Aroused from their sleep and alarmed by this uproar, the balance of my men sprang up and followed the example of the refugees. There was an end to all discipline. Pandemonium seemed to have been let loose, and a disgraceful rout seemed inevitable. The officers sustained me nobly, but their voices could not be heard. Fortunately, the horses were so frightened that very few of them could be caught. Had the men been able to get their horses, they would doubtless have nearly all run away. Most of those that did get their horses, did run away. Some of these reached Buffalo, 25 miles distant in two hours and reported that I and my command were all being slaughtered and that they had come for reinforcements. At last only half a dozen men were left with me. I then grew desperate and told them that they might go, too, if they wished;—that I would remain there alone and die defending our camps. They replied that they would remain and die with me. We took our places, therefore, behind the fence, prepared to fire upon the enemy should they charge upon our camp as we expected they soon would. Even then, we could see a small party of them outlined against the sky upon the high point already mentioned.

Presently a few more men, unable to catch their horses, came back and took their places with us; then a few more, and so on until all my men but about a dozen were in their places eager to atone for their bad conduct. A very few also of the refugees remained. I was now really eager for the enemy to come. It spoils a good story for them not to come. Were I writing a novel, I would have them come my way, and would whip them like blazes. As it is, however, I can not do this. They did not come. The bright morning came, and not a drop of blood stained the grass upon which we sat to eat our early breakfast. I felt disappointed; but, maybe it is better that no one was slain there that night. Some of Maybry's men told me afterwards that the reason they gave up their intention to attack us was that the reconnoitering party that had seen our camp in the time of our greatest confusion, had reported that we were evidently aware of their intention and were prepared to receive them. They supposed that our noise was the noise of preparation. It was well, perhaps, that they did not know any better. On that evening, we reached Buffalo, having taken a few more prisoners on our march. I made my report in accordance with the facts, and my superior officer fully approved of all that I had done, and even congratulated me upon the skill with which, in so critical an emergency, I had managed my undisciplined men. And thus ended my first military expedition. It was fuller of instruction than of glory.

Soon after my return from this expedition, my wife gave birth to a son. He was a beautiful child and we called his name Ianthus. On his death a year later, I wrote the poem that bears his name.[26] From this time on till the beginning of August, we did but little more than patrol the county in every direction, arrest suspicious characters, seize rebel arms, and preserve order. During all this time, I rapidly grew in favor with my men and with the loyal people generally. In a corresponding ratio, I came to be feared and hated by the disloyal portion of the people. I now see some mistakes that I then made, but my intentions were always good. Though I had always deprecated civil war, now that it was inevitable, I entered into it with all the energy of my restless nature. I was now regarded as an able leader,—a kind of modern Francis Marrion, and I was proud of the distinction.[27] It is generally thought to be the proper thing to condemn men for ambition. For my own part, however, I have very little use for any man, and no use at all for a soldier, that has no ambition. Ambition is the essence of energy.

26. On Ianthus, see chap. 8, note 9, below.

27. Francis Marion (1732–95) was a Revolutionary War hero known as the "Swamp Fox," who harassed British troops in South Carolina with small militia forces that would strike quickly and then seem to disappear. See Hugh F. Rankin, *Francis Marion: The Swamp Fox* (New York: Crowell, 1973), and Paul David Nelson, "Marion, Francis," in *American National Biography*, www.anb.org (hereafter *ANB*).

2. The Battle of Wilson's Creek and the First Spy Mission

August to September 1861

Early in August, I was sent with a wagon and a small escort to Springfield to obtain a supply of ammunition for our regiment. The journey thither required two days and was attended with a good deal of danger, the rebel army commanded by Gen[.] Price being then only a few miles from Springfield. We arrived in safety, however, but found great excitement and anxiety prevailing among the Federal troops and the loyal people of that place. General Lyon was in command. He was a brave and efficient officer, but he had only about 3500 men with which to face about 23000 under Gen. Price.[1] Many have argued that, under the circumstances, Gen. Lyon should

---

Source: Kelso, "Auto-Biography," chap. 10, 716–23.
1. Brig. Gen. Nathaniel Lyon's strategy was to move in three columns against the enemy, two from St. Louis and one coming from Fort Leavenworth, Kansas. One force would take the capital, Jefferson City, in the center of the state. Another would move to Rolla and then to Springfield and the southwest corner. The three would unite at Springfield. Two wings of Lyon's forces (two thousand troops) left St. Louis on June 13; they arrived at Jefferson City the same day, but Gov. Claiborne Jackson and the State Guard had withdrawn. The opposing forces skirmished at Boonville on June 17, and the State Guard, commanded by former governor Sterling Price (1809–67), again withdrew. In early July, State Guard forces were gathering at Cowskin Prairie in the southwest corner of the state. They would be joined by Confederate troops from Arkansas led by Brig. Gen. Ben McCulloch (1811–62). Lyon's command reached Springfield on July 13. By late July he was estimating that the enemy had 30,000 troops (they had about 13,500); Lyon had 5,800 (*OR*, ser. 1, vol. 3, 9–52; Phillips, *Damned Yankee*, 215–47; William Garrett Piston, " 'Springfield Is a Vast Hospital': The Dead and Wounded at the Battle of Wilson's Creek," *MHR* 93 [July 1999]: 345–66; Piston and Hatcher, *Wilson's Creek*, 45–145; Gerteis, *Civil War in Missouri*, 32–65).

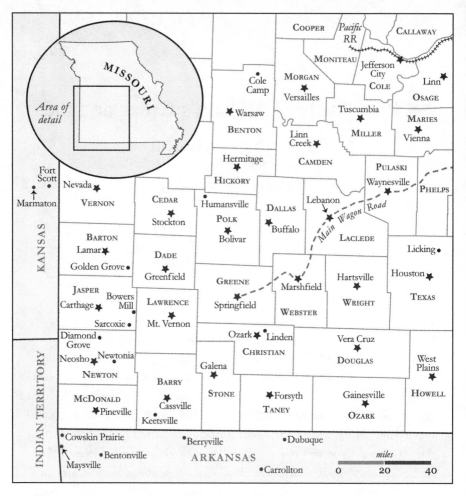

Figure 2. Southwest Missouri during the Civil War. Drawn by Rebecca Wrenn. Map source: "Southwest Missouri in 1864," parts 1 and 2, in Bruce Nichols, *Guerrilla Warfare in Civil War Missouri*, vol. 4, *September 1864–June 1865* (Jefferson, N.C.: McFarland, 2014), 12–13.

have evacuated Springfield and retreated without venturing a battle. Such a retreat, however, would have been regarded as a virtual abandonment of the cause of the Union in Southern Missouri. Tens of thousands of brave, but then wavering men, who finally became good Union soldiers, would have gone to the other side. It was better that Lyon fought as he did; better that he almost drove from the field a force seven times as numerous as his own;— better that he died like the hero he was; better almost any thing that would call forth admiration and sympathy for the defenders of the Union and for their cause, than a bloodless retreat which would have had an opposite effect.[2]

When I met Gen. Lyon, he seemed to be very nervous from over-work and anxiety. He was giving all his orders verbally. Among other orders given in my presence was one to issue as much ammunition as possible to the troops and to throw all the balance into Wilson Creek. Another was to take all the money out of the banks, pay out of it as much of it to the troops as was due them, and load the balance into wagons, and thus have it ready to be carried away at a moment's notice. From these orders I understood that he regarded his position as a desperate one.[3] He let me have more ammunition than I called for and would have no receipt for it, as it would otherwise have to be destroyed any way. He said, however, that it would not be safe for me to attempt to reach Buffalo with my ammunition wagon, that I would be almost certain to be captured; that I must remain where I was; and that he would send for my regiment. He asked me if I thought a written order to Col. Edwards would be necessary. I replied that I thought not;—that I thought a letter from me would be sufficient. He then directed me to send such a letter as soon as possible, and I did so. Col. Edwards, however, justly regarding this as an inexcusably loose way of doing business, refused to move on such information. He wrote to Gen. Lyon asking orders and desiring that I be sent on at once with the ammunition of which he was sadly in need. The orders

2. The wise choice, critics at the time and since have said, would have been for Lyon to withdraw to Rolla and fight another day. But Lyon had concluded, he said, that "to abandon the Southwest without a struggle would be a sad blow to our cause, and would greatly encourage the Rebels. We will fight and hope for the best" (quoted in Phillips, *Damned Yankee*, 251; see also Piston and Hatcher, *Wilson's Creek*, 133–34).

3. Temperatures had soared to well over one hundred degrees. Lyon's troops were exhausted from marches and from being on alert. Supplies, especially of food, were very low, as was morale. He was losing troops as the ninety-day enlistments of many had expired. His new commander, John C. Frémont, had just arrived in St. Louis on July 25 and told Lyon no reinforcements would be coming, as troops were needed in New Madrid. Other observers noted that Lyon was getting little sleep and losing weight. See Phillips, *Damned Yankee*, 245, and Piston and Hatcher, *Wilson's Creek*, 132, 145.

were sent, and I was hurried on with the ammunition.[4] The delay, however, prevented our being present on the day of battle to aid the heroic but ill-fated Lyon.

As we approached Springfield three days later, we met crowds of fugitives fleeing before the victorious rebel army. The desperate battle of Wilson Creek had been fought; Lyon had fallen while leading one of the most gallant charges ever recorded in history; and the remnant of his little Spartan band were in full retreat toward Rolla. Some time after the battle, Mrs. J. S. Phelps found the body of Gen. Lyon entirely buried under the bodies of brave men that died fighting over him after he fell.[5] Learning from the fugitives that to advance any further would be to seek certain capture or destruction, we turned about and returned to Buffalo. Here we remained one day preparing for a retreat further northward. That was a day of trial. A few prepared to take their families with them on the retreat. Most of us, however, were compelled to leave our families to the mercy of the enemy and of the guerrilla bands that were already swarming over the country. On the next day, we began our sad retreat in a north-easterly direction. At night, we encamped on the Big Niangua near Bennet's Mill. Here, contrary to my judgment, it was decided to remain one day. I feared that inaction would demoralize our excited and undisciplined men. The result fully justified my worst fears. For some reason, I do not remember what, Col. Edwards left us and went on to Jefferson City. Lieut. Col. Hovey went on with his family to Illinois and did not return till he could do so in safety. The Captains quarreled, four of them determining to go to Rolla, the other four to Jefferson City. Having already determined to enter the regular volunteer service of the United States at the

---

4. Gen. Nathaniel Lyon, Springfield, Mo., to Col. William B. Edwards, Dallas Co. Home Guards, Aug. 9, 1861, Missouri History Museum, Civil War Collection, http://collections.mohistory.org/archive/ARC:A0286_6908: "I am surprised that orders here to you given were not sufficient to cause your command to repair to this point. I therefore direct that you repair here as heretofore directed with all possible dispatch and bring all the available force at your command with all the provisions you can bring without causing unnecessary delay. Arms and due equipments in the hands of your men are of course indispensible. . . . P.S. cause your men to wear a strip of white cloth on their hats."

5. The State Guard and Confederate forces defeated Lyon's army at the Battle of Wilson's Creek, twelve miles southwest of Springfield, on Aug. 10, 1861. The Union's Army of the West had 258 killed, including Lyon; 873 wounded; and 186 missing, for a total of 1,317 casualties. The Confederate and State Guard had 277 killed, 945 wounded, and none reported missing, for a total of 1,222. It was the second major battle, and second Union defeat, of the Civil War, having followed the Battle of First Bull Run on July 21. Lyon, the first Union general to die in battle, was hailed as a martyr in the northern press. See OR, ser. 1, vol. 3, 53–130. For the fullest account of the battle, see Piston and Hatcher, *Wilson's Creek*; on Mrs. Phelps and Lyon's body, see Phillips, *Damned Yankee*, 258–61.

first chance, I very easily became disgusted and unwisely resigned. The Captains being now at full liberty, and being unable to agree, each took his own course.

On the next day, our regiment divided, never again to be reunited. I accompanied the division that retreated in the direction of Jefferson City. I do not now remember the number of days we were upon the route. Nothing of special interest occurred during that time. When we arrived at the City, we were quartered, together with great numbers of other Home Guards in the buildings at the Fair Grounds. Here every thing was in confusion.[6] The men were all grumbling, the officers nearly all intriguing. The time for which the Home Guards had enlisted was about out, or rather, it was very indefinite. It was very uncertain, too, whether we should ever receive any pay for our services, while in that organization. Under these circumstances, the men generally wished to quit this non-descript service and enter the regular volunteer service of the United States. Most of those who held offices in the Home Guard organization, wished to retain these same offices after entering the volunteer service. These, therefore, very naturally wished the volunteering to be done by companies, the present organization of each company to remain unchanged. Another set of office seekers, who would be cut off by this plan, contended for a reorganization of the companies, upon entering the volunteer service, letting the present officers stand their chance for election the same as any other candidates. The wrangling was very warm and the intriguing very active, many of these ambitious patriots declaring that the Union might go to h—l before they would enter the service without a certainty of an office.

I was offered a Majorate in one of the new regiments about to be formed. Declining this offer—very unwisely, no doubt—I declared that I would show to the world that my patriotism was entirely above selfish personal motives;—that I would volunteer as a private. I immediately made

6. Brig. Gen. Ulysses S. Grant to Capt. Speed Butler, Jefferson City, Mo., Aug. 22, 1861, John Y. Simon, ed., *The Papers of Ulysses S. Grant*, vol. 2, *April–September 1861* (Carbondale, Ill.: Southern Illinois University Press, 1969), 128: "During yesterday I visited the camps of the different commands about this city and selected locations for troops yet to arrive. I find great deficiency in everything for the comfort and efficiency of the army. Most of the troops are without clothing, camp and garrison equipage. Ammunition is down to about ten rounds of cartridges and for the artillery none is left. . . . The Post Quartermaster and Commissary have not been here since my arrival . . . [and] are apparently in a bad condition. There are no rations for issue; the mules, sent some time since, are being guarded in a lot, no effort being made to get them into teams; and a general looseness prevailing."

my words good, having myself sworn in by an officer recruiting for Mulligan's Irish Brigade.[7] My old friend, John McConnell, and a few others followed my example.[8] In the evening, there was a pretty general call by the men for me to make them a speech. I complied, describing the circumstances we were in, condemning the conduct of the officers and office seekers, and advising them all to volunteer independently as I had. My speech was loudly applauded, and great enthusiasm prevailed. Just as my Demosthenian eloquence was having its finest effect, however, Major Hall, the Officer of the Day, came up and declared that I was inciting the men to mutiny.[9] My stream of eloquence was instantly interrupted, and I quickly found myself marching out of the Fair Grounds in front of several bayonets. The guards, however, who thus escorted me out, apologized for what they were doing, declaring that they held me in much higher esteem than they held Major Hall whose orders they were compelled very reluctantly to obey. I told them that I did not blame them,—that they were simply doing their duty. Many of the men declared that they would follow me. The gate closed, however, behind me, and the guards were ordered not to let any others out. Several did climb over the wall in another place, however, and go with me to Mulligan's camps which were on the heights south of the city.

At first, we were scattered among various messes of Mulligan's men. To us, this arrangement was very unsatisfactory. In a few days, we were supplied with tents and placed in a camp to ourselves, I being put in command. Here we had a good enough time, having nothing to do but drill and guard our own camp. I soon became popular with the men, and, when we became sufficiently numerous to be entitled to a Lieutenant, I was unanimously elected to that office. I never received my commission, however. Why I did not, I never knew. Immediately after my election, Mulligan was sent with his brigade to Lexington where he was soon after captured,[10] and I with my recruits was sent to Saint Louis under the command of a villainous looking Captain who refused to recognize me as an officer or to answer any questions in regard to

7. Col. James A. Mulligan commanded the 23rd Illinois, then at Jefferson City, "a regiment raised in Chicago and locally known as the Irish Brigade" (Gerteis, *Civil War in Missouri*, 79).
8. Pvt. John N. McConnell, Cos. F and H, 24th Regt., Infantry Volunteers. He was probably also the John W. McConnell listed as 1st sergeant in Co. C, Dallas County Home Guards, with service preceding his enlistment in the 24th ("Soldiers' Records," MDH; NPS Soldiers' Database).
9. Maj. John K. Hall, Osage County Regt., Missouri Home Guard ("Soldiers' Records," MDH). Demosthenes (384–322 BCE) was a prominent Greek orator and statesman.
10. Mulligan was forced to surrender to a much larger Confederate force after the siege of Lexington, Mo. (Sept. 13–20, 1861). See *OR*, ser. 1, vol. 3, 171–93. For a concise account, see Gerteis, *Civil War in Missouri*, 108–9.

the disposition that was to be made of us. Not liking this phase of our affairs, McConnell and I obtained permission to join the 24th Mo. Infantry, which was largely made up of our friends.[11] I now very much doubt if the man who took us to St. Louis had any authority to do so. I think he simply stole that many recruits for his own benefit. What became of most of the balance of them, I do not know. Soon after I left Jefferson City, Major Hall, who had put me out of the Fair Grounds,[12] was tried for some grave offense, and was degraded by having his straps taken off in presence of the men. So my revenge came, but not, as I had intended it should, by my own hand.

While we were lying at Jefferson City, I often took long rambles alone among the beautiful hills and forests which surround that pleasant city.[13] Pawpaws were ripe, and were very abundant. Of these, I usually carried a good supply for my men. On one of these rambles, I came upon an orchard of over a hundred acres of very large fruit trees all bending under their loads of fine fruit. I knew that the proprietor was a wealthy secessionist who was selling several wagon loads of fruit every day, at enormous prices, to our soldiers. My long walk had made me hungry, and I wanted to taste a few specimens of this fine fruit. I passed up through the orchard, therefore, to the house and asked the proprietor for a few peaches, pears, &c. to eat. He treated me in a surly manner, told me that he had no fruit ripe enough to eat, and pointed me to a little peach-tree in his yard which, he said, contained as ripe peaches as he had, and from which I might help myself. I stepped to the tree and examined the peaches. They were of a late variety and were as hard as green peaches could well be. I felt that I was insulted and I told the man so. I told him that I had come up through his orchard and knew that he had hundreds of bushels of fine ripe fruit; that, in coming so far through the orchard to ask for the fruit, I had acted the part of a gentleman; and that I did not now propose to be treated otherwise than as a gentleman. I went back, therefore, right before his eyes into the orchard, took off my shirt, made a bag of it, and filled it with fine ripe pears. Fixing my blouse in the same manner, I filled it with fine ripe peaches. Then telling the man— who was watching me through the fence—that this was the way that a *gentleman*

11. Kelso enlisted on Aug. 18, 1861, in Dallas County, Mo., and was mustered with the official organization of the regiment (also called the "Lyon Legion") on Oct. 14, 1861, at Benton Barracks, St. Louis ("Soldiers' Records," MDH).

12. Benton Barracks was located in what became Fairground Park, a couple miles north of downtown.

13. On Jefferson City, Mo., see Gary R. Kremer, "'We Are Living in Very Stirring Times': The Civil War in Jefferson City, Missouri," *MHR* 106 (Jan. 2012): 61–74. See also Eldon Hattervig, "Jefferson Landing: A Commercial Center of the Steamboat Era," *MHR* 74 (April 1980): 277–99.

should be treated, I wished him a good day and departed. My bags were heavy and inconvenient, but I reached camp with them at last. My men were hugely delighted with the fruit, and with my account of the manner in which I had obtained it. I felt, however, that I had not yet received full satisfaction for the affront I had received from that miserly old fruit man. I went back, therefore, next morning, taking with me six strong men each carrying a large sack. I found my old friend, the miser, in his orchard with his negroes filling his wagons for market. Setting my men at work to fill their sacks, I had a very friendly conversation with my old friend; or rather, I had a very friendly talk *to* him, he not speaking a single word during the whole time. I expatiated upon the excellence and the abundance of *our* fruit, the fine weather *we* were having in which to gather it, the good price *we* were likely to get for it, &c. &c. growing more pleasant all the time as I saw the corners of his mouth draw down. Whenever they could do so without letting their master see them, the negroes would tell me by their looks that they were immensely delighted with what I was doing.

When McConnell and I reached the 24th Mo. Infantry, which was then in training at Benton Barracks, we at first entered the company of one of my late Captains of the Dallas County Home Guards. Afterwards, we were transferred to Co. F commanded by Captain Barris.[14] In this company, I served till March of the next year, McConnell till the close of the war.

It was now September which is usually a sickly month near the Mississippi River. The water at Benton Barracks was bad, and malarial fevers, diarrhea, and cholera-morbus prevailed among the men.[15] There was a great

14. Capt. Samson P. Barris, Co. F, 24th Regt., Infantry Volunteers ("Soldiers' Records," MDH).
15. Benton Barracks was a military camp four to five miles outside of St. Louis. Chaplain Frederich F. Kiner, serving in the 14th Regt., Iowa Infantry, was impressed in the late fall/winter of 1861: "Benton Barracks is situated upon a very flat piece of land. . . . The buildings, so far as comfortable quarters for the soldiers was taken into consideration, I think were well designed. Good cook houses, with suitable furnaces for cooking were conveniently arranged in the rear of the Barracks.—As to water, nothing could have been better looked to than the water conveniences. . . . [Water was] carried into the camp by the means of pipes leading from a large reservoir situated upon an elevated part of the city. . . . The camp was well drained, consequently it never remained muddy any length of time after heavy rains and spells of wet weather. Upon the whole, I never saw any better in all my travels as a soldier" (Kiner, *One Year's Soldiering* [Lancaster, Penn.: E. H. Thomas, 1863], 11–12). The Western Sanitary Commission, however, described conditions that decimated the nearly twenty thousand troops that filled the camp by December: "The most prevalent diseases were measles, pneumonia, typhoid fever, and diarrhea. . . . The barracks being rough buildings, with many open cracks, and floors without any space beneath, were far from comfortable. . . . The consequence was that many of the measles patients were afterwards attacked with pneumonia, and died" ([Jacob Gilbert Forman], *The Western Sanitary Commission: A Sketch of Its Origin, History, and Labors for the Sick and Wounded of the Western Armies* [St. Louis: R. P. Studely, 1864], 13). Kiner's regiment shared in the suffering: "Some time in December the measles broke out among the troops, and its ravages were very fatal among us" (Kiner, *One Year's Soldiering*, 13).

deal of grumbling, all being eager to get away,—eager to win laurels upon the glorious battlefield. I did much to cheer the drooping spirits of the homesick men, and soon grew more popular with them than ever. The officers treated me with the respect due to an officer, and not as a private soldier. I was rarely put on duty, and had an unlimited pass to go whenever I pleased and wherever I pleased. Col. S. H. Boyd, the commander of our regiment, volunteered the promise that I should be made a captain just as soon as we had recruits enough to form a new company.[16] I was still called Major Kelso, and soon came to be regarded with great partiality by our Commander-in-Chief, Maj. Gen. S. R. Curtis.[17] Indeed, it became a common remark among the men that I had more influence at Head Quarters than all the officers of our regiment put together. While lying here, I usually brought in a shirt-full of fine apples to my comrades every day. Most of the apples I obtained from the orchard of a wealthy old rebel, in the neighborhood, who was wont to set two large fierce dogs upon all those who undertook, without pay and permission, to test the quality of his really fine fruits. As soon as I heard of him, I determined to give him a call. When I arrived at his orchard, he was just in the act of hissing his dogs after two young soldier boys. The boys being unarmed, had a hard time trying to escape by climbing a high fence. Seeing these boys sufficiently terrified, the old man called off his dogs and returned to the house. I then entered the orchard and went down near the house so that he should be sure to see me. When he did see me, he returned and hissed his

16. Col. Sempronius H. "Pony" Boyd, 24th Regt., Infantry Volunteers ("Soldiers' Records," MDH). Boyd (1828–94) was a lawyer, slaveholder, and staunch Unionist who served as mayor of Springfield, Mo., in 1856. He resigned his command on April 18, 1863, to serve in the 38th Congress (March 4, 1863–March 3, 1865). Kelso would challenge and defeat him for the seat in the next cycle; Boyd challenged the election, but the result was upheld. Boyd would serve another term in Congress (1869–71) and finish his political career as President Benjamin Harrison's minister resident and consul general to Siam. See *Biographical Directory of the United States Congress,* http://bioguide.congress.gov; Holcombe, *History of Greene County,* 743; and *Pictorial and Genealogical Record of Greene County, Missouri* (Chicago: Goodspeed, 1893), 215–19.

17. Maj. Gen. Samuel R. Curtis (1805–66) graduated from West Point in 1831 and served as adjutant general of Ohio and colonel of the 3rd Regt., Ohio Infantry, during the war with Mexico. He practiced law and served in Congress (1857–61). He began the war as colonel of the 2nd Regt., Iowa Volunteer Infantry, and brigadier general of Volunteers in the spring of 1861. In Dec. 1861, he was put in command of the District of Southwest Missouri. After the March 1862 victory at Pea Ridge he was promoted to major general. In Sept. 1862, he became commander of the Department of Missouri. He was unable to work well with the conservative governor H. R. Gamble, and President Abraham Lincoln, who could not remove Gamble, instead removed Curtis in May 1863. Reassigned to the Department of Kansas in early 1864, he again defeated the Confederate Army of Sterling Price in October. See *Biographical Directory of the United States Congress;* William L. Shea, "Curtis, Samuel Ryan," *ANB;* and Beckenbaugh, "The War of Politics."

dogs upon me. I sat quietly down with my back against a large apple-tree, cocked a formidable Colt's dragoon that I carried, and then began to eat an apple.[18] When the dogs drew near, I drew a bead upon the leader, then spoke to them kindly. They wagged their tails and made friends with me. The man then approached, seeming to be in quite a rage about something, and carrying a formidable club which he was using as a walking stick. "Good morning," said I kindly and cheerfully as he drew near, "won't you sit down by me and eat some of my fine apples with me? They are really delicious." "No," said he, with a look of disgust upon his face, "I don't care for any." Then, without so much as thanking me for my kind invitation, the ill-bred fellow turned and left me.

About the close of this month, Gen. Curtis called upon me to go secretly to South West Missouri and ascertain the numbers, the intentions, &c. of the rebel forces then lying at Springfield.[19] I went by rail to Rolla, which was then the terminus of the rail road.[20] From this place, Springfield is distant about 120 miles, over a rough, hilly and sparsely settled country. After leaving Rolla, I did not dare long to keep the road. I took to the forest, keeping near enough to the road to see it occasionally and thus avoid getting lost. During the first day, a cold rain fell nearly all the time. By this, and by the water from the bushes among which I made my way, I was soon wet to the skin. When night came, I sat down in the intense darkness, under a tree that afforded me some shelter, drew my single blanket over my head, ate a little "hard-tack," which was all the food I had, then placed my face between my knees and listened long to the dreary patterings of the rain-drops and the sad moaning of the winds of night.[21] I dared not kindle a fire, and I was much too chilled to sleep very much. That dreary night seemed like one of the longest I ever knew.

---

18. Colt's dragoon: a .44 caliber revolver designed by Samuel Colt and produced for the U.S. military, 1848–60. See Stephen Van Rensselaer, *American Firearms* (Watkins Glen, N.Y.: Century House, 1947), 11–13.

19. Springfield in late Sept. 1861 was occupied by about five hundred State Guard troops under the command of Col. Theodore T. Taylor (Wood, *Civil War Springfield*, 52, 57–58).

20. On Rolla, see John F. Bradbury, Jr., *Phelps County in the Civil War* (Rolla, Mo.: N.p., 1997).

21. Hardtack: "A bland and very hard cracker made of flour and water, it was roughly three inches square and perhaps half an inch thick. Hardtack, when properly dried, had a very long shelf life, so that soldiers swore that the 'B. C.' stenciled on hardtack boxes was not the contractors' initials but rather proof that the crackers had been prepared before the Christian era" (Scott Nelson and Carol Sheriff, *A People at War: Civilians and Soldiers in America's Civil War* [New York: Oxford University Press, 2007], 215).

The second day was nearly a repetition of the first, though so much rain did not fall. I spent this night, as I spent the night before, sitting with my blanket over my head and my face between my knees. I had no tree for shelter, and the rain fell in torrents. A small band of prairie wolves insisted upon keeping me company, their howlings greatly heightening the dreariness of this long weary night. Whether they were howling because of their pity for my lonely condition, or for some great sorrow of their own, they did not see fit to inform me. I did not sleep much. When morning came, they left me, intimating that they loved me well enough to eat me up. The rain ceased, the clouds dispersed, the sun shown out brightly, and I moved on. The bushes were still wet, the rain drops upon the leaves sparkling like gems in the bright morning sunshine. I soon began to grow so sleepy that I could hardly travel. I therefore sought a sunny spot in a hazel thicket and lay down therein to sleep and to dry my clothes and my blanket. I slept till late in the afternoon. Then, feeling greatly refreshed, I moved on. When night set in, I did not stop. I came out into the road, near which I had been traveling, and kept that till morning, leaving it only once to lie down while a small body of rebel horse-men passed by me. I was now in a well-settled portion of the country, in which I would be likely to be recognized by any one who might see me. I therefore again hid myself in the forest and slept. During the succeeding night, I again cautiously advanced.

Morning found me in the vicinity of Springfield. Here I made myself known to the family of one of my comrades. I was securely concealed, furnished with a good warm bed, and bountifully fed, for a couple of days. Then, having learned the strength of the rebel forces, and their probable intentions, I turned northward toward Buffalo, distant 35 miles. Traveling, as I did, without a road, through a rough country, I was nearly 24 hours making that distance. I walked all night. In the morning, I reached the house of a friend a few miles from Buffalo. Here, safely concealed, I spent the day eating and sleeping. When darkness came on, I moved on cautiously toward my own home. When I arrived, it was nearly midnight, and my family were all asleep. When aroused, my wife seemed surprised and displeased at my coming. She said that, by this imprudent act, I was greatly endangering the safety of the family. Time proved that, in this belief, she was correct. Without coming to kiss me, or calling me to her for that purpose, she told me where to find some blankets to make me comfortable, and urged me to get out into the forest as soon as I could, telling me that the house was liable to be surrounded at any moment by bands of rebel guerillas. I followed her instructions, feeling more chilled by her manner than I had felt from the cold rains of the previous nights. I lay alone in the dark forest so near the ones I loved, and thought bitterly that she could so quietly resume her slumbers with me thus so near her. Why did she not at least go with me for half an hour to my lonely bed in the forest, and hear me tell of my dangers, and of my sufferings? My love had received a great wound. It survived many such wounds in the days that were coming, but it died at last. I did not sleep at all that night.

In the morning, my wife came to meet me, and we had a long conversation, which would have been a pleasant one had it not been for the bitterness in my heart caused by the unloving reception of me the night before. When she returned to the house, she sent the children to me, and their real love did much to dissipate the gloom from my mind. During that day, I slept much, receiving, however, several visits from my wife and children. The next night, I spent alone in the forest, receiving the benefit of a hard rain. On the next day, the rain still fell in torrents. Believing that, on such a day, very few people would be out, I determined to make a detour around Buffalo and visit an important friend a few miles on the other side. With the exception of half a mile, I would have the shelter of the forest. In crossing the open space, I would run some risk, as it was near Buffalo, was occupied by several houses, and was intersected by two well-traveled public highways. I hoped that the rain would be pouring down when I reached this open space. As if the fates were all against me, however, the rain ceased just before I reached that space. At first, I could see no one on the open ground. When I reached the road, however, about the middle of this space, I saw two bodies of horsemen, one on each side of me, approaching the spot where I was. They were both still several hundreds yards distant, and did not seem to notice me. I kept right on, therefore, at a brisk walk, across the road, toward the forest on the other side. Presently, however, a third party of horsemen came from that very point on a road that lay only a few rods to my left. Why should so many parties happen along just then and there. Seeing that I could not entirely evade this party, who evidently already saw me, I stepped a few yards further from the road to a clump of small persimmon trees that were loaded with fruit. By busying myself picking fruit and eating it, I meant to appear like some innocent person that did not care who saw him. Had I continued this ruse, it probably would have been the wisest thing I could have done. The horsemen, however, had to pass down out of sight, for a few moments, in a deep gulley. While they were thus out of sight, I concluded to conceal myself under some long drooping grass and reeds that grew close by on the bank of a small stream. I soon heard the horsemen approaching, and, from their words, I learned that my sudden disappearance had greatly excited their curiosity. They left the road and came out to the persimmon trees. They trampled around over the ground, swearing that they had certainly seen a man there, and that he must have sunk at once into hell, they seeing nothing under which he could conceal himself. When they had gone, I came out of my hiding place, and, in safety, reached the shelter of the friendly forest.

Every bush that I touched let fall upon me a shower of cold raindrops. Indeed, the rain itself had again begun to fall. I was soon wet to the skin and chilled to the bone. To avoid the cold wet bushes, I finally concluded to risk following a pathway upon which I was not likely to meet anyone on such a day. I did, however, very soon meet a rebel lad who at once recognized me. I knew he would report me, and that a party would be likely to follow me. I therefore left the path, made many meanderings over rocky places to spoil my trail, and then concealed myself on a high point from which I could see the pathway that I had left. In a short time, three armed men, did, sure enough, go dashing along at a gallop in the direction I had been going. In about an hour they returned. Not supposing that any other party would be likely to come out, I returned to the pathway, and proceeded to the house of my friend. With him I made arrangements to bring letters next day to my house from various families to their friends in the army at St. Louis. Favored by the darkness, I returned home that night, passing through the out-skirts of Buffalo. I again slept in my lone forest-bed. It was now necessary for me to get away just as soon as I could.

The next day was clear, and my wife hung my blanket to dry with several of her own on a fence near the house. My blanket was covered with green burrs from the forest. While it was hanging there, some little girls, the daughters of a rebel lady living near, called, and seeing the burrs on the blanket, were very curious to know how they came there. My family would not give them the desired information. Toward evening, their mother came almost bursting with curiosity. While she was still present, quizzing my family, my friend came with the letters. He was not acquainted with my family, and, supposing that all the parties present were members thereof, he inquired for me and stated his business. With a prudence that could hardly have been expected of one so young, my little daughter, Florella, then hurried to me and made known to me what had happened. I went to the house at once determined to detain the woman till night, even if I had to employ force to do so. I detained her simply by telling one story after another just as fast as I could.

When night came on, I put out in a direction nearly opposite to the one my enemies would naturally expect me to take. They would expect me to go due northward, and, as I learned afterwards, they did send out a party of mounted men to search for me in that direction. I went to the south-east, and was soon in a rough hilly country. When morning came, I hid myself and slept during the day. During the next night, I traveled northward on a line about half-way between Buffalo and Lebanon. As before, I hid myself and slept during the day. At night, I again moved on following a road that would have lead me to Linn Creek. Early in the night, I suddenly ran into the camp of a rebel train that was carrying away the goods of J. W. McClurg, a wealthy merchant of Linn Creek, and afterwards Governor of Missouri.[22] Leaving the road, I fled precipitately into the forest. The night being cloudy, I became lost, and wandered about sometimes entangled in vines and briers, sometimes stumbling over fallen trees, and once tumbling from a perpendicular bank about eight feet high into water about four feet deep. When morning came, I had no idea toward what point I ought to travel. I had to risk making inquiries of some one. Coming upon a country house, I found the woman out milking. She proved to be the wife of a Union officer with whom I had some acquaintance. This was a fortunate meeting. She gave me a good breakfast and wisely instructed me in regard to the route I was to take. Sleeping, as usual, most of this day, I traveled the next night and reached the Osage

22. Joseph W. McClurg (1818–1900) was a merchant in Lynn Creek, Camden County, Missouri. His business with his father-in-law and brother-in-law—McClurg, Murphy, Jones, and Company— "became a major merchant-distributor of all kinds of trading goods throughout the upper Ozarks region" and by "1860 the company was carrying $100,000 in stock and $300,000 in accounts receivable." The census taker in 1860 estimated McClurg's personal property at $95,000 and recorded him as the owner of six slaves and the co-owner of two others. In 1861, he organized seventeen companies as the Osage Regt. of Missouri Volunteers in which he served as a colonel, and spent eight thousand dollars to supply the regiment. Supporting emancipation, he freed his slaves in the fall of 1863. "Twice during the war, his business fell victim to raids from pro-Southern guerrillas, who attacked and burned his storehouses at Linn Creek." McClurg served three terms in Congress, 1863–68, as a Radical Republican and was governor of Missouri, 1869–71. See William E. Parrish, "McClurg, Joseph Washington," *ANB* (quotations); Floyd C. Shoemaker, ed., *Missouri, Day by Bay* (Columbia: State Historical Society of Missouri, 1942–43), 142–43; 1860 U.S. Census, Linn Creek Township, Camden County, Missouri, family no. 35; 1860 U.S. Census, Slave Schedules, Linn Creek/Osage Townships, Camden County, Missouri; "Soldiers' Records," MDH; and Lynn Morrow, "Joseph Washington McClurg: Entrepreneur, Politician, Citizen," *MHR* 78 (Jan. 1984): 168–201.

opposite Warsaw. Not finding any boat on my side of the river, I had to risk waiting till morning and crossing on the ferry. Having reached the other side, I left the road, took to the hills and traveled all day. I was very hungry and my provisions were gone. Early in the evening, therefore, I supplied myself with a couple of ears of corn from a cornfield, a dozen potatoes from a potato field, and a dozen apples from an orchard. Taking these into a wild canyon, I kindled a fire and put them to roasting. This was the only occasion on all my secret service in which I ventured to kindle a fire. While my provisions were cooking, I fell asleep. When I waked, I ate the done portion of them, and then slept again while more was cooking. And thus I spent the night, a feeling of indescribable loneliness oppressing me.

Next day, I traveled without much effort at concealment, and, at night slept at the house of an absent rebel soldier. On the following day, I reached Jefferson City and took a train to Saint Louis. Although I had not conquered any body, I was welcomed back as a hero. Gen. Curtis was well pleased with my report, and said I should be well paid for my services. I never did receive any thing, however, for this trip or for any of my other secret service expeditions. Before I applied for this pay, Gen. Curtis died, and I could not sufficiently prove my claim. Then, from some neglect of my officers, I lost three months of my pay as a private in the 24th Reg. Mo. Infantry. This pay I am now trying to secure. That for my secret services, I have long since abandoned.[23]

23. General Curtis died on Dec. 25, 1866. Kelso's service record for the 24th Regt., Infantry Volunteers, notes that his "Date of discharge not available," although he mustered into the 14th Cavalry MSM on March 24, 1862. As an amendment to an appropriations bill, Congress approved "Arrears of pay and bounty" for Kelso on March 2, 1889 (*List of Private Claims Brought before the Senate of the United States from the Commencement of the Forty-Seventh Congress to the Close of the Fifty-First Congress* [Washington, D.C.: Government Printing Office, 1895], 2:354).

3. Big River and Scouting the Southwest Corner

August to September 1861

Soon after my return to Saint Louis, our regiment was sent, in great haste, to Big River, some 50 miles or more south, on the Iron Mountain Rail Road, to help repel an attack which was being made upon the bridge across that river by the notorious rebel leader, Jeff Thompson.[1] The moon was shining brightly, and the train that carried us almost flew. We were in open cars, and, as we instantly dashed from the bright moonlight of the open spaces into the dark shades of the forest, and from the dark shades into the bright moonlight again, the scene was wild and weird beyond description. Presently, however, danger made us slacken our speed, and we were enabled to warm ourselves by the glowing fires of half consumed farm houses and villages to which the rebels had put the torch.

When we reached Big River, the fight was over, and the bridge was already nearly consumed. Its defenders were all either killed or captured.

Source: Kelso, "Auto-Biography," chap. 11, 724–31.

1. Meriweather Jeff Thompson (1826–76), brigadier general in the Confederate Missouri State Guard, First Military District (southeast Missouri), was nicknamed the Swamp Fox after Revolutionary War hero Francis Marion, for his ability to move his forces rapidly over difficult terrain, strike quickly, and then disappear. Thompson had advanced north on Oct. 11, 1861, in hopes of disrupting federal forces, recruiting for the Confederacy, and taking supplies. A detachment of five hundred dragoons on Oct. 15 defeated the federal detachment at Blackwell, Mo., and burned the Iron Mountain Railroad bridge across the Big River. "It was a large three-span bridge," Thompson reported, "and cannot be rebuilt in months" (M. Jeff. Thompson, Report, Oct. 15, 1861, *OR*, ser. 1, vol. 3, 225, and see 201–36). See also Gerteis, *Civil War in Missouri*, 27 (on Thompson), 112–16 (the expedition and battles).

The wounded of both sides had been carried to neighboring farm houses. The rebel dead had also been removed. The Union dead still lay in the little stone pen in which they had intrenched themselves while living. Most of them had been shot in the head as they stood on their knees firing over their low wall. They had fallen backward, and I shuddered as I gazed upon their ghastly upturned faces and their glassy eyes gleaming in the moonlight. Nearly the whole party had fallen thus at their post; and of the few that did not fall, the greater portion left a puddle of blood where they stood before they surrendered. On the outside of the stone pen, were great numbers of blood puddles, not yet cold, which had been drawn from the veins of brave rebels who had fallen there. The combatants had been only a few rods apart, and the slaughter had been fearful. Being more exposed, the rebels had suffered more severely. By vastly superior numbers, they had gained a very dear victory.

Here we lay till morning, trying to learn what had become of the rebels, and hoping that they would give us battle. I was one of those sent out to reconnoiter the neighborhood. I followed the trail of the enemy some distance, and satisfied myself that they had fled. Leaving the road on my return, and cautiously making my way through the forest, I discovered a rebel who seems to have been left to watch our movements. From his position he could see our regiment, and he was so absorbed in his watching, that he did not notice my approach from the opposite direction. Stepping up to him as noiselessly as a ghost, I clapped the muzzle of my gun to his back and told him to drop his gun quick or I'd drop him into hell. He dropped his gun, and came very near going to hell from sudden fright. Taking up his gun, I conducted him in and gave him up to our commander who seemed pleased with my little exploit. Morning was now dawning.

Boarding a train on the other side of the river, we proceeded some distance further south. Here we were divided into three parties and placed to guard three bridges which were not over a mile apart. The equinoctial storms were now past, that delightful period called Indian Summer had come, and the leaves of the forest had put on a thousand gorgeous dyes. At such a time and in such a place, it was a real delight to be permitted to spend the days, as McConnell and I did spend them, scouting about the neighborhood in search of apples, rebels, paw-paws and other such things. I do not now remember how many days we remained here. The enemy gave us only one call. That was at night and they did us no harm. We were in rifle pits, and their bullets simply whistled over our heads, making us flatten ourselves a little more than necessary. The enemy, too, being invisible in the dark forest, were not liable much to suffer from our random shots. Presently the firing ceased. We waited an hour or more to see if it would be renewed. Hearing nothing, I crept silently around and came up in the darkness behind the position which had been held by the enemy. As I was creeping into this position, I could hear my own heart thumping. I was expecting every moment to feel the bodies or hear the whisperings of enemies. All was still as the grave. The enemy were evidently gone. Creeping on a little further, however, I did perceive a man's head protruded a little into a spot of moonshine. My heart thumped louder than ever, and drops of cold sweat began to roll off my body. For a moment I did not move a muscle. Then I crept a little closer, intending to shoot this man, and trust to the darkness to escape from his comrades, if they were still there. But why did the man keep his head so perfectly still? Why did he keep it so flat upon the earth and in the moonlight? Could he have fallen asleep? I would soon know. I crept closer. He did not stir. His face was flat upon the ground. He *was* asleep. I touched him. I turned him over. He was covered with blood. He would never wake again. My heart ceased its thumpings. My cold sweat ceased to flow.

Soon after this affair, we moved still further south to Iron Mountain. Here, for two or three days, McConnell and I, as usual, were permitted to scout about the country. We made one trip to the top of the celebrated Pilot Knob.[2] This is a conically shaped mountain, about 500 feet high, composed of nearly pure iron. The view from its summit was the finest I had then ever beheld. After our usual day's ramble, McConnell and I, on a certain occasion, were called upon to go secretly to a place, Farmington I think it was called, and learn what the rebels at that place were doing. We started about sun-set, and reached the point of our destination, nearly forty miles distant, and did our reconnoitering before morning. We kept the main road all the way, leaving it only for a few moments at a time when we were obliged to do so to avoid interrupting certain bodies of rebel cavalry that came meeting us. Until we had performed our mission, we were peaceably inclined, and did not wish to interrupt any body. Had we felt ourselves at liberty to do so, we would

2. Pilot Knob, the site of the southern terminus of the Iron Mountain Railroad, was the place of an important battle on Sept. 27, 1864 (Gerteis, *Civil War in Missouri*, 182–88), part of Confederate Maj. Gen. Sterling Price's fall 1864 expedition into Missouri (see *OR*, ser. 1, vol. 41, 303–729).

have bush-whacked some of these parties. Having performed our mission, we started back, keeping the road till it became day. Then we left the road and struck as straight a course as we could through the mountains, determined to give battle to any party we might meet of the enemy if their numbers were less than double our own. We saw only one man, however, and he fled at our approach. When within about four miles of our own camp, we came upon a miserable looking little cottage in the forest. The wooden chimney was burning on the outside. We knocked at the door and it was opened by one of the most beautiful girls I ever beheld. She was about seventeen years of age, and wore a dress faded and worn, but neat and clean. We told her of the fire, and helped her put it out. I found her quite intelligent and witty. On departing, I told her that I proposed some day to come back and make her my wife. She said: "All right." McConnell said the same to her sister, who was scarcely less beautiful, and received the same reply. Indeed, McConnell was now so nearly given out, that he came very near remaining there. We reached our camps, at last, however, about sun-set, having walked nearly 80 miles over a rough country in 24 hours. Of course, we were nearly exhausted. While we were making this trip, the desperate little battle of Frederickton, in which many of our friends were engaged, was being fought, and we were losing our share of the glory of that battle.[3]

Having rested and slept one night and one day, I was called upon by Col. Boyd to go out in disguise and pass along the entire southern border of Missouri to the South West corner, and see if it would be possible for his regiment alone to march through on that line.[4] Having disguised myself as well as I could, I started early in the evening and walked all night. McConnell wished very much to go with me, but I would not permit him to do so. It was no use to risk two lives when one would do just as well. Being weary and hungry when morning came, I stopped at a little log house near the road and asked for breakfast, truthfully telling the people that I had no money with

3. Thompson's force of about 2,000 men moved south; engaged and was defeated by a combined federal force of 4,500 at Fredericktown, Mo., on Oct. 21; and then retreated further south (*OR*, ser. 1, vol. 3, 225–30; Gerteis, *Civil War in Missouri*, 113–16).

4. After his victory over Union forces at the Battle of Lexington, Mo. (Sept. 18–20, 1861), General Price withdrew to the southwest corner of the state, amassing forces, as Governor Jackson's rump legislature, meeting at Neosho (seventy miles southwest of Springfield), passed a secession bill (Oct. 28). Forces with Confederate Brig. Gen. Ben McCulloch, who had also been stationed in Springfield, had pulled back to northwest Arkansas. About 1,000–1,200 Confederate troops were in Springfield by Oct. 25 (Holcombe, *History of Greene County*, 369–72; Gerteis, *Civil War in Missouri*, 109–18; Wood, *Civil War Springfield*, 55–78).

which to pay for it. Being told that I could have breakfast, I sat down to rest while it was being prepared. I felt very ill at ease. Besides the man of the house, there were some half dozen other men present. They seemed to be a sober honest set, fairly well dressed for country people, and all were armed. They evidently regarded me with suspicion, but, instead of questioning me, as I expected they would, they preserved an ominous silence, occasionally conferring together in tones too low for me to hear. The lady of the house, sharper than any of the men, seemed to read me at once. The side pockets of my coat were so full of "hard tack" that the tops of the pockets stood open, thus disclosing the ends of the "hard tacks," as the soldier biscuits were called. Seeing the kind of food I was carrying, the woman took her husband outside to communicate to him her suspicions. When he returned, his eyes fell at once on my pockets. I now felt that I had been very imprudent in carrying such provisions thus exposed. My breakfast was now ready, but my appetite was gone. I hastily bolted a few mouthfuls and started, not feeling at all sure that I would be permitted to go. By a few questions that I asked, however, I had made the impression that I was a southern man, and as I was going in the right direction, no effort was made to stop me. Had I been going in the opposite direction, I would undoubtedly have been stopped.

Strangely enough, I feared the woman in this case more than I did the men. I feared that, after my departure, she would communicate to them her suspicions, and induce them to pursue me. So soon as I was out of sight of the house, therefore, I left the road and struck into the thick bushes with which the mountainsides were covered. Presently, I struck an obscure road that led in the direction I wished to go. I took this road, having carefully concealed my revolvers and thrown away my "hard tack." At the first house I came to, I found a large and active looking young man making inquiries about the road. He was going my road for some fifteen miles. We therefore walked on together. He was very reticent and non-committal. His company was a burden to me. I concluded to break the ice at once by letting him know that I was a southern man and that I was neither afraid nor ashamed to own my principles. Without exhibiting in his countenance the least expression of surprise or pleasure, he gave me a strange look that I did not like, and simply replied: "That is my ticket." Determined, if possible, to remove the suspicion with which he evidently still regarded me, I began to pour out a tirade of abuse upon the abolition Yankee government, the "lop-eared

Dutch" &c.[5] Seeing him occasionally glancing at me still with a blood thirsty look in his keen black eyes, I felt very ill at ease, and rapidly grew more bitter in my denunciation of the Union and of all its friends. We were now at a distance from any habitation, in the midst of a dense forest. All at once, with remarkable dexterity, he whipped out his revolver, and held it, cocked, uncomfortably close to my head, saying: "I'll let you know that I am a Union man. Now what have you got to say?" "I have to say," replied I, "That I have never injured any Union man, and I never expect to; I simply claim the right to express my honest sentiments in regard to these matters." "Well," said he, "you might express your honest sentiments without so much uncalled for abuse, and without telling so many _____ lies." Knowing that any attempt to draw my revolver would be instant death, I simply looked him steadily in the eye and said nothing. He hesitated a moment, almost resolved to shoot, then letting his revolver fall to his side, but still holding it in his hand, he turned and started on. I did the same. He now did all the talking. I said nothing. I thought it would be folly to try now to convince him of my true character. All I wanted was to get rid of him. Presently we came to a place at which our road forked. Seeing that he was taking the left hand fork, I silently took the other. Thus ended a very disagreeable adventure.

By noon, I found myself in the midst of by far the finest pine forest I had then ever seen. The trees were very high and straight, and they stood very close together. The lowest limbs were from 50 to 80 feet from the ground. The tops of the trees were so dense and so close together that they almost entirely shut out the rays of the sun. A kind of twilight gloom prevailed. The smooth trunks of the trees looked like columns supporting the roof of a vast cathedral. The ground was entirely free from under-brush, and was beautifully carpeted with the clean leaves or needles of the pine. Having now walked for about twenty hours, I was very weary and sleepy. I left the road, therefore, and finding a sunny spot in a secluded part of this grand forest, I rolled myself in my blanket and went to sleep, holding my revolver in my hand. After some hours of sound sleep, I dreamed that I was standing on the corner of the public square of Springfield and Saint Louis Street, watching our army coming in, and listening to the cheerings of the men. Becoming half awakened and partially aware of my surroundings, my

---

5. "Lop-eared Dutch" was a common slur against German immigrants. Most Germans supported the Union.

dream changed and I thought the noise I heard was the cries of a party of rebels who had found me asleep in the forest. I sprang up, presented my revolver, and then, becoming fully awake, knew that the noise which had disturbed me was simply the howlings of the autumn winds in the tops of the pines. The former part of this dream was afterwards literally fulfilled. I did actually stand on that very corner, and did see our victorious troops marching in, and did hear their exultant cheerings.[6]

It was now nearly sunset. I started on, and though I was very hungry, I walked all night. In the morning, a heavy frost was upon the ground, and ice covered the ponds. I had now to pass up the valley of a little river—Current River, I think it was—and had to cross it many times by wading. While I was sitting down putting on my shoes after my tenth wading, I was overtaken by a good looking Confederate officer who was riding a magnificent charger. I asked him if he could tell me where I could get something to eat. He said he could. He said, if I would jump upon his horse behind him, he would take me to the house of an uncle of his who lived not far away and who would entertain me in a hospitable manner. I did as he directed, and we were soon at the house of his uncle, where we were entertained in true southern style. While on the way, I had told my benefactor my plausible little story, and had learned from him that he was engaged recruiting for the Confederate service. I also learned that he intended, after resting a few days with his uncle, to go on one or two days journey in the direction I was going. Having gained his confidence, and knowing that his presence would shield me from suspicion so long as I was with him, I determined to wait for him and go in his company. I really liked him, and, when looking into his frank open countenance, I felt very sorry that I had to appear before him under a false character. He was one of nature's true noblemen.

Our host was a genial, well-made, and well-preserved man of about 55 years. He was a farmer in good circumstances. He was a remarkably fine

6. A cavalry force of 300, led by Maj. Charles Zagonyi, commander of John C. Frémont's Body Guard, routed the 1,200 Confederates at Springfield on Oct. 25, 1861. The Union Army, led by Frémont, reoccupied Springfield on Oct. 27. Maj. William Dorsheimer, a Frémont aide-de-camp, described the scene: "As we approached, Colonel Marshall dressed the ranks, the colors were flung out, the music struck up, and the cadets marched into Springfield in as good order as if they had just left camp. It was a gala-day in Springfield. The Stars and Stripes were flying from windows and house-tops, and ladies and children, with little flags in their hands, stood on the door-steps to welcome us" (Dorsheimer, "Frémont's Hundred Days in Missouri, Part III," *Atlantic Monthly*, March 1862, 372–85, 375 [quotation]). See also *OR*, ser. 1, vol. 3, 249–53; Dorsheimer, "Frémont's Hundred Days in Missouri, Part II," *Atlantic Monthly*, Feb. 1862, 247–59; Holcombe, *History of Greene County*, 372–87; Wood, *Civil War Springfield*, 55–77; and Gerteis, *Civil War in Missouri*, 117–19.

shot, too, and kept our table well supplied with fat wild turkeys, all of which he shot in the head. His wife was a fine motherly woman and a first-class cook. She told me that she had five good manly sons in the southern army, and that she was now preparing her baby boy, a fine lad of sixteen, to go to his brothers. Thinking that he was too young, the other boys had left him to comfort their mother, but he said he could not bear to stay at home any longer, and must go to their "boys," as he called his big brothers. This good mother said that, dear as her noble sons were to her, she would cheerfully give them all up to the cause of the South, if that cause needed them. With such mothers, it is no wonder that the men of the south fought so valiantly.

Leaving these good people, after a couple of days, we went on to my friend's first recruiting station which was distant about 15 miles. The people met here by appointment, and all seemed glad to see my friend. He introduced me, and let them know that I was a good southern man, well posted, and a good talker. Then I must make them a speech: They would hear no excuse. I complied, though I knew I was running great risk in doing so. My name was simply John Russell, but what if some one in the crowd should recognize me as John Russell Kelso? I showed them how fully the Bible approved and authorized the practice of slavery, and how utterly the North, by opposing this divine institution, were defying God and trampling the Bible under their feet.[7] In all this, I spoke nothing but the truth. I also showed them that the Constitution of the United States guaranteed to us the right to hold slaves, and that the North, by nullifying this constitutional guarantee, had herself broken the bond that held the several states in the Union,—had thus released us from all moral and political allegiance to that Union, and by making war upon us, had rendered it our duty to defend ourselves with all the means which God had placed in our power. What I said about the Constitution, was mostly true. It was a pro-slavery document unworthy, in that regard, of

7. Proslavery Christians frequently referred to the following scriptural passages: Gen. 9:25–27 (Ham's descendants [through his son Canaan] are cursed to be servants); Gen. 17:12 (God sanctions Abraham's slaveholding); Deut. 20:10–11 (God sanctions Israel enslaving its enemies); 1 Cor. 7:12 (Christian slaves should not mind their enslavement); Rom. 13:1, 7 (Paul teaches Christians to honor the powers that be, even harsh Roman slaveholders); Col. 3:22, 4:1 (Paul offers guidelines for the master-slave relationship, rather than denouncing it); and 1 Tim. 6:102 (Christian slaves do not need to be emancipated). See Noll, *Civil War as a Theological Crisis*, 34–35. See also Daly, *When Slavery Was Called Freedom*.

the respect of mankind.[8] My speech was well-received, and several volunteered into the service of the Confederate States.

On the next day, we visited another recruiting station a dozen or more miles further on. Here I repeated my little rebel speech to an enthusiastic audience of secessionists. As before, several enlistments were made. When I ceased speaking, many gathered around me to take me by the hand. Among these was a fine looking elderly man who exclaimed: "I always knew that we were right. I always knew that our cause was a just one. But I never before heard the facts so connected and the case made so plain. How strange it is that, with all these facts before them, any intelligent person can be in favor of the Union!" He then invited me to his house, saying that he wished his wife to hear me talk. I accepted his invitation and was entertained with that magnificent hospitality so prevalent in the south. I found the wife a highly educated and very intelligent lady. Free from the prevailing prejudices of the South, she held far more nearly correct views of the situation than were held by her husband and her neighbors. She held that secession was a great mistake, and her husband and her friends had not been able to convince her to the contrary. Hence his desire to have her hear me talk. After supper, we sat some hours before the fire eating apples, drinking cider, and talking. The wife and I skirmished over the whole secession ground, I contending for secession and she against it. Whenever I gained a point, the husband's eyes sparkled with pleasure, for he loved his cause and wished his wife to be converted to that cause. Whenever she gained a point, his eyes sparkled with equally great pleasure, for he adored his wife, and was proud of her ability as a debater. So he was bound to be highly pleased any way. Between the wife and me, it was a drawn battle. Neither made a convert of the other. She said, however, that now, since her people of the South were bound to fight, she would do her best to sustain them. The only drawback to the pleasure of that evening was the thought that I was deceiving these excellent people whose hospitality I was enjoying. I was in the battle of deception now, however, and I must fight it through on that line.

8. The U.S. Constitution prevented Congress from interfering in the international slave trade before 1808, counted slaves as three-fifths of a person, provided for the return of fugitive slaves, and promised that the federal government would help states suppress slave rebellions (Art. I, sec. 2, para. 3; Art. I, sec. 9, para. 1; Art. I, sec. 8, para. 15; Art. IV, sec. 2, para. 3; Art. IV, sec. 4; Art. V). See Paul Finkelman "Garrison's Constitution: The Covenant with Death and How It Was Made," *Prologue Magazine*, Winter 2000, www.archives.gov, and James Oakes, *Freedom National: The Destruction of Slavery in the United States, 1861–1865* (New York: Norton, 2013).

Next morning, this good woman, fearing that I might become hungry when at a distance from any house, put up some choice biscuits, a baked chicken, a cup of preserves, and some other delicacies for me to carry as lunch. Handing me these, she invoked God's blessing upon me, and parted with me as with a valued friend. I have rarely met two more charming people than she and her husband were. Leaving them, I was soon alone in a wild and sparsely settled country. I felt greatly relieved. I knew that, for the last few days, I had been playing a very dangerous game; and though there was a kind of wild and romantic fascination in the very danger I was facing, I was glad when the long nervous tention of the trial was over. I now determined to avoid, as much as possible all public places. Indeed I felt so much safer in solitude than in company that I concluded not to be seen at all while my provisions held out. I acted upon this conclusion, avoiding the roads and making my way, by course alone, through the forests. On the second evening, however, hunger and the coming on of a cold rain-storm compelled me to seek shelter. I stopped with a poor fellow who never could have owned a decent horse, much less a slave, and yet who was almost furious because, as he declared, the abolition Yankees were trying to free "*our* niggers." He seemed to fully believe that, should these abolition thieves succeed in their nefarious undertaking, the "buck niggers" would at once marry off all the white girls and thus force "*us*" to either do without wives or to put up with "she niggers." And he was a sample of a large portion of the men of the South,—of that portion who did most of the fighting. I afterwards knew men to run their grown daughters away, upon the approach of our army, to prevent those daughters from being married by the "free niggers" who accompanied that army. I am aware that this statement will appear almost incredible to those who never knew any thing of the gross ignorance and the absurd prejudices that prevailed among the poorer classes of the south. The people of these classes were not afraid of *losing* their *negro property*, for they *had* no *such property* to *lose*. The great fear that made them so willing to fight was the fear of "*nigger equality*,"—the fear that, if once freed, the "buck niggers" would successfully compete with us in courting and marrying white girls. About the only arguments ever advanced upon the subject by these classes of men were: "How would you like for a big buck nigger to step up by the side of your sister or your daughter and ask her for her company? How would you like a big buck nigger to marry your sister or daughter? &c." These arguments were always supposed to be, and generally actually were, unanswerable. Those who were well acquainted in the South at that time know that I have not over-drawn this picture. Of course these remarks do not apply to the higher classes of the South, who were generally well educated and intelligent. These classes felt themselves too far above the negroes, and too far above the "poor white trash," too, to fear equality with either of these classes.

By adapting my conversation to all the prejudices of my host, I easily won his admiration. He was a hunter acquainted with the country for a day's journey on every side. He gave me very useful directions in regard to my route, and advised me to spend the next night with a friend of his who lived about 20 miles away. I did stop with his friend whom I found to be an intelligent man and who, in his turn, gave me directions for the next day and advised me with whom to stop. And thus it was for several other days. The weather was now bad and my progress was slow. Twice I was stopped by parties of rebels and was closely questioned by their officers. These were critical moments. The least hesitation or faltering on my part would, I well knew, cost me my life. My perfect self-possession, however, and my very plausible story, from which I never varied, carried me safely through. Having at last reached the south-western part of the state, and having learned all there was to learn about the rebels, I turned my steps toward Rolla which was the nearest post occupied by Federal troops. As I drew near the Federal lines, every body grew more suspicious of me. I would have traveled entirely in secret and lived upon corn taken from the fields, had it not been for the inclemency of the weather. On the last evening that I was out, I called at several houses, but was turned away from them all. I was very weary and hungry, but I had to stagger on through the dense darkness, the cold rain and the deep mud. At last, when almost exhausted, I reached another house and asked to be taken in. The woman who answered my call said that she did not know that she could keep me over night, but that I might warm myself a little while by her fire and dry my dripping clothes. She asked me several questions, and having satisfied herself that I was a good southern man, she said that I might stay till morning,—that she would have taken me in at the start, had she not been afraid that I might be a Union man,—that she would not feed a Union man on any occasion.

My hostess proved to be the wife of a rebel Captain of whom I had often heard. Perceiving that she was a very religious woman, I suddenly became very religious, too, having a great deal to say about the Lord, what he would do for us, &c. She was greatly pleased with my godliness. At breakfast next morning, she requested me to ask the blessing. I complied, this being the last time I ever enacted that farce. I told her that I wished to make part of a circuit around Rolla and reach a certain point on the other side. She said that, if I traveled on any of the roads, I was liable to be captured by the Federal cavalry that were almost constantly scouting about the country. In order to save me from so great a misfortune, she would have her little son go with me upon a pony to guide me eight miles through the forest. Not wishing to walk these eight miles for nothing, I made an excuse to step out of sight a few minutes into the bushes, then meanly deserting my friendly little guide, I struck straight for Rolla.

When I arrived at the first picket station, about three miles from Rolla,[9] it was evening, and all the pickets but one had gone into the town to get feed for their horses and provisions for themselves. The one remaining man had imprudently left his carbine hanging upon the bow of his saddle, and had gone twenty yards away to pick wild grapes. Slipping up to his horse on the other side, I took his gun, rested it upon his saddle, drew a bead upon him, and then gave a keen Indian war whoop. He turned in a frightened manner, saw how he was situated, and turned deadly pale. "Ah ha!" said I, "I've got you at last." "Well," said he, "I reckon you have." "I do not *reckon* any thing about it," said I, "I *know* I've got you. Walk up here!["] He approached, looking mean and miserable. "Did you not know," I asked, "that, while on duty, a guard should never, not even for one moment, put his gun out of his hands?" He replied that he did know this. "Then," said I, ["]here is our gun. Take it. I am a Federal soldier. But do not forget this lesson. The next bush-whacker that comes along may be a real one, and may not let you off so easily." He took his gun and looked serenely happy.

When I arrived in Rolla, I found my regiment already there, waiting orders to move on toward Springfield with Frémont's army which was then moving in that direction. Not receiving such orders, I obtained permission, after two or three days' rest, to go alone into Dallas County and watch the course of events there, and encourage enlistments.

---

9. A picket station was a small detachment of troops sent out to watch for the approach of the enemy. On Rolla, see John F. Bradbury, Jr., " 'Good Water and Wood but the Country Is a Miserable Botch': Flatland Soldiers Confront the Ozarks," *MHR* 90 (Jan. 1996): 166–86: "The four-year-old town of about six hundred citizens sported a motley collection of seventy-five unpainted buildings scattered along the railroad tracks in what one soldier said resembled 'the effects of a recent earthquake.' The new two-story brick courthouse and county jail were the only buildings of note. Siege guns and an earthen fortification overlooked everything. The army's log headquarters building was usually awash in a sea of choking dust or churned mud" (169).

4. Federals in Retreat, Refugees in the Snow, and Vengeance in Buffalo

October 1861 to February 1862

Leaving Rolla in the morning, I struck through the forest, by course alone, and walked all day, stopping over night at an isolated Union house in the hills. Next day, I moved on in the same way. On this day, while crossing a public road in a somewhat open space, I saw a large body of cavalry approaching upon the road I was crossing. They were several hundred yards away yet, and did not seem to have seen me. I sprang, therefore, behind a large log, that lay in ten feet of the road, and hid myself. Here I underwent another experience of heart thumping and cold sweating. I soon learned that this body of men was Freeman's regiment of half-robber rebel cavalry.[1] Many of the men knew me, and would have made short work of me, had they

---

Source: Kelso, "Auto-Biography," chap. 12, 732–44.

1. Col. Thomas Roe Freeman's regiment of seven hundred men was camping about thirty miles south of Rolla on Oct. 30, 1861 (*OR*, ser. 1, vol. 3, 537, 557). Freeman (1829–93), a prewar judge from Phelps County, helped organize the first regiment of pro-southern State Guards in southeast Missouri. He served as lieutenant, captain, and then colonel of the 1st Regt., Cavalry, McBride's Division. The "notorious" Freeman was captured by federal troops in Feb. 1862 (*OR*, ser.1, vol. 8, 269), imprisoned for eight months, and then exchanged in the fall of that year. He was then commissioned by the CSA to organize a brigade (Freeman's Brigade), which operated on the Arkansas-Missouri border by mid-1863. He sent out small squads of bushwhackers to rob stagecoaches and conducted raids with larger forces. Union Army reports connect his brigade to "guerillas and horse thieves" (*OR*, ser. 1, vol. 22, part 1, 548; see also 746). "Soldiers' Records," MDH; Nichols, *Guerilla Warfare in Civil War Missouri*, 2:esp. 146–49, 242–45; James E. McGhee, *Guide to Missouri Confederate Units, 1861–1865* (Fayetteville: University of Arkansas Press, 2008), 111.

discovered me. They seemed to take a very hopeful view of their affairs. They seemed to understand that Fremont's army was to be permitted to reach Springfield unmolested; that it was to be there cut off and captured, and that the rebel army was then to go into winter quarters in Saint Louis.[2]

When this party had passed, I proceeded upon my way, stopping over night at the house of one of my comrades. Here I learned that my house had been burned soon after my departure on my former trip; that nothing had been saved from the flames; and that the rebels had threatened to burn the house of any one that gave my family shelter. Though this news did not surprise me very much, it did trouble me very greatly. I could not sleep for thinking. Besides the sufferings of my family, I deeply felt the loss of my neat little home, my library, my pictures,—many of which could never be replaced—, of my own writings, and of many other things. Hitherto, I had been making war from motives of pure patriotism alone. I now felt that, from this time on, a new, a less noble, but a no less powerful feeling would control my conduct. That feeling was an intense desire for *revenge*,—a desire which, intensified by additional wrongs, became at last with me an all-absorbing passion which nothing but blood could ever appease.

Reaching home late in the evening, I found that my family, furnished by the neighbors with a few clothes and blankets, had taken shelter in a little hovel that stood on a distant part of my farm. The cheerful fortitude with which I found my wife bearing her wrongs and her misfortunes made me very proud of her and rendered her dearer to me than ever. She now began to appear a heroine in my eyes,—my ideal, a second Mima,[3] and my love, always intense,

2. Maj. Gen. Sterling Price outlined such a plan in a letter to Gen. A. S. Johnston, commander of Confederate Forces, on Nov. 7, 1861, *OR*, ser. 1, vol. 3, 731–32: "In my last letter I informed you that I was slowly falling back towards the Arkansas line before a large force of the enemy, under the command of Major-General Frémont. . . . The withdrawal of this large force from St. Louis leaves this former point almost defenseless. . . . Is it not the day and the hour to hasten a movement on Saint Louis, the possession of which is of such vast importance to the South? . . . Your movement threatening St. Louis will of course compel the Federal commander to hasten to that point. Should his force be too large for us to risk a general engagement, we can with our mounted men follow him, harassing him, and impeding his movement by firing the prairies and attacking him from every skirt of timber and every hill until you reach St. Louis, when, having him between us, his capture will be certain."
3. In the summer of 1856, as Kelso's first marriage was disintegrating, he had fallen in love with Mima Snyder: "She was like a single bright star in my dark and stormy sky. She was the most wonderful learner of all the female pupils I ever taught. Indeed, in the most lofty flights that my own intellect was capable of taking, hers was capable of accompanying it. She was rather under medium size, remarkably well formed, and very active. Her eyes were light hazel, her hair and complexion light. Magnetically she was my exact opposite. Her fore-head was too prominent to be consistent with perfect beauty; but her

began to assume for her the form of adoration. Henceforth, she would be my guiding angel. I would try to be worthy of her,—try to make her proud of me. The thought of her would give me comfort in time of sorrow, strength in time of temptation, and courage in time of danger. Oh! why did she, afterwards, blight her own life and mine by driving from her so true a devotion!

In one or two days more, a large portion of Frémont's army began to pour through our town on their way to Springfield.[4] They made a splendid appearance. The loyal people were jubilant. They believed that their trials were over. Many, even, who had been afflicted with the secession mania, now, all at once, began to exhibit symptoms of loyalty.[5] Several Union men who had been plundered by the rebels now proceeded to collect the value of their several losses, real or imaginary, from the wealthy secessionists of the county.[6] I helped make some of these collections. We had no doubt that Fremont, with his magnificent army, would sweep all the rebel forces west of the Mississippi before him to the Gulf. What were our disappointment, chagrin, and dismay, then, when, a few days later, we learned that Fremont had been removed from the command of this army, and that the troops, in a demoralized and half mutinous condition, were in full retreat before a comparatively feeble force of the enemy, and that, too, without having fired a single gun.[7] The enemy, exasperated by the advance of this army, and emboldened by its disgraceful retreat, would now wreck their

---

modesty, her gracefulness, her sweetness of disposition, her cheerfulness, and her wonderful brilliancy of intellect combined with her sympathetic and affectionate nature, rendered her the most charming woman I ever met. In short she was my *ideal* in all its perfections. And yet, for a long time, I had thought of her only as a perfect lady, a true friend, and an excellent pupil. The thought of loving her would have shocked me as very wicked. . . . Indeed, our minds soon came to be so thoroughly *en rapport* that our thoughts and emotions were as fully known to each other as they could have been had they been expressed in words. I felt that she shared my great sorrow and that she would give her life to make me happy" (Kelso, "Auto-Biography," 697).

4. John C. Frémont's army of five divisions had left St. Louis on Sept. 27 and then moved south to Springfield slowly. The press inflated the size of his force to 20,000, 40,000 (which is what Price believed he had), or even 60,000 troops. He claimed only 6,800 were on the rolls in St. Louis. Men joined the ranks as he moved south; when he relinquished command at Springfield, his successor reported 18,000 (*OR*, ser. 1, vol. 3, 569). See Nevins, *Frémont*, 523–25, 531–33. See also Parrish, *Turbulent Partnership*, 68.

5. Probably Oct. 24. Frémont's troops were led by his bodyguard, "distinguished from ordinary Union troops by their plumed hats and dark blue uniforms" and "matching chestnut horses" (Gerteis, *Civil War in Missouri*, 118).

6. Not far from Buffalo, on his way toward Springfield with Frémont, Maj. William Dorsheimer saw a crowd, with the help of some Union soldiers, take revenge on the house of a local secessionist who had killed his Unionist neighbor when the region had been controlled by rebel forces (Dorsheimer, "Frémont's Hundred Days in Missouri, Part II," 248).

7. Abraham Lincoln's order relieving Frémont of command was delivered on Nov. 2; his replacement, Maj. Gen. David Hunter, left Springfield on Nov. 8 and withdrew troops back to Rolla and Sedalia (*OR*, ser. 1., vol. 3, 553–54, 559–61, 569; Gerteis, *Civil War in Missouri*, 119, 123; Nevins, *Frémont*, 539–42).

insatiate vengeance upon the forsaken and helpless Union people, men, women, and children, who were left behind. For me, I could scarcely believe that we were being thus so nefariously betrayed by the friends we had trusted,—by the government we had loved, and for which we had freely offered our lives and all else we possessed. And yet it was only too true.

Why the fatal mistake—the atrocious crime, rather, of removing Fremont at that time, and of recalling his army, was committed, and who was responsible for that crime will probably never be made satisfactorily known to the world. My own opinion is that the whole thing was a wicked conspiracy, concocted by ambitious men high in authority at Washington, to crush Fremont, of whose rising prestige they were jealous. These men knew that Fremont was an ambitious man and that he had his eyes upon the presidency of four years ahead. They knew, too, that, if left alone, he would be likely to sweep the rebellion west of the Mississippi out of existence. They knew, further, that the glory of such a campaign would give him a prestige which would almost insure his election and the election of his friends to places now occupied or coveted by the conspirators. They knew, finally, that their own base personal interests would be best promoted by cruelly and treacherously crushing him just as they did. To them, these base personal interests were worth far more than were all the fond hopes that were crushed in our bosoms, by their wicked actions, all our homes that were thus given up to plunder and to flames, all the hundreds of loyal lives that were thus sacrificed.[8]

8. John C. Frémont, famed explorer, "Pathfinder of the West," and Republican candidate for president in 1856, had taken command of a very difficult situation one hundred days earlier. The enemy controlled southwestern Missouri and also threatened from the east. His own troops were poorly trained, disorganized, and meagerly supplied. But Frémont, never having been in charge of more than a few hundred men, was in way over his head. He spent extravagantly and unwisely, secluded himself behind a bloated staff, seemed more concerned with the pomp of his Body Guard than with decisive action, quickly alienated the politically powerful Blair family (Congressman Frank and his brother Montgomery, in Lincoln's cabinet), and developed a grandiose plan to drive the enemy all the way to New Orleans, convincing his generals—including Kelso's admired Gen. Samuel Curtis—that Frémont was incompetent. On Aug. 30, without consulting Washington, Frémont had issued a proclamation authorizing his army to shoot anyone found with arms north of Union lines and to emancipate the slaves held by rebels. The first provision would have invited Confederates to kill prisoners of war; the second leaped far ahead of what Lincoln, anxious about keeping slaveholding border states in the Union, was yet ready to do about slavery. Political machinations did help bring down Frémont, but these had to do with power in Missouri and Washington in 1861 and not primarily with the next presidential election (Frémont was nominated by a convention of Radical Republicans in 1864 but he withdrew his name). Yet Frémont was popular with his troops and had with his emancipation proclamation become a hero to Radicals. At the news of his removal, his camp was briefly "in a semi-mutinous condition. . . . Several regiments threw down their arms and refused to serve under any other commander" ("Our Southeast Missouri Correspondent," *New York Herald*, Nov. 7, 1861). On Frémont's hundred days in Missouri, see Nevins, *Frémont*, 473–549. See also Parrish, *Turbulent Partnership*, 48–76; Rolle, *John Charles Frémont*, 190–213; Connelly, *Schofield and the Politics of Generalship*, 23–40; and Boman, *Lincoln and Citizens' Rights*, 36–62.

Be all this as it may, however, the terrible fact was staring us in the face that we were abandoned to the mercy of an infuriated and relentless foe. Union women and children, with scared faces, crowded the road sides and eagerly questioned the last stragglers of the retreating Federal army. When all were gone, a terrible and un-namable dread began to prevail. Some who had been foremost to seize rebel property, now hastened to give it back, and, with white lips, to beg pardon for what they had done. They were now willing to do any thing, however mean and cowardly it might be, to win rebel favor and rebel protection. Some even renounced their pretense to loyalty and insolently declared themselves, henceforth, on the side of the rebellion.[9] One, to whom I had always been a friend, and to whom I had done many favors, told me that he was going to seize upon my farm immediately; that it would now be confiscated, and that he meant to have the first claim upon it. He did this, as soon as I was gone, taking my chickens, my potatoes, my corn, my farming implements, &c. Most of the loyal people, however, both men and women, in this time of trial, displayed a truly noble heroism. Many of them determined to take their families and flee away for safety. I determined to remove my family. I did not dare leave them behind. I feared that, upon their defenceless heads, the enemy would wreak their vengeance against myself.

We did not expect the rebel forces to reoccupy our town for several days. I therefore instructed those who meant to leave, to make their preparations but not to move till my return. I then put out upon a good horse to meet my regiment which I had learned was marching toward our part of the country. If it came on, we would all rally to it and not leave. If it did not come on, we would leave as soon as I returned. I reached the regiment, 75 miles away, the first day. I found that the regiment had been stopped and ordered back to Rolla. Col. Boyd instructed me to have the loyal people seize

9. In Nov. 1861, a committee of citizens in southwestern Missouri sent the new commander, Maj. Gen. Henry W. Halleck, a petition complaining of rebels "laying waste to the whole country and subjecting women and children to destitution and starvation." Noting "that the recent retrograde movement of our army from Springfield has been the cause of from 3,000 to 5,000 men, women, and children leaving their homes, without money and many in a suffering condition," the citizens pleaded for fifteen thousand troops for protection (*OR*, ser. 1, vol. 8, 370–71). In a letter to Confederate Gen. Sterling Price, Halleck subsequently charged that "you subsist your troops by robbing and plundering the non-combatant Union inhabitants of the southwestern counties of this State. They say that your troops robbed them of their provisions and clothing, carrying away their shoes and bedding, and even cutting cloth from their looms, and that you have driven women and children from their homes to starve and perish in the cold" (*OR*, ser. 1, vol. 8, 515).

as many rebel teams as they needed, and to get away as soon as possible. I made most of the return journey that same night, my horse failing and falling under me about six miles from Buffalo. My return was anxiously expected. Having no team of my own, I acted upon my Colonel's instructions, and seized from a wealthy rebel officer's farm, a light wagon and a yoke of small young oxen.

Next morning, quite a train of us started, moving slowly, all the wagons but mine being heavily loaded with provisions, household goods, &c. We took a north-easterly direction on a road that was but little traveled. It was dark when we reached our camping place, about 20 miles from Buffalo. Our hindmost wagon, a large heavy one, did not come in. We waited an hour or more for its arrival, and then went in search of it. We found that, in the darkness, it had strayed off, on a wood road, into the forest. We followed it two or three miles, and then found it overturned in a gully. It belonged to a man by the name of Humphrey, a helpless, fat, old beer-tub weighing about 300 pounds. We found him sitting down in the dark by his wagon, puffing like a young steam-boat, and trying to quench his raging thirst with heavy drafts of vinegar from a jug which he had managed to fish from his wreck. Peter H. Humphrey, his son, a grown man and after-wards a good soldier, being sick, had been upon the wagon when it upset.[10] He was now almost crushed and suffocated under the load of goods that had fallen upon him. We could just hear his feeble voice. He spoke calmly, however, and gave us good instructions, the old man being of no service at all. I had only two men with me, and we had a hard time righting the wagon, so very heavy, in darkness so dense, turning it around, and getting it upon ground upon which it would stand, and reloading it. Much of the loading consisted of heavy boxes of pork. It was nearly morning when we reached camp.

At first we had thought to avoid Lebanon which might be in the hands of the rebels before we could pass through it. Finding the road we were upon impassable, however, we turned to the right and struck the main road leading

10. John Humphrey was a fifty-six-year-old farmer. His son Peter, thirty-two, had worked as a clerk in a store. Peter had been a private in the Dallas County Home Guard from its organization on June 24, 1861, until it was disbanded in August; he would join Kelso's company as a corporal on April 7, 1862, and would be promoted to sergeant a year later (1860 U.S. Census, Benton Township, Dallas County, Missouri, family no. 242; "Soldiers' Records," MDH).

from Buffalo to Lebanon.[11] We camped at a place which we could have reached the first day, had we taken this road at the start. We had lost one day of hard traveling. Next morning, soon after we started, when we were about three miles from Lebanon, we were met by a strange man on horse-back, who seemed considerably excited, and who, dashing in amongst us, advised us to turn back, stating that a rebel flag had already been hoisted over the Court House in Lebanon, and that a body of rebel cavalry were only a few miles away, advancing upon the Springfield road out into which our road would soon lead us. We regarded him with suspicion, and all declined to turn back. "Then," said he, "rush your teams and get through as quickly as possible." Having said this, he dashed away and was soon out of sight. We did rush our teams, but in vain. The man was hardly gone, when a body of rebel cavalry dashed out of the forest all around us. Unfortunately for me, I wore my uniform. We were captured so quickly that I had no time to get my musket which was in the wagon. I felt so reckless after the disgraceful retreat of our army, that I would have thrown myself away on this occasion by fighting, could I have got at any gun in time. Besides this, I knew that I would be killed any way, if these chanced to be Missourians from whom I had helped take property. They turned out to be Texas Rangers and, for enemies, behaved very well.[12] They took all the arms in the train except my fine new musket, upon which my wife and her sister were purposely sitting. When called upon for my arms I pointed to an old musket which had just been taken from another wagon, and replied that that was all the arms I had. They took a few of the best horses from the train, and a few blankets. When they were going to take some of our few blankets, my sister-in-law told them that these were all we had,—that our house had been burned, and that we suffered cold even as it was. Hearing this, they let us off. They seemed sorry that the union

11. Lebanon, Laclede County, was on the main wagon road to Springfield. It was a very small village prior to the war but a busy one due to a branch store of J. W. McClurg being located there (see chap. 2, note 22, above). Lebanon had been occupied by Home Guard/federal troops from the early summer of 1861 under Capt. Samuel Flagg, but they withdrew after the defeat at Wilson's Creek in August. About 250 men from Laclede County fought for the Confederacy, including one company organized at Lebanon that fought against Frémont's Body Guard outside Springfield (Oct. 25). See *History of Laclede, Camden, Dallas, Webster, Wright, Pulaski, Phelps and Dent Counties, Missouri* (Chicago: Goodspeed, 1889), 63–72. Lebanon was "a town so alternately plundered by both sides as early as the beginning of 1862 that it was entirely destitute of even the most common domestic goods" (Bradbury, "'Good Water and Wood,'" 171).
12. Confederate correspondence of Nov. 5, 1861 reported, "Three detachments of the Texas regiments had been near Springfield" (*OR*, ser. 1, vol. 3, 739).

families should regard them with so much fear, and advised all these people to turn about and go home. No one being willing to do this, all were permitted to go on but myself. I, being a soldier, was kept.

When my friends were all gone, I began to feel quite serious. I was not much afraid of these Texans, but I feared the Missourians who, I understood, would soon arrive. I did not let my captors know, however, that I felt at all uneasy. I joked with the men, argued with the officers, and tried to make myself agreeable generally. After being detained several hours, I was released on parole, and permitted to depart; and, from what I learned afterward, I was not gone any too soon, since the officer whose wagon and oxen I had taken reached Lebanon in pursuit of me that evening. When he learned that I had escaped him for the present, he struck the butt of his gun upon the ground and swore that he would never rest until he had shed my blood. I suppose he has never rested yet. "There is no rest for the wicked."

The train had traveled well that day, and it was some hours after dark when I reached their camp. They had been doubtful about my fate, and were greatly rejoiced to see me among them again. A heavy snowstorm was falling, but we had a good camping place, and spent the night quite comfortably. Next morning the snow was nearly a foot deep and greatly impeded our progress. During the day, the cold became intense. The country being comparatively open, the wind, which blew almost a hurricane, hurled upon us great billows of drifting snow that almost blinded and stifled us. When night was approaching, we passed two large and comfortable looking houses. At both of these, I stopped and begged shelter for our sick and for our women who had young babies. No men were at home at either house. At the first house, the woman said that she did not propose to put herself to any trouble to save "black abolition enemies from the sufferings they had brought upon themselves." I left without reply. At the other house, the woman said that all her "späh rooms had Tuhkey cahpets upon them," and that she "could not receive sick company on her Tuhkey cahpets." I asked her if she thought her "Tuhkey cahpets" were worth more to her than our wives and babes, who were perishing in that storm were to us. She said that she was not responsible for our being out in the storm. I told her that I wished the day might come when she should suffer as our loved ones were then suffering. She said that that was not a Christian wish. I replied that hell was full of such Christians as She was. I then proposed to my friends to take possession of these houses any way. They all objected, however, saying that the result of such a procedure would probably be the murdering of us all by some band of armed rebels before we could get beyond their reach. We struggled on, therefore, through the dense darkness, the drifting snows, and the fearful cold, our weary and discouraged animals sometimes almost refusing to move any further.

About midnight, we reached a high open flat sparsely covered with small post oak trees. Here we stopped. Chopping by feeling and not by sight, we felled many of these trees, and carried them together into several piles. We were working for life and we worked with a will; but our axes were few, and in the dense darkness, our progress was slow. It was two hours before our fires were burning. During these two hours, the women and children remained in the wagons, some of them, poorly clad, becoming actually frost-bitten. Even now, our fires burned badly. The wood was all green and covered with snow. On the side next the wind, great billows of snow were rolled by the wind upon the feeble flames, and, on the other side, the smoke and sparks were carried right into the faces of those who took shelter there. That was a truly fearful night. No one tried to cook anything. All went supperless to their miserable rest. I placed our few old blankets upon the snow, on the side of my fire opposite the wind, under the canopy of smoke and sparks. Here I put my family to sleep. My wife cared for our little four month old infant. I took our little two year old daughter, Iantha, in my arms, and opening my bosom, tried to warm her against my body. She would cling close to me and shiver. Her bowels were troubling her, however, and I had several times to take her out into the terrible cold. Presently all but myself fell asleep, mourning in their sad dreams.

I could not sleep. I lay there thinking;—thinking thoughts of unutterable bitterness. What had I done that my life should be hunted as it had been? What had my poor wife and babes done that they should be thus driven from home to perish in the storms of winter. Had they all been at rest in their graves, instead of lying there sighing in their sleep, my thoughts could not have been more bitter than they were. The blood in my veins seemed to grow hot. My whole nature was changing. All in it that was gentle was dying. I found myself thirsting for blood. I forgot how many of the rebels were good and kind people, faithfully giving their lives for a cause which they believed to be right. I forgot everything only that my family were there perishing in that awful night storm of winter, and that the rebels were responsible for this. In my madness,—what else shall I call my condition?—I vowed to slay twenty five rebels before I cut my hair. If it was madness to *make* such a vow, what was it to *keep* it, as I *did?*

I arose from my bed. I wandered about the camp. I wanted to see all there was to see of suffering. Most of the people were sleeping. A few women were still up at some of the fires, caring for their sick children or for those whose limbs had been frosted. These women were nearly all crying. At a distant fire, I found the saddest case of all. A young woman, scarcely more than a child herself, was confined in child-birth. Her bed was on the snow upon the windward side of the fire. Her young husband and a few women were trying to so hang up blankets about her upon sticks as to protect her from the terrible blasts and the drifting snows. I helped them a little in this. The blankets, however, were swept down every few minutes by the storm, and great billows of drifting snow came upon her. And there amid the howlings of that fearful winter storm, by the dim fitful light of that smoky log fire, her child was born, and there they both died, and there, too, on the cheerless morrow, they were laid to rest in the cold ground. A sad, sad closing of the young life of that poor little girl mother. She had fondly looked forward to the time when her infant, loved before it was born, should nestle in her bosom. When she heard its faint cry in that awful storm, she fervently prayed "God" to spare its life for her sake, and to spare her life for its sake;—to spare both for *Christ's* sake. But he did not hear her. He was not out in that storm. Is he ever out in such a storm? Is he ever present where he is really needed? Does he ever hear the cry of the poor and the perishing? Why is he always present in gorgeous churches among the rich who do not need him? Why is he never present in the hovels of the poor who do need him? Why does he always hear the prayers of well-paid, well-dressed, and well-fed priests—the Cooks, the Beechers, the Talmadges—who, in gorgeous bazaars of pride and fashion, pray for money and fame, with their lips alone?[13] Why does he never hear they [*sic*] prayers of the worthy poor, who, with their whole hearts, pray for all they have—their lives and the lives of their loved ones? Why did he not hear the fervent prayer of this poor dying woman that night? Was he busy with the fat and lazy priests of some grand church or cathedral? Why did he not hear the earnest prayers of the heroic De Long and his comrades

---

13. Joseph Cook (1838–1901), Henry Ward Beecher (1813–87), and Thomas De Witt Talmage (1832–1902) were prominent and popular Protestant preachers. See articles by Allen C. Guelzo (Cook), Clifford E. Clark (Beecher), and Donald J. Bruggink (Talmage) in *ANB*.

who so recently perished of cold and hunger on the dreary plains of Siberia?[14] Does he never venture so far north? I myself have prayed—oh! so earnestly! for him—if there were any such being—to spare some of my own children when they were dying. Why did he not hear me? Was it because I was poor? If he be, as he certainly seems to be, the god of the rich alone, then let the rich alone serve and support him. I have no use, no love, no respect for any such god.

Several months afterward, I saw that homeless, wifeless, childless young man, far away upon the tented field. Like myself, he had vowed vengeance, and was successfully seeking it. And why should he not seek vengeance? I know, that when we are calm, when no war excitement is upon us, when no wrong has been done us, it is easy to moralize. I now do this myself. I know that it is easy to say that a soldier should have no animosity against those whom he may be killing, or who may be killing him. I know that it is very easy to say that, when killing one another, brother Christians—the common followers of the "meek and lowly Jesus"—should do their mutual work on one another in a *"spirit of love;"*—to say that they should *lovingly* shoot one another with *smooth bullets* which will not tear the flesh;—to say that they should *affectionately* cleave one another's skulls with *dull sabres,* or *caressingly* cut one another's throats with *dull butcher knives* which will not feel so uncomfortably keen when they touch the skin.[15] Probably I might now do these things myself in—*talk*. At the time of which I am speaking, however, I did not have quite grace enough to do them in—*deed*. Very few men ever have so much grace.

During the balance of our journey, which lasted several more days, we suffered a good deal from cold, but never so much as we did on that dreadful night which I have just described. On this night, though I was not at the time aware of the fact, my own toes were severely frosted. Afterwards, my toes became very sore, and the nails of some of them came off. My children had

14. George W. De Long and nineteen others died in the fall of 1881 while on a scientific expedition to the Arctic. See George W. De Long, *The Voyage of the Jeannette: The Ship and Ice Journals of George W. De Long, Lieutenant-Commander of the U.S.N. and Commander of the Polar Expedition of 1879–1881,* ed. Emma (Wotton) De Long, 2 vols. (London: Kegan Paul, Trench, 1883).
15. Clergy in both the North and South urged early in the war that soldiers fight without malice or revenge in their hearts. But as "the Civil War escalated in scope and intensity, the fury of hatred and revenge against the perpetrators of death and destruction crowded out Christian charity" (McPherson, *For Cause and Comrades,* 148, and see 71–74). See also Woodworth, *While God Is Marching On,* 139–41; Stout, *Upon the Altar of the Nation;* Miller, *Both Prayed to the Same God,* 133–37; and Rable, *God's Almost Chosen Peoples,* 67.

no shoes and were thinly clad. Sometimes they had to walk up long, icy and dangerous hills bare foot, or stand in the snow till I could go back to carry them, after I had driven the team to the top. At last, crossing the Mississippi River at Saint Louis, we reached Illinois, and stopped in a large town called Collinsville, where we found Dr. Hovey and family, and several others of our old friends from Buffalo, who had left there on the first retreat. Here I remained about a week, providing fuel and other necessaries for my family. Then I returned to my regiment. Before I left, however, there was sown in my heart the germ of a great sorrow from which I have never fully recovered.

I have spoken of Dr. Hovey. He was a handsome middle-aged man, highly educated and very intelligent. He was always kind, obliging, and generous. He was a fine musician, and was one of the best conversationists I ever knew;—always cheerful, always sparkling with wit and humor. In gracefulness, in the inimitable polish of his manners, he was a very Chesterfield.[16] Men, in spite of their just jealousy of him, liked and admired him. Women, in spite of their conscientious scruples, fell madly in love with him. He possessed every desirable quality of glorious manhood except *honor*. Of this most important quality of manhood, he was woefully in want. More than one hearth-stone had he already desolated by leading the wife's heart, if not her whole person astray. In the presence of this magnificent man, this unscrupulous home-destroyer, I felt as awkward and uncouth as the rudest rustic would feel in the presence of an emperor. I felt that in contrast with him I appeared at a disadvantage in the eyes of my wife. In only two things, was I decidedly his superior. These two things were honor and courage; and, with some women, they weigh less than does a well-fitting coat, an oily tongue, or a silken moustache. My wife was now more beautiful than ever; and, as I have already said, my love for her was becoming a kind of adoration. I could see that she was pleased with the evident admiration of this wonderfully pleasing man, and grateful for his many little kind attentions. I had read in his glance that he loved her, as such men do love, and intuitively I felt that he would win her from me if he could. I was going away. My presence could no longer shield her. She would be among strangers. He would be the kindest, the most considerate, and, apparently, the most unselfish of friends. He would win her gratitude, then love, for such a man, would almost

---

16. Chesterfieldian: suave, elegant, polished—a reference to Philip Dormer Stanhope, 4th Earl of Chesterfield (1694–1773), a writer on manners and etiquette.

inevitably follow; and then,——I could not endure to think further. Was I jealous? Yes. But my jealousy was such as a loving angel might feel when he sees a woman, pure as an angel, dearer than his own life, blindly approaching a precipice of the existence of which he dared not warn her. I dared not even hint to her my fears. All I could do was to hope that she herself would discover the fatal precipice before it was too late.

When I reached Rolla, I found my regiment in camp upon a bleak naked hill, exposed to the full force of the winter winds. Considerable sickness was prevailing among the men. Several deaths were occurring almost every day.[17] Here I remained some two or three weeks, cheering the men and making myself a general favorite. Most of the time I spent in the study of the German language, of which I already had some knowledge, and in which I made fine progress.[18] Toward mid-winter, the weather moderated and the snow disappeared from the ground. Then, having been duly exchanged, I went with Burch to the north east corner of Dallas County.[19] This was a rough mountainous locality in which the few hardy inhabitants were all true to the Union. Here feeling comparatively safe, we stopped with an aged couple who had no children, and who lived in the most secluded portion of this secluded locality. Here we lived in good style, having fine hot biscuits, tea, cold milk, chicken, fresh eggs, fresh fish, game, &c. in abundance every day. Burch, being lame, remained indoors most of the time. I, to the contrary, wandered to my heart's content among the romantic hills of this wild region. Occasionally, I extended my rambles beyond my protecting mountains into

17. Taking command of the troops at Rolla on Dec. 28, General Curtis found that they had "made very little defense against the cold, and some of them on bleak hills will be ordered into timber valleys for the purpose of better providing against cold" (Gen. Samuel R. Curtis to Capt. J. C. Kelton, Rolla, Dec. 19, 1861, *OR*, ser. 1, vol. 8, 472).

18. Holcombe, *History of Greene County*, 477: "It is said that he [Kelso] always carried a book of some sort in his saddle pockets, and frequently engaged in the study of mental philosophy and the subtleties of metaphysics while lying in the brush by the roadside waiting to 'get the drop' on a 'rebel!'" Britton, *Civil War on the Border*, 2:205–6: "He [Kelso] always carried a book with him, and was always pouring over its pages when he was not occupied in attending to his regular duties. . . . After the most fatiguing scout or march, on halting his command to rest and feed, he soon stretched himself upon the ground on his blanket with his head slightly elevated against a tree or on his saddle, with his book in his hands, earnestly perusing its pages until the bugle-call sounded the march. . . . When in camp he paced back and forth in front of his tent with a book in his hand."

19. On prisoner exchanges, see James M. McPherson, *Battle Cry of Freedom: The Civil War Era* (New York: Oxford University Press, 1988), 791: "The relatively few prisoners captured in 1861 imposed no great strain on either side. . . . Field commanders sometimes paroled captives or worked out local exchanges on the spot after a skirmish." A more formal arrangement between the Union and Confederacy went into effect at the end of July 1862.

localities in which the rebel element prevailed. I learned all that was going on in the county. On one occasion, I was gone two or three days. On this occasion, I visited my old home near Buffalo. At midnight, I crept out of the darkness of the forest, took a drink from my own spring, stood upon the ashes of my dear old home, visited the little play-house of my loved little ones now so far away. As I stood there, among those scenes, in the moonlight, in the deep silence of that midnight hour, a feeling of unutterable loneliness came over me, and feelings of uttermost bitterness welled up in my bosom. I took off my hat, called the moon to witness, and repeated my vow of vengeance. Then, reentering the darkness of the forest, I was soon far away on my return to my comrade and to the safety of the hills. While at my old home, I noticed that most of my fine young fruit trees were destroyed, being barked by the sheep of the good neighbor that had so kindly taken possession of my farm, stolen my chickens, my potatoes, &c.

A few days after this, in company with Burch and two other good men, Amos Norton and Jasper Hensly, I made a night scout to Buffalo, intending to kill or capture any straggling rebels we might meet.[20] We met no such rebels, but we visited several good Union families, and had a real pleasant time. Soon after this, I left my comrades, and went into hiding all alone only a few miles from Buffalo, and in a rebel locality. Sometimes I ventured out at night to some Union house to get food. Sometimes I subsisted on raw corn taken wherever I could find it. Sometimes I suffered much from hunger and cold, but these things I did not mind. I had learned the names of several of the parties who had burned my house. Some of these men were still in the neighborhood. Most of them were men that I knew, men that I had never harmed. I now wished to see each of these men privately on *important business*. I did thus see some of them, and did transact with them some *important business,*—the most *important* of *their* lives. For reasons of my own, I will not describe these business transactions in detail. Of this period of my life, I wrote to my wife: "Suffice it to say that, for nearly three weeks, I wandered about the country, taking both friends and foes by surprise. Like an evil spirit,

20. Amos Norton, a thirty-nine-year-old farmer when the war began, was a corporal in Co. G of the Dallas County Home Guards and then would become a second lieutenant in Co. H, 14th Regt., and first lieutenant and regimental quartermaster in Co. M, 8th Regt., MSM Cavalry. Jasper Hensley, twenty-eight, also a Dallas County farmer, was a private in Co. F, 24th Regt., Infantry Volunteers. He would be listed as absent without leave and with loss of pay from Nov. 11, 1861, to May 9, 1864 ("Soldiers' Records," MDH; NPS Soldiers' Database; 1860 U.S. Census, Benton Township, Dallas County, Missouri, family no. 4).

I appeared and disappeared, leaving them wondering whence I came and whither I went. I watched the roads, sometimes by day and sometimes by night. Sometimes my 'tracks' have been seen around certain houses in the morning, and fear has spread like the wind. Report says '*Kelso* has been seen,' in many places where he never was, and many daring deeds are attributed to him that he knew nothing of till the report reached him." One at a time, I captured several armed rebels who proved not to be the men I mistook them for, and that I wanted. These I released, promising them certain death, if through their contrivance or information any attempt was made to hunt me down. Before finally leaving this field of labor, I concluded to call upon the good neighbor who claimed my farm, and who as I had learned, was now at home. I hoped that he would make some war-like demonstration that would justify me in punishing him as he deserved. In this, I was disappointed. When I surprised him by my sudden appearance, he turned deadly pale, shook like a leaf, and, for a time, was speechless. Then, recovering himself a little, he said that he knew my business, that he was sick and I would not shorten his life much. He then opened his bosom, told me to shoot, and blubbered like a whipped school boy. I had never beheld so utterly abject a wretch. Of course, I would not hurt so mean a *thing*. He lived till the close of the war and then with his eldest son, "a chip out of the old block," was hanged for theft by vigilantes. My vengeance came, but not by my own hand.

When leaving the army, Gen. Curtis requested me to bring him upon my return, as full information as possible of the doings and the intentions of the rebel forces at Springfield.[21] I now concluded to obtain this information and then return to the army. Leaving my present haunts, therefore, I bent my steps south-ward, and prowled around, secretly, for several days, in the vicinity of Springfield. Having learned all I could concerning the rebels, I turned my steps toward Rolla. During the first night, I traveled, hoping by

21. Gen. James H. McBride of the pro-southern State Guard reoccupied the city on Dec. 1, 1861, and Maj. Gen. Sterling Price, commander of the Guard, was there by Dec. 23. Price spent January recruiting for the Confederacy and asking for reinforcements (*OR*, ser. 1, vol. 8, 729–31, 736–37, 741–42, 745, 747–48, 756–57). On Feb. 7 Confederate Maj. Gen. Earl Van Dorn wrote Price about a campaign he hoped would begin in late March in which combined forces of 45,000 troops would march on St. Louis (Van Dorn to Price, Feb. 7, 1862, *OR*, ser. 1, vol. 8, 748–49, and see Van Dorn to Price, Feb. 14, 1862, *OR*, ser. 1, vol. 8, 750–52). But by Feb. 12, Price and his army had evacuated Springfield and were falling back to Arkansas in the face of Curtis's advance. See also Albert Castel, *General Sterling Price and the Civil War in the West* (Baton Rouge: Louisiana State University Press, 1968), 64–69; Robert E. Shalhope, *Sterling Price: Portrait of a Southerner* (Columbia: University of Missouri Press, 1971), 191–99; Holcombe, *History of Greene County*, 403–8; and Wood, *Civil War Springfield*, 78–81.

morning to be beyond the usual range, in that direction, of the rebel scouting parties. Becoming bewildered, however, in the darkness of a cloudy night, I made much less progress than I expected. In the morning, I hid myself in the forest, not thinking it safe to be out at all, in that locality, by daylight. A regular "norther" was blowing, however, and I could not endure the cold while lying still. I moved on, therefore, carefully avoiding the public highways. The very inclemency of the weather made me feel more secure. I did not think many scouting parties would be out on such a day. Toward noon, however, while I was crossing a large open space, I discovered a large body of rebel cavalry approaching. They saw me at the same time, and sent a large squad after me. Seeing that escape was impossible, and knowing that resistance would be worse than useless, I surrendered at discretion. I hoped that these might be, like my former captors, men from the far south who would not know me. This body, however, proved to be composed of mixed troops: some Texans, some Arkansans, and some Missourians. I was soon recognized, and my prospects for life began to grow very gloomy.

My captors went into camp in a corn-field near by. Taking down the fence and using the rails for fuel, they made a long line of fires on the edge of the field about a rod from the thick brush that grew on the outside of the fence. Here, we were quite comfortable, being protected by the brush from the fierce winds that were blowing. Having fed their horses and eaten their dinners, they organized an irregular court martial to try my case. During the hour or more that elapsed, after my capture, before the meeting of this court, I had kept the men about me in a roar of laughter by telling them some really ludicrous anecdotes. Knowing that I was talking for my life,—making them feel kindly toward me, I threw my whole soul into my stories, and never talked better. The Texans had me in charge, and seemed to bear me no ill will. Indeed, some of them tried to convince me that I was on the wrong side, and to persuade me to join them. I replied that if the United States Government sustained Fremont's emancipation proclamation, I would join them;—that I had volunteered to fight for the preservation of the Union, but that I did not propose to fight for the freeing of the negroes. The latter part of this statement was not true, but it was good policy in me to make it.

Knowing that every thing I had done would be proved against me, and knowing the good effect that perfect candor is sure to have upon brave men, I promptly admitted every thing with which I was charged. I admitted that I had "jay-hawked" some of the rebels of Dallas county; and that I had "bush-whacked" some of those who had burned my house and driven out my family.[22] I contended, however, that in all this, I had done no more than any southern man would do to Union men, if they should treat him as these men had treated me. I admitted that I had been a spy on former occasions, that I was the man who had spoken at the recruiting stations in South-East Missouri, that I was now in disguise as a spy. I reminded them, however, that some of the bravest and best men they had were spies on their side;—that only the bravest of men ever undertook this necessary service so full of danger. I told them that I knew my danger when I un[der]took this service; that I had entered upon it with my eyes open; that I knew the laws of war condemned me to die; that I expected to die; but that I should die, as I had lived, a man. I told them that my trial, though irregular, had been perfectly fair and that I had no complaints to make.

Having heard me through, they left me in the hands of four guards, and drew aside to hold a consultation among themselves. A Texas Captain, who had favored me all he could during my short trial, seemed now to be pleading my case with the other officers. At the close of their consultation, he returned to me, bringing his own blankets for me to sit upon. I asked him the result of their consultation. He evaded my question, but his face, in which I could see sorrow depicted, told me that I was doomed. He retired and did not come near me again. A general discussion of my case seemed to [be] also going on among the men. From remarks that I occasionally overheard, it seemed that the Texans were not going to have any thing more to do with the case;—that the Missourians and Arkansans claimed me of right, and that I was to be delivered into their hands to be disposed of as they saw fit. This, of course, meant death. I heard one man say that it was a "d——d pity for so brave a man to be strung up like a dog!" And am I to die by *hanging?* I asked myself

22. Both "jay-hawker" and "bush-whacker" were terms that came to prominence in the Kansas territorial warfare of the 1850s. The first term likened violent Free-Soilers "to a mythical hawk that was said to harry its prey as it killed it." The second term "initially referred to men who cheated when hunting by whacking the bushes for quail rather than waiting for them to emerge; it broadened to connote rural poverty and criminality" (Nelson and Sheriff, *People at War*, 99, 97). In Civil War Missouri, "Bushwhackers were, strictly speaking, lone gunmen who 'whacked' their foes from the 'bush.' However, the name also became a pejorative term for anyone who apparently killed people or destroyed property for sport, out of meanness, or in a personal vendetta." "Jayhawker" initially referred to violent Union partisans, "although like bushwhacker, [it] gained more universal application" (Sutherland, *Savage Conflict*, xi). Kelso may here be using "jay-hawked" to refer to the appropriation of rebel property and "bush-whacked" to surprise revenge killings by a lone gunman from the woods.

this question. In my own inner consciousness, I answered—*no!* Am I to *die* at *all?* No! I am to live to perform an important work after the close of the war.

With his strangely expressive eyes, one of my guards made me know that he was a friend to me, and that he would aid me all he could to escape. With my eyes I replied that I understood him. He looked pleased. He then glanced toward the middle of the field where preparations were being made for my execution, and then at the dense brush thicket so close on the other side. Seeing that I again understood him, he drew a little further from the fire, and placed himself more directly in my way than were any of the other guards. All was now ready. A few minutes more and it would be too late. I must go. But how was I to start? My heart seemed to cease beating. Just then, some one a little to my left called another "a d——d liar!" A blow was struck. That was for me. I felt it. The guards turned their eyes in that direction. I sprang up, I know not how, so quickly. I darted past my friend. He was just stumbling in the way of the other guards. At the second bound, I was in the thicket. I heard the four muskets roar out after me. I was not hurt. I knew that one of them would be sure to not hurt me. I was then very active. Few men were equal to me on foot. I stooped forward so that the top of my head and not my face should take the the [*sic*] thorns and the briers. I fairly dived through the thicket. I was out of sight. My pursuers would have to follow by sound. They would have to stop to listen. No foot man could overtake me. The bugles sounded, and a great uproar followed. The men were mounting to chase. But their horses were to bridle, and no mounted men could chase in so dense a thicket. I was free. I would escape.

How far I ran, I do not know; but, when I stopped, perspiration, mixed with blood from scores of scratches, was trickling freely down my body. My hat was gone and my clothes were torn to tatters. I felt like running further, but I had reached the limit of the friendly brush thicket. It would not do for me to venture into the open ground beyond. Finding as good a place as I could, I hid myself and lay there straining my ears to hear the sounds of my pursuers. I heard nothing. The darkness of night would soon bring additional safety. I felt a wild joy hard to describe. But, after the heat of my race, I soon became chilled to the bone. Besides this, a heavy snow storm came on. What should I do? By night, an inch or more had fallen. Knowing that they could easily trail me in this snow, would not my enemies be likely to send out a party on the morrow to search for me? I believed that they would, and I knew that recapture would be certain death. They would not be likely, however, to look for me so close to the scene of my recent great danger. They would look for me farther on. I would be safer here, and here I would stay till the hunt was over. They would not be likely to continue the hunt for more than one day. Setting to work in good earnest, collecting boughs, I soon had a fair shelter from the wind and the snow. I slept most of the night. Next day, I kept still, anxiously listening for any sounds that indicated danger. I heard nothing, the weary day passed, and I resumed my journey.

Avoiding all settlements as much as possible, I stumbled along in the darkness, through snow about four inches deep.[23] My course was devious, and my progress slow. When morning began to dawn, I found as good shelter as I could and stopped. I tried to sleep, but I was too cold and too hungry to do so. The hours dragged on with intolerable slowness. At last, about two o'clock, my hunger became so intense that it over-mastered my fear of recapture. I had not eaten a morsel since I ate with my captors fifty hours before. I must have food now. I struck out in the direction of the main road. This I reached in about one hour. Finding a house soon afterwards, I asked for food and was told that some would be prepared for me. I asked the distance from Lebanon, and what was going on there. I was told that the distance was only about three miles, that Gen. Curtis was there with his army, and that, from where I then was, I could see the smoke from the camp fire of the nearest picket station.[24] The gladness which this information brought can be better imagined than described. I told the good woman of the house not to go to any trouble to prepare food for me;—that I would go to the picket station and get food there. I started on and was soon seen by the pickets. They mounted their horses and came dashing down upon me, each with a revolver in his hand. As they drew near, I held up both hands and spread out my fingers to show that I was unarmed, and that I did not propose to make any resistance. I was a little afraid that they would shoot me any way. I was bare-head,—my hat having been lost in my race for life through the brush. My shoes were full of holes, and my clothes were in tatters. My new captors surveyed me with a look of mingled wonder and merriment. They all commenced talking together. "Give up your arms!" "Who are you?" "Where's your hat?" "How much did your coat cost?" "Where are you going?" "What'r you doing here?" "What'l you take for your boots?" &c.

23. On Jan. 31 General Curtis noted that the severe cold and four inches of snow made it difficult for the mules and horses to pull the wagons (*OR*, ser. 1, vol. 8, 538).

24. General Curtis sent cavalry to occupy Lebanon on Jan. 22 (twenty rebels evacuated at their advance). He intended to make Lebanon his main supply depot to support his army marching further south to Springfield and beyond. Curtis and half of his command (six thousand troops) left Rolla on Jan. 26 and were in Lebanon by Jan. 31 (*OR*, ser. 1, vol. 8, 56, 513, 526, 527). Kelso probably arrived in camp by Feb. 7.

They searched my pockets and my whole person and found nothing. They then took me to their camp which was in an old vacant farm house. Here the Sergeant asked me a good many questions, most of which I either evaded or plainly refused to answer, stating that I would answer Gen. Curtis's questions on the morrow when taken to him. I told the sergeant, however, that I was a farmer, a stone-cutter, a school-teacher, and a preacher. He said that they had no farms for me to cultivate just then, no stones for me to cut, and no children for me to teach; but they would like to have a little preaching. He said that they had some fat chickens already dressed, and that, if I would preach for them, they would prepare one of these for my supper. I replied that I would preach. I told him, however, that I was extremely hungry, and that I could preach a great deal better if I could see the chicken cooking. He ordered one of the men to put the chicken to cooking, then ordered me to mount a large table that stood in the middle of the floor and go to preaching.

As yet, I had made it impossible for them to guess to which side I belonged, and I did not intend that my sermon should aid them in guessing this. At first, I bore down pretty heavily on the Union side. This made them eye me with unfriendly looks. Then I bore down just as heavily on the rebel side. This pleased them. Finally I concluded with a comic exhortation that made them lie down on the floor and yell with laughter. This exhortation brought me into great favor with them. When my chicken was ready, I ate it nearly all, besides some good fresh sausage and a liberal amount of other food. When thoroughly stuffed, I became so sleepy that I could hardly hold my eyes open. The Sergeant said that I might sleep there before the fire, on blankets which he furnished me, that they would not tie me, but that if I made the slightest attempt to escape, they would "jog my memory by quietly putting a bullet through my head." Perfectly satisfied with these conditions, I fell asleep, and scarcely dreamed till I was awakened for breakfast in the morning.

After breakfast, the Sergeant himself took me into the town and directly to Gen. Curtis' head quarters. A council of war was being held in the general's office, and nearly all the officers of the army were present.[25] When I was

25. The officers in Curtis's Army of the Southwest on this campaign were Brig. Gen. Franz Sigel, Brig. Gen. Alexander Asboth, Col. Peter J. Osterhaus, Col. Nicholas Greusel, Col. Frederick Schaefer, Col. Jefferson C. Davis, Col. Thomas Patterson, Col. Julius White, Col. Eugene A. Carr, Col. Grenville M. Dodge, and Col. William Vandever. Asboth and Sigel had just arrived with their men on Feb. 6, bringing Curtis's troop total to 12,095 (*OR*, ser. 1, vol. 8, 204–6, 545, 553).

brought in, the general rose to meet me, took me by both hands, and treated me as if I had myself been a Major General. He then, with some very complimentary remarks, introduced me to such of the officers I had not before met.

When the meeting had adjourned, I had a long conversation with Gen. Curtis alone, in which I gave him a full account of all my doings, all my dangers, all my sufferings, and all the information I had obtained. His grand old face lighted up with pleasure and approbation. He said that upon my information he would at once prepare to act;—that he would march against Springfield just as soon as possible.[26] He said, however, that I had ventured too much;—that, while he admired such daring, he could not advise its practice. He urged me to say nothing to any other person about my having been captured and condemned to die as a spy. He said that a general knowledge of that fact, even in our own army, might greatly endanger my life. I promised silence, and, during the war, and for some time afterwards, I did keep silence. I did not tell even my wife of this matter. I did not wish to inflict upon her the additional anxiety of knowing that I was fighting as it were with a halter around my neck. A large reward was offered by the enemy for my head, and that offer was kept standing till the close to the war. Almost every body knew of that offer, and yet very few knew why it was made. Many a rebel afterwards tried to get my head for that reward; and many a one lost his own head in the attempt. Indeed, from that time on, when I was done with a rebel's head, it was usually of no use to any one else. As to my own head, it was a

26. Kelso may have told Curtis what the general reported on Feb. 9 as "Latest news from Springfield: [General Sterling] Price was still there. General [Daniel M.] Frost arrived Friday or Saturday with a few men, and his battery, with about 400 men, was expected within four days" (Curtis Report, Feb. 10, 1862, *OR*, ser. 1, vol. 8, 59). Or it may have been the information that Curtis relayed to Capt. J. C. Kelton on Feb. 10: "[Gen. Earl] Van Dorn is moving up [from Arkansas] to join Price. . . . Van Dorn has promised 30,000 or 40,000 at Springfield very soon. Expects to be there with 10,000 by the 15th. These are the hopes and expectations of the enemy" (*OR*, ser. 1, vol. 8, 551). But Curtis had other sources. "I see men every day direct from Springfield," he wrote. "Of course I interrogate scouts, deserters, and all kinds of witnesses" (Curtis to Franz Sigel, Rolla, Jan. 25, 1862, and Curtis to Kelton, Lebanon, Feb. 2, 1862, *OR*, ser. 1, vol. 8, 526, 541). The general's son and aide-de-camp, Lt. Samuel Prentis Curtis, wrote in 1866 that Lt. Col. Clark Wright, a resident of southwestern Missouri, had "established a system of scouts and spies to ascertain the movements and condition of the enemy. He reported to Curtis that he had six different lines of communication direct from Springfield. . . . There were additional means of receiving information from Springfield, through Colonel Phelps, through spies who reported directly to the commanding General, and through other sources" (Samuel Prentis Curtis, "The Army of the South-West, and the First Campaign in Arkansas: Chapter Second," *Annals of Iowa* 4 [July 1866]: 673–88, 678 [quotation]).

present to me from my mother; I liked it; it exactly suited me; I wanted to keep it; and, though it cost me a great deal of trouble to do so, I did keep it. My toes had been again frosted and were very sore. A few days of rest, however, made all right. I was again ready for duty.[27]

27. Curtis and Kelso may have had a good idea of what was happening at Springfield, but the average soldier did not. Robert Pinckney Matthews, a private in Co. D, Phelps Regt., Missouri Infantry, camped with Curtis's army at Lebanon, recalled the rumors that circulated daily: "One day there would be a report in camps that Price had 50,000 men concentrated at Springfield awaiting to give us battle. The next day, we would hear that the rebels had fortified that place on every side, that forts and rifle pits extended five miles out from the town, and to take the place we would have to assault a strong line of earthworks every few hundred yards, this whole distance. The next day we would probably hear something else" (Matthews, *Souvenir of the Holland Company Home Guards*, 36).

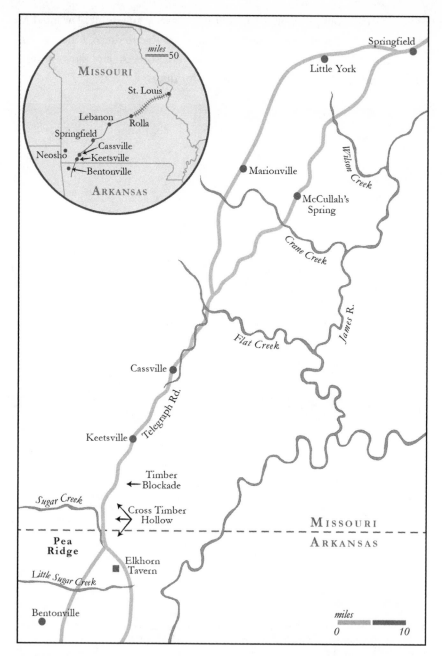

Figure 3. The March to Pea Ridge, Arkansas, February 1862. Drawn by Rebecca Wrenn. Map source: William L. Shea and Earl J. Hess, *Pea Ridge: Civil War Campaign in the West* (Chapel Hill: University of North Carolina Press, 1992), 31, map 2.1.

5. The March to Pea Ridge

February 1862

It was now sometime in February of 1862.[1] The men were ordered to parch large quantities of corn and have it ground in a large mill in the vicinity of our camp. When mixed with one third as much ground sugar, the meal of this parched corn makes a very palatable food, and contains much nutriment in a small bulk. With our haversacks filled with this mixture, we received orders to march in the direction of Springfield.[2] I do not now remember how far we marched that day, nor do I remember the name of the place in

Source: Kelso, "Auto-Biography," chap. 13, 744–51.

1. In February 1862, Maj. Gen. Henry W. Halleck understood the larger strategic problems that Union forces faced. Halleck had taken over as commander of the Department of Missouri on Nov. 19, shortly after the Frémont fiasco. (The Department of Missouri included the states of Missouri, Iowa, Minnesota, Wisconsin, Illinois, Arkansas, and the portion of Kentucky west of the Cumberland River.) "Halleck recognized that [Gen. Sterling] Price's amalgam of Confederate and state guard troops was much more than a local threat. St. Louis was the primary base of operations for projected offensives on the Mississippi, Tennessee, and Cumberland rivers. Every Federal soldier stationed in Missouri to counter the state guard and protect St. Louis was one less soldier that could be used in the upcoming river campaigns. . . . This was an intolerable situation. Price's ragtag Missouri army was paralyzing Federal operations from Kentucky to Kansas. Like Lyon and Frémont before him, Halleck realized that he must go on the offensive in Missouri and harry the rebels out of the state as quickly as possible" (Shea and Hess, *Pea Ridge*, 3).

2. Special Orders No. 75, issued for Gen. Samuel R. Curtis on Feb. 7 while the troops camped at Lebanon, ordered the preparation of six days of light rations for the upcoming forced march: "hard bread, flour, hominy, rice, desiccated potatoes, and mixed vegetables, sugar, coffee and salt. Pinole (ground parched corn and sugar) ought to be procured. . . . The rations can only be cooked of nights, and some beef should be jerked (dried over a slow fire) to carry in the haversacks, to be eaten with the pinole." Because the flour mill at Lebanon had stopped grinding due to a broken cog wheel, Curtis also reduced the ration of flour and substituted corn meal (*OR*, ser. 1, vol. 8, 548–49).

which we camped. The same is true of the next day and the next camping place. If this history be ever published, let these facts be supplied if possible. Also, let dates and all else necessary be supplied when practicable.[3] I find that, after more than twenty years, many important facts have faded from my memory.

At our second camping place, I think it was—, we were supplied with a mess of execrable unmasticatable cartilage mis-called beef. After a long and unsuccessful attempt to disintegrate a mouthful each of this vile stuff, the men spewed it out, then rose up and blasphemed aloud.[4] I therefore announced that, in thirty minutes, I would be at the slaughter ground close by to preach a funeral sermon of the ancient bovine from whose mortal remains this embodiment of toughness had been obtained. This announcement flew like the wind, and soon thousands of men and officers were congregating about the slaughter ground. When the time arrived to open the services, I, in a very solemn manner, took my station in front of a head which, from the appearance of its horns, must have belonged to an ox of immense age. Taking off my hat and casting a sad look around upon my vast audience, I said:—

> Fellow Soldiers:—We have assembled here to perform the last solemn rites to the memory of the venerable Old-buck who, at the advanced age of sixty nine years, eleven months, and seventeen days, yielded up the ghost, only a few hours ago, on this sanguinary field, beneath the folds of our glorious Star-Spangled-Banner. He was born toward the latter part of the last century, of poor but respectable parents. When a calf, he gamboled joyfully, in the sun-shine, upon the beautiful blue-grass pastures of his native hills;—the hills of Old

3. The main body of the army left Lebanon (fifty-five miles northeast of Springfield) on the morning of Feb. 10, 1862. By 5:00 p.m. they were camping at Copley, eighteen miles closer, and by the end of the day they were at Marshfield (another ten miles). See Curtis correspondence and reports, and orders issued by Acting Assistant Adjutant Gen. T. I. McKenny, *OR*, ser. 1, vol. 8, 58–59, 550–54. For a detailed narrative of the movements of both armies before the Battle of Pea Ridge (March 6–8, 1862), see also Shea and Hess, *Pea Ridge*, 27–61.

4. Curtis had reduced the soldiers' rations of flour (hard to procure) and salt pork (perhaps because of expense) but had doubled their ration of fresh beef and pork, which he said was "abundant in the country" and would be supplied through the commissary (*OR*, ser. 1, vol. 8, 548, and see 549). He was wrong about the abundance: the men foraged "'by regiment, by company, by platoon, squad and by individual—to find something to eat in the adjoining country.' What they found was not always of the most desirable quality or quantity, for the area between Springfield and Fayetteville had been picked over by the Confederates for months. The surgeon of the 18th Indiana noted that 'what beef we get it takes two men to hold up while one knocks them down.' He worried that 'it looks like starving if we do not save rations'" (Shea and Hess, *Pea Ridge*, 51).

Kentucky;—the hills of the proud state that has given us a Clay, a Wickliffe, and the most famous brand of Bourbon Whiskey.[5] At an early age, the lamented Old-buck experienced a change of *heart*—a change of *something*, any way, that tended greatly to preserve his virtue. Indeed his strict chastity—the result of this change—was a model for the imitation of all young bulls and all young men. Would that more of them would follow his noble example. So of his temperance. He never befouled his mouth, his breath, or his morals with intoxicating drinks or with tobacco. His piety, too, was never questioned. Though he was never heard praying aloud,—as men often pray to be heard of their fellows—, he was often heard to groan—to say "*um-m-m*," as the most godly men often do in the amen corner of the church. Besides this, he was never known to lie down to rest, or to rise up from rest, without bowing a few moments upon his knees. Ah! My friends, could the same be so truthfully said of you? Born, as he was, a slave and in a state where slavery prevailed, he meekly bowed his patient neck to the yoke, and never, throughout his long and useful life, questioned the divine right of his master to the proceeds of his labor. Thus, with him, the years came and went. Men, who were infants when he was born, grew old and died. Nations arose and fell. Still, in the state of his master's adoption, our beloved Missouri, he toiled on. Two or three generations of masters had passed away. He had grown feeble with great age. His eyes—these eyes which you now see looking so appealingly to heaven, had grown dim. His ears—what was left of them after various markings, had grown dull. His teeth had long since departed. He had become so emaciated that he could scarcely cast a shadow when standing in the sun-shine. He was calmly waiting for the messenger of death to come and take him to his everlasting home. Just then our beef contractor came along. Seeing this poor emaciated creature, standing thus with three feet in the grave, and being prompted by the devil, he, in cold blood and with malice aforethought, brought the said creature to the seclusion of this place, and here—foully murdered him. (Here I wept.) Murdered him that he might sell for us to eat the few pounds of cartilage that covered

5. Henry Clay (1777–1852), U.S. senator, speaker of the House, secretary of state, and presidential candidate, was one of the most significant U.S. politicians in the first half of the nineteenth century. Charles A. Wickliffe (1788–1869) was a congressman, governor of Kentucky, and postmaster general of the United States. See articles by Robert V. Remini (Clay) and M. Philip Lucas (Wickliffe) in *ANB*.

the aged bones of this ancient bovine. "Oh! What a fall was there, my countrymen?"

Turning, however, from the contemplation of these meager remains of the Sainted Old-buck, who is doubtless now a calf again, gamboling upon the green pastures that surround the gates of the New Jerusalem, let us take a brief view of the latter end of this bloody beef contractor; whose cadaverous countenance methinks I see in the audience before me. That latter end is awful to look upon. The wretched cow-killer is haunted. The gaunt form of the murdered Old-buck, stands before his affrighted eyes, and bellows, "*um-m-m-m,*" in his agonized ears. Whole regiments of gaunt soldiers, made miserable dispeptics by eating his beef, tramp to the death march before his vision and bellow "*um-m-m-m*" in his ear. He tries to scream but can only bellow, "*um-m-m-m.*" He is changed into an emaciated old ox, toothless, deaf, and blind. He chews his cud but imagines that he is trying to chew some of his own beef. What a terrible warning this ought to be.

This short sermon called forth enthusiastic applause from the audience, and we were never afterwards furnished with beef quite so bad.

On the next evening, after a hard day's march, we encamped upon a small creek some seven or eight miles east of Springfield on the Marshfield road. After a rest of about two hours, we were called out for a night skirmish two or three miles nearer Springfield. Having driven the enemies' skirmishers in, we returned, about midnight, to our camp and slept without tents.[6] Indeed, I do not remember that we spread our tents any more till we reached Pea

6. At 7:00 a.m. on Feb. 12, the army marched to Pearson's Creek (eight miles from Springfield), except for the 3rd Division, which took a different road and camped a mile closer. As they marched, at 10:30 a.m., their advance cavalry was fired on by scouts. Curtis answered with his howitzers. The front guards had sporadic fire through the afternoon. At nightfall 1,500 Confederate cavalry lined up across the road behind sharpshooters and attacked Curtis's outer picket at Pearson's Creek. Curtis's troops returned fire again, killing two and wounding several, Curtis thought, though another soldier estimated eight to ten killed and ten wounded. The Confederates then pulled back to Springfield. See *OR*, ser. 1, vol. 8, 58–59, 550–54; see also Lyman G. Bennett, "Route of the Army of the Southwest. Commanded by Major General Samuel R. Curtis . . . 1862," a volume of maps and cartographic sketches of Curtis's pursuit of Price, in Samuel R. Curtis Campaign Books, [not before 1862]–1865, Military History Collection, Kansas State Historical Society, Topeka. The first map is a sketch of the skirmish at Pearson's Creek, on which Bennett gives the higher estimate of enemy casualties. Bennett was a corporal in the 36th Regt., Illinois Infantry, who was following a few weeks behind Curtis's army, catching up right before the Battle of Pea Ridge. See also Bennett, Civil War Diary, Dec. 1861–April, 1862, R274, Western Historical Collection, MDH.

Ridge in Arkansas, about a week later. As we were on our return from our skirmish, I made the acquaintance of a chicken near a farm-yard, and invited it into my camp.[7] I was very hungry, and this chicken did me good. My conscience condemned me a little for taking it in the way I did; but I soon grew so much in grace, that I could eat a rebel chicken without remorse, no matter how it was taken.

Next day, we reached Springfield, the enemy having evacuated that place during the previous night.[8] When I reached the edge of the public square, at the head of St. Louis Street, I stopped and saw the troops marching in, and heard their wild cheering, just as I had seemed to see them and to hear them, long before, in my dream in the lone pine forest of the Current River hills.[9] For a few moments, we halted upon the public square and heard a speech from Gen. Sigel. His speech was loudly applauded. Any speech would have been. In my own opinion, however, Gen. Sigel was better as a fighter than as a speaker.[10] After the close of the speaking, we marched to the southern part of the town and encamped in and around the college grounds. We were all in fine spirits.

Next day, we moved southward in pursuit of the rebel army, on the Fayetteville road. Having one day the start of us, Gen. Price, the commander of the rebel army, might have escaped us, had he so desired. He seemed, however, to prefer fighting over all the ground as he retreated. At any rate, every evening for a whole week, he let us run upon him. Every time, he gave

---

7. The skirmish had taken place right next to E. R. Danforth's farm, probably the source of Kelso's chicken. Danforth was wealthy and owned fifteen slaves, but it is not clear if he supported the Confederacy. See Holcombe, *History of Green County*, 207, 247, 265, 406, 602, 706, 903; Bennett, sketch of the skirmish at Pearson's Creek, "Route of the Army"; 1860 U.S. Census, Slave Schedules, Jackson Township, Greene County, Missouri, family no. 1.

8. After the skirmish at Pearson's Creek, Price evacuated his army from Springfield and moved south. Curtis and his troops entered Springfield at 10:00 a.m. on Feb. 13 (*OR*, ser. 1, vol. 8, 59).

9. A private in Phelps's Regt., Missouri Infantry, described the scene: "It was an hour of joy. It was an hour of triumph to the Phelps men and the 24th Mo. There is a language of the heart which speaks when all words fail to convey the thought. So with the members of our regiments whose homes and friends were here" (Robert P. Matthews, quoted in Wood, *Civil War Springfield*, 82).

10. Franz Sigel (1824–1902) was born in Sinsheim, Grand Duchy of Baden. He had been a lieutenant in the Grand Duke Leopold I's army and then held a command in the German revolutionary army of 1848. After the failure of the revolution, he lived in Switzerland and New York City before moving to St. Louis in 1857 and establishing strong ties to the German community there. Inept at the Battle of Wilson's Creek, he nonetheless became a darling of the German American press, a pattern that would continue throughout the war. See Earl J. Hess, "Sigel, Franz," *ANB*, and Gerteis, *Civil War in Missouri*, esp. 67–70.

us a lively reception, for a few minutes,—sometimes for an hour or more, and then retreated. This evening, we had some lively cavalry skirmishing and artillery practice. The enemy had gone into camp. When they fled, they left us their campfires and a large quantity of corn. These things we thankfully received at their hands. They also left us about twenty beeves all nicely skinned. These, we were afraid to use.[11] Many of our men, however, did drink hot coffee which they found steeping upon the coals at the campfires. Moving on a few miles further, the rebel army made another camp.

As we marched out next morning, I noticed a beautiful and bright little boy, about six years of age, coming out of the rebel slaughter ground carrying his arms full of butcher-knives, which, in their hasty departure on the preceding evening, the rebel butchers had left behind. I think I never saw a happier child than he seemed to be. Looking up in my face as I smiled upon him, he said, in a sweet glad voice; "I've got a whole lot of butcher-knives. I'm taking them to my mamma!" I asked him if he would not let me have one. He said he would, and I selected a very fine one almost equal to a bowie knife. No sooner had I done this, than the men commenced stepping up to him as they passed, and taking a butcher-knife each till all were gone. The poor little fellow stood there, then, with tears in his eyes, looking after his departing treasures, as if all his faith in humanity were gone and all his hopes departed. It costs me a pang, even yet, to think of his unutterably grieved look, and to know that I unintentionally helped bring upon him his great grief.

Terrible rumors were now flying in advance of us. It was said, and it seemed to be pretty generally believed among the terrified rebel country people, that we were killing all the male rebels from ten years old up;—that we made those whom we captured dig their own graves and then kneel in them to be shot. There was also another rumor, not so generally believed, however, that we were killing the old ugly women and giving the young and

---

11. Gen. Samuel Curtis to Capt. N. H. McLean, Feb. 22, 1862: "Most of our provisions for the last ten days have been taken from the enemy." But two days later, Curtis reported that forty-two of his men were poisoned at Mud Town from eating food the enemy had left behind. Several men died and others suffered terribly, according to a report on Feb. 27. See *OR*, ser. 1, vol. 8, 562 (quotation), 68 (Curtis report of the poisoning), 570 (report of deaths). Henry Perrin Mann, who rode with Curtis as a member of the 15th Illinois Cavalry, attributed the deaths to poisoned whiskey (Henry Perrin Mann, Civil War diaries, 1862–65, R 455, entry for Feb. 21, 1862, typescript p. 6, State Historical Society of Missouri, Rolla).

handsome women to our free negroes. Who started these absurd rumors, no one will probably ever know. They seem to have been started, for fun, by thoughtless rebel soldiers. Be this as it may, the affair had no fun in it for the poor frightened people.[12] They hastily threw a few necessaries into their wagons, and precipitately fled. As we pressed them closely, they lightened their loads by throwing out sacks of flour, bacon hams, cooking utensils, bedding, &c. Sometimes, for miles, both sides of the road were lined with such things as these. The provisions were a god-send to us, for our own provision trains never came up with us on that whole long chase. These poor foolish people whom we would not have molested, being still closely pressed, would often take their horses from their wagons, and, escaping themselves upon these, would leave their women and children behind in their abandoned wagons. It was pitiful to see so much unnecessary waste and so much uncalled for terror. In a panic, people never reason.

On this evening, after a little fiercer fight than on the preceding evening, we again took the enemy's camp. Indeed, we did this nearly every evening till the end of the chase. We considered it much easier and much pleasanter to thus drive the enemy out of their camp and get their wood and their corn than it was to procure these things for ourselves. Every succeeding evening, however, we had to fight a little harder, and, toward the last, our camps came to cost us pretty dearly.

On this evening,—I think it was—, after we had gone into camp, I saw a large crowd of soldiers gathered in the road laughing very loudly at some object in their midst. Forcing my way in to see what the show was, I perceived a poor old woman who was so fat that her limbs could scarcely support her. It seems that she had been running, and even now she thought she was running. Her feet, however, did not move. She did all her running with her head, neck and hands. These she kept going very rapidly, her whole body

12. General Curtis, in camp near Fayetteville, Ark., on March 1, 1862, circulated an address to the public that began by quoting a letter he received from a local man: "We, as citizens, have left our homes and firesides for the purpose, as we supposed, of having to defend ourselves against a soldiery that would lay waste our humble homes and outrage the chastity of our wives and daughters and place our own lives in jeopardy." Curtis answered that the "falsehoods circulated concerning us have driven thousands from their homes . . . [and] have involved the whole community in the troubles which [the writer] seeks to mitigate." His army needed supplies, and if people stayed home, the army would pay for them instead of just taking them. Military prisoners were not mistreated, peaceable private citizens would be left alone, and there had been no complaints about his soldiers mistreating women. See OR, ser. 1, vol. 8, 577–78. See also Mann, Civil War diaries, entry for Feb. 26, 1862, typescript p. 7.

shaking like a mountain of jelly. The men, mostly thoughtless young fellows, were yelling with delight and suggesting ludicrous things that she should do. I reproved them, saying: "Boys, do not laugh at the poor old woman! Do you not see that she is frightened?" Then addressing her, I said: "Old woman, do not be frightened! No one is going to hurt you." Looking at me without any expression of comfort in her countenance, she wheezed out with a long pause between the several words: "You—kee-e-ul—ld—all—l—the—we—e—men—and che—e—ldren?" No, said I, we have not killed any women and children. She did not believe me, however, and instinctively spreading her huge feet farther apart to get the benefit of a wider base, she began to make her head and neck go with wonderful rapidity, and to paddle the air with her hands like a seal fighting flies with its flippers. The men screamed with laughter and I must confess that my own risibilites were considerably wrought upon. "Hold on!" said I, "you can not out-run us at that rate. If we wish to hurt you, you may as well stand and take it. You can not escape by running." Just then, I saw two well-dressed intelligent-looking young ladies approaching in the company of two of our young officers. Beckoning them to come in, I requested them to speak to the old woman who was frightened out of her wits. They did so, telling her that there was no danger and that they would take her with them out of the crowd. She knew them, and, seeing that they were safe, she recovered at once from her terrible fright. Her great fat face lighting up with joy, she said: "The Lord know I never was so scart so bad in all my life."

If I remember correctly, the events of the next day were nearly a repetition of those of the two preceding days;—hard marching till evening, and then a little recreation in the way of hard fighting. We encamped near a hill of considerable height. While the men were cooking their supper, I climbed this hill alone and looked down upon the camp which covered some forty acres. At least a thousand bright fires were burning upon this space. Not a breath of air was stirring. The smoke rose straight upward into a vast column to the height of a mile or more, then, reaching a rarer atmosphere, it spread out into an immense canopy gorgeously illuminated by the flames below. A little way to my right, the rebel camp, about the same size, presented a similar scene. It was the finest night scene I had then ever beheld. Since then, I have seen few that have surpassed it.

Of this chase, I briefly wrote as follows: "Of course you have learned through the news-papers something of the chase we made;—a chase scarce equaled in American history.[13] To attempt, by letter, to relate all the adventures, the exciting, the amusing scenes I have passed through would be in vain. It would have done you good to see our boys sometimes. After a long march all day, they would be so weary that many seemed scarce able to drag along; but, when the roar of cannons was heard in advance, all would spring forward, at double-quick, seeming strong as ever, while loud cheers echoed along our ranks. At such times, we plunged through creeks, tore through bush, all regardless of consequences, our only feeling being one of wild gladness at the prospect of getting a fight. At night, our trains would be behind, and without food or blankets, we would drop down upon the frozen ground and sleep sweetly."

This brief letter, written to my wife, March 4th 1862, is the only writing I have to aid my memory in giving this portion of my history. I may not, therefore, specify the correct number of days occupied in this chase; and, in some instances, I may give, as occurring on one day, events that actually occurred on some other day. Were I writing a history of the events themselves, such probable inaccuracies in chronology would be entirely inadmissible. As it is, however,—as I am giving an account of the events that have occurred in my own life, such inaccuracies, though to be regretted, do not make so much difference. So the events described did actually occur in my life, at about the time stated, it does not make any great difference upon what particular days they severally occurred. Should you, however, to whom this history is bequeathed, conclude to have it published, it would be well to obtain from the heirs of Gen. S. R. Curtis, or from the records at Washington, the full official account of this remarkable campaign. So of many other events yet to be described, in connection with my military career, in which the chronology may be at fault. Correct the chronology whenever it requires correction, and place the events in the order in which they ought to stand.[14]

---

13. For press coverage in Missouri, see for example, "From Rolla," St. Louis *Daily Missouri Republican*, Feb. 4, 1862; "The Army in Springfield—Price Running—Curtis Pursuing," *Daily Missouri Republican*, Feb. 21, 1862; "The Movement South," *Daily Missouri Republican*, Feb. 24, 1862; and "The Pursuit of Price," *Daily Missouri Republican*, Feb. 27, 1862. Two journalists embedded with the army filed regular reports: William L. Fayel of the *Daily Missouri Republican* and Thomas W. Knox of the *New York Herald* (Shea and Hess, *Pea Ridge*, 15, 399).

14. By the evening of Feb. 14, 1862, Curtis was about thirty miles southwest of Springfield at McCullah's Spring. His advance cavalry was attacked at Crane Creek, and his troops made a stand until other forces joined them and the enemy retreated. When Curtis reported on the evening of Feb. 15, he was at Flat Creek, nearing Cassville (sixty miles southwest of Springfield). They had engaged the enemy again,

On the next day, if I remember rightly, we made a forced march, pressing the enemy closely all day and picking up a good many of their exhausted stragglers. Many of our own men fell out of the ranks and threw themselves down to rest by the side of the road. During the whole following night, these men were coming straggling in. This occurred on several successive days and nights. Many of these stragglers, however, never overtook us at all. They made their way back to Springfield, and formed a straggler's camp. On this occasion, the inevitable daily skirmish began a little earlier than usual, continued longer, and approached more nearly to a real battle. The cavalry and the artillery were all engaged. The hills re-echoed grander thunderings than had ever been heard in that part of the country. It was only when our infantry began to come into action, that the enemy sullenly retired. We had a few men killed and several wounded; and we inflicted a still heavier loss upon the enemy. Among the prisoners taken by us, was a brother of one of my comrades. I saw these two brothers meet. Both were very young men. Both seemed embarrassed, and neither of them had much to say. We were very hungry, and few of us had anything to eat. Utterly exhausted, most men sunk down upon the ground, almost helpless, and begged their stronger comrades to bring them water. I went out alone to hunt food, and, after a tramp of five miles, returned with a fat pig weighing about eighty pounds. I, too, was now nearly exhausted. I tumbled down to rest while very grateful comrades dressed and boiled the pig. Having eaten our meager allowance of pig, we slept sweetly upon the bare frozen ground.

Next day, we made another forced march, skirmishing a little with the enemy, occasionally, throughout the day. Over half our infantry men

---

driving them from their entrenchments at 3:00 p.m. The army moved out at 4:00 a.m. on the morning of Feb. 16. A running battle continued as the troops crossed the Arkansas line. On Feb. 17, there was another engagement at Sugar Creek Crossing in Arkansas, one hundred miles from Springfield and six miles across the state border. A cavalry charge drove the Confederates from their high ground; the Federals lost thirteen men killed and fifteen to twenty wounded. On Feb. 18, a cavalry detachment routed a small Confederate force and took control of Bentonville, Arkansas. By Feb. 20, Curtis had moved his army to Osage Springs, just south of Bentonville. On the morning of Feb. 23, they took Fayetteville, Ark., pushing out the Confederate picket guard who set fire to the main public buildings before they left. Curtis then established his camp twenty-five miles north of Fayetteville, his left flank on Cross Hollow (previously a Confederate cantonment) and the White River Mountains, and his right on Osage Springs five miles west. On March 3, Curtis reported that the main force of the enemy was in the Boston Mountains, gathering reinforcements to attack him. On March 4, the Confederates burned a mill and all the forage sixteen miles to the southeast. See relevant reports and correspondence, OR, ser. 1, vol. 8, 59–76, 186–89, 554–83.

straggled from the ranks. Seeing a great crowd of men surrounding an apple cellar, I, for the first time, left the ranks to get some apples for Captain Barris, who was ill.[15] By reason of the great crowd around the cellar, I was a long time reaching the door, and when I did reach it, I did not venture to enter. The air inside was stifling. The apples seemed to be under the floor. A layer of men had got down upon their bellies to reach these apples through a trap door. Another layer of men had thrown themselves down upon their bellies, on the top of the first layer, and were trying to reach down after apples, past the shoulders of the first layer. Sometimes, even a third layer threw themselves, in like manner, upon the backs of the second layer. As fast as the members of the upper layers departed, other fresh arrivals took their places, thus giving the members of the lower layer no chance to get up at all. These poor fellows were nearly suffocated and were pleading pitifully to be allowed to get up and depart. Not caring to be caught in this trap, I slowly worked my way out of the crowd.

When I again reached the road, the army had all passed except the stragglers who, in marching, observed no order at all. With these, the road was literally packed. Nearly every man, notwithstanding he had ostensibly quit the ranks because he was exhausted, was carrying some kind of plunder;—generally something to eat. One had his bayonet run through two large middlings of bacon, and, with his gun thus loaded upon his shoulders, was marching vigorously along as if he had never known any such thing as weariness. Another marched thus with two geese, tied together by the necks, slung across his gun. Another with two turkeys. Another with half a dozen chickens. One carried upon his shoulder a sack of flour, another a sack of meal, another a sack of dried fruit. Hundreds were thus loaded. A few carried plunder not in the usual line. Of these, one had a large earthen jar full of some kind of preserves. From the mouth of this jar, which he carried under his left arm, he constantly kept taking handfuls of preserves and cramming them into his mouth. Another carried a large wooden churn full of buttermilk. This he carried by locking both arms around it and hugging it to his bosom. Another, a kind of Oscar Wilde, nearly seven feet in height, who

15. Capt. Sampson P. Barris had joined the Greene and Christian County Home Guards as a forty-two-year-old private in July 1861 at Springfield, and then reenlisted with the formation of the 24th Regt., Infantry Volunteers, in August, serving as captain of Co. F. He mustered out in Oct. 1864 ("Soldiers' Records," MDH.).

cared more for the beautiful than for the useful, wore upon the lower part of his body, the immense hooped skirt of some gigantic female; upon his shoulders, a large striped shawl; and upon his head, a huge, funnel-shaped, Leghorn bonnet of the style fifty years ago.[16] Thus attired, this remarkable aesthete marched proudly on, contemplating his various charms in a large looking-glass which he carried in both hands directly in front of him.[17]

By the time I had fully taken in all these things, the thunders of heavy cannonading began to reverberate among the hills. By one common impulse, the whole vast mass of stragglers started forward on a run. The swinging of middlings of bacon upon bayonetts, the flopping of geese, chickens, and turkeys hung upon guns, the bobbing up and down of sacks of flour, of meal, &c. upon men's shoulders, made a novel and ludicrous sight. The man with the jar of preserves ran as fast as he could, taking out a handful of preserves every few jumps, cramming them into his mouth and daubing them upon his face. He meant to go into battle with a full stomach. The man with the churn of butter-milk ran well, but labored under a good deal of disadvantage. He had to lean back as he ran, so as to keep the center of gravity within his base, and this made his running resemble that of Parson Bullin, when the lizards under his clothes made him disrobe himself in church and flee into the woods.[18] The butter-milk splashed up through the dasher hole, and around the edges of the lid, and came down in quite a shower upon the face and bosom of our hero, leaving many little lumps of butter entangled in his beard. He did not propose to fight for fame alone. Our seven foot aesthete took longer strides than had ever before been taken in that monstrous hooped skirt. Running so fast against the wind made the front part of the skirt come down against his legs, while the stiffness of the hoops and their great size

16. As Kelso wrote his "Auto-Biography" in California in the spring of 1882, the national press was avidly covering the American tour of the Irish writer Oscar Wilde (1854–1900), remarking on his flamboyant appearance and "effeminacy." Kelso may have seen articles in the California papers such as "The Latest Pen Portrait of Oscar Wilde," *San Francisco Bulletin*, Feb. 21, 1882, reprinted from the *New York Herald*. Wilde came to California in March: "Oscar Wilde: His First Appearance before a California Audience," *San Francisco Bulletin*, March 28, 1882.

17. Robert Pinckney Mathews, a private with the Phelps Regt. on the same march, seems to be remembering the same scene: "I saw some cavalry, who had confiscated a lot of ladies bonnets from a small store by the road side, riding along with the feminine head gear on their own heads, the ribbons fluttering like streamers in the air. I also saw another carrying a large looking glass and he amused himself, while the thunder of the artillery was shaking the hills, by holding it before the faces of his comrades to let them see how pale they were" (Matthews, *Souvenir of the Holland Company Home Guards*, 45).

18. George Washington Harris, "Parson Bullen's Lizards," in *Sut Lovingood. Yarns Spun by a "Nat'ral Born Durn'd Fool." Warped and Wove for Public Wear* (New York: Dick and Fitzgerald, [1867]), 48–59.

made the back part rise high up and stick far out behind. This hero carried no gun. He would run a few rods holding his looking-glass in one hand by his side. Then he would throw it up in front of him, seize the other edge with his other hand, and look at his image in it as he ran. He wanted to regale his vision upon his own beauty before it was spoiled forever, as he very well knew it soon might be, by some stray bullet carelessly fired in his direction by those naughty rebels.

About 300 yards from our battle line, we met all the regimental Adjutants, calling aloud the position of their several regiments. This enabled every straggler to find his own proper place in the battle line. I heard the Adjutant of my own regiment calling: "Twenty Fourth Missouri, extreme right!" Bearing off toward the right, I and the other stragglers of our regiment were soon in a squad to ourselves, all the balance having found their proper places in the line as we passed along behind it. When I perceived myself to be in the company of several comrades that I knew, I suggested to them that we go a little beyond what seemed to be the extreme right of the line and get behind a number of little trees that we saw growing there. They liked the suggestion, and away we went to the trees. Upon our arrival, however, we found to our great disgust that every tree and every bush already had a man or officer behind it, who did not propose to give up his place for our benefit. The result was that, much against our wishes, we had to stand out in open spaces and be shot at by an enemy that was pretty well sheltered. As the storm of bullets whistled about our ears, it was amusing to see some of the men and officers, behind saplings not larger than a man's three fingers, trying to draw themselves in from both sides and to make themselves as slim, respectively, as were their protecting saplings.

This was by far the most important skirmish that we had yet had. It was the only one in which the infantry, generally, had taken part. For a time it seemed that the enemy were going to give us a pitched battle. They soon retired, however, leaving us masters of the field. They left their dead, their wounded, and several prisoners in our hands. We also lost a few in killed and wounded. For a hospital, we took possession of a large farm house in the vicinity.[19] This ended our chase. We fell back a little from the battle ground and went into camp. Why we did not pursue the enemy any further, I never

19. The Battle of Little Sugar Creek, Ark., Feb. 17, 1862, on Dunagin's Farm. See *OR*, ser. 1, vol. 8, 61, 270, 559. See also Shea and Hess, *Pea Ridge,* 39–44.

knew. As we turned back, every turkey, goose, chicken, churn, and other article of plunder, thrown down by the stragglers in the rear of the battle line, was picked up by the first man that came upon it. Then was heard a great deal of first-class cursing. One, forgetful of how [he] himself had obtained the plunder, was loudly proclaiming: "Some d——d thief has stolen my two turkeys!" Another, equally forgetful, was proclaiming: "Some d——d thief has stolen my butter-milk!" And so on for a thousand other things. One half the army seemed to be accursing the other half with being d——d thieves. Those who now had the plunder did not seem to hear the invidious remarks of their less fortunate comrades. They were extremely quiet, and their countenances were a charming expression of innocence and contentment. Most of those who had no plundered provisions, got nothing to eat at all that night. I was so fortunate as to steal an ear of corn for my supper from a poor half-starved mule. As the mule saw me robbing him of his own scant fare, he seemed to reproach me with his eyes, but he did not say anything out of the way to me.[20]

After the fight was over, and the wounded had been carried off, myself and several comrades were strolling about the battleground and looking at the enemy's dead that had not yet been removed.[21] Most of them looked pale and lay in puddles of blood. Among them, however, was one corpse that had a good healthy color, and about whom no blood was to be seen. I felt of this corpse's wrist. Its pulse was strong and good. I put my ear to its nostrils. It held its breath for about one minute, then let up with quite a puff. It was a strange corpse. We rubbed some prickly pear leaves briskly under its nose. Its eyes flew open, a kind of sheepish smile lit up its countenance, and it exclaimed: "Hold on! boys, I'm not dead!" It then proceeded to inform us that it had happened to stumble and fall while closely pursued by a body of

20. T. I. McKenny, Special Orders No. 90, Sugar Creek, Ark., Feb. 18, 1862, OR, ser. 1, vol. 8, 560: "You have moved in the most inclement weather, over the worst of roads, making extraordinary long marches, subsisting mainly on meat, without salt, and for the past six days you have been under the fire of the fleeing enemy. . . . In your rapid pursuit of the foe and the cravings of actual hunger, the peaceable citizens through whose country we have passed should forgive some acts of spoliation which are incident to war under such pressing circumstances, but . . . let us show the people everywhere that our tents and knapsacks are not disgraced with plunder."
21. Shea and Hess, Pea Ridge, 43: "Curtis's men carried the wounded to Enoch Trott's store in Little Sugar Creek Valley, buried the dead, and gawked at the shattered trees and telegraph poles, the patches of blood on the frozen ground, and the dozens of dead horses lying about. 'For the first time [I] saw men [who] were killed in battle and it was a nasty sight,' George A. Cummins of the 36th Illinois scribbled in his diary. 'I hope to see but few of such.'"

our cavalry, who were cutting down everything they over-took;—that while down, this body of cavalry passed over it; and that it had then concluded to lie there, if permitted to do so, till dark, when it could escape. We put this corpse among the prisoners. On another part of the field, we found the body of quite an elderly looking man. He lay upon his back. He had been shot through the brain and his silvered locks were dabbed with blood. The fierce look of battle was still upon his rigid countenance, and his stiffened hands still clutched his musket. As we were gazing upon him, we were startled by the strange cry of one of our comrades: "By G-d! boys, he's my daddy!" And so he was. The father and the son, two as brave men as ever fought, had met thus after years of separation. You will not wonder when I tell you that we all shed tears as we saw that son wiping the blood from that cold face, and heard him pitifully calling the name of the father he had always loved. Oh! war! war! what untold sorrow thou dost produce. We helped the son bury the father with the honors of war.

During the next three days, most of the men got but little to eat except a small quantity of cornmeal that was distributed among them. This they made into dough, as well as they could, on flat stones, pieces of bark, &c. and baked it in the hot ashes of their camp fires. I fared a little better. Being permitted, as usual, to scout about the country every day with a few comrades, I frequently made the acquaintance of pigs, chickens, turkeys, &c. which I kindly invited to my camp and to my table. I soon grew weary, however, of this comparatively inactive life. I therefore called upon Gen. Curtis and asked him to permit me to go with two comrades, McConnell and Garrison, into the enemy's camp and try to kidnap and bring away their Commander-in-Chief, Gen. Price himself.[22] We had talked the matter over and had come to the conclusion that we could accomplish this dare-devil undertaking. Gen. Curtis, however, refused to permit us to undertake any enterprise so full of hazard. At first he said that I might go alone simply to get information. Then, after thinking a moment, he recalled even that permission, saying that I was too well known to the enemy and that he could send other men who would not run half the risk that I would run, and that he wished me to help him fight.

22. Sgt. James H. Garrison, Co. F, 24 Regt., Infantry Volunteers. He would be discharged to accept a commission as captain in Co. G, 8th Missouri Cavalry Volunteers, in Sept. 1862 ("Soldiers' Records," MDH).

Disappointed in regard to this affair, I asked permission to return to Missouri to raise recruits for my regiment. This request was granted. I started next day.[23] By this departure, I missed a chance to participate in the terrible battle of Pea Ridge, which was fought soon afterwards. Had I thought that a battle was near, I would not have gone.[24]

23. This was on or near Feb. 20, 1862. Curtis was beginning to see that the enemy was retreating further into Arkansas than his orders or his supply line would allow him to follow. Shea and Hess, *Pea Ridge*, 52: "Curtis faced a strategic dilemma as a result of his success in clearing the rebels out of southwestern Missouri and a large part of northwestern Arkansas. Price and McCulloch had joined forces and had moved just out of his reach into the Boston Mountains thirty miles to the south. The Federal commander had three options, none of them attractive. First, he could advance into the Boston Mountains and risk the loss of his army either in battle or through starvation. Second, he could fall back toward Springfield in order to improve his supply situation and risk encouraging Price to return to his old mischief in Missouri. Third, he could attempt to hold his ground in northwestern Arkansas and keep the enemy at bay. Curtis reluctantly settled on the third option as the only feasible course of action. He knew that as soon as the Federals assumed the strategic defensive, the initiative would pass to the enemy, but he felt he had no other choice."

24. The Battle of Pea Ridge, or Elkhorn Tavern, Ark., March 6–8, 1862. See *OR*, ser. 1, vol. 8, 189–330. There have been several studies of this battle; the best is Shea and Hess, *Pea Ridge*. For an assessment of human costs and strategic importance, see 270, 334, 308: "The Federals lost 1,384 men at Pea Ridge: 203 killed, 980 wounded (of whom perhaps 150 later died), and 201 missing and presumed captured, roughly 13 percent of the 10,250 troops engaged. . . . Confederate losses are less certain. . . . Approximately 16,500 Confederates . . . set out on the campaign from the Boston Mountains and the Indian Territory; fewer than 14,000 reached Pea Ridge, and fewer than 13,000 were engaged. By a conservative estimate, the Army of the West suffered approximately 2,000 casualties during the battle, a loss of at least 15 percent of the troops engaged." Kelso's regiment, the 24th Missouri, had three killed, sixteen wounded, and seven missing. "Pea Ridge reshaped the strategic balance in the West. . . . Curtis's victory at Pea Ridge was the turning point of Federal efforts to dominate the Trans-Mississippi."

6. Scouting, Recruiting, and the Cavalry

February to May 1862

It was now near the close of February, 1862. Leaving the army about four miles south of Bentonville, I started, early in the morning, due northward toward Missouri. Having no suitable food to carry with me, I carried none at all. I trusted to chance to obtain food somehow upon the way, although I had not a cent of money. My pockets were filled with letters which I was to carry to Springfield. The day was clear and delightful. The early spring birds were twittering about me. The country was beautiful, and it seemed strange that men should be seeking one another's lives;—men, too, of the same race, the same nationality, the same religion, the same language, the same laws, and the same customs. But so it was; and knowing that almost every man I might meet here would be a deadly enemy, I avoided the roads and the settlements as much as possible, and kept to the hills and forests. During the day, I saw several small parties of men at a distance, but did not directly meet any one. Being fresh from rest, I felt vigorous, and did good walking. I walked all day, and over half the night. After it was dark, I kept the road, leaving it and lying down whenever I heard any body coming. About 2 o'clock, I began to grow weary and my feet were severely blistered. I lay down upon the ground, but soon became too cold to sleep. I must have some kind of shelter. Finding an old empty corn crib, I entered it, and slept a short time upon a small pile of corn shucks that it contained. Even here, however, I soon became too cold to

Source: Kelso, "Auto-Biography," chap. 14, 752–59.

sleep. I waked, but felt too weary to go on. I lay there shivering. Presently, I heard the sound of a large body of horsemen passing upon the road. Not supposing that so large a body of the enemy would be likely to be so close in the rear of our army, I concluded that they must be friends. At any rate, I lay still and let them pass. Soon after the sound of their marching had ceased, another party arrived that left me in no doubt in regard to its being an enemy. It entered the crib, and, finding me there, claimed that I had invaded its premises, and gave me to understand that I must depart at once or take the consequences of refusal to do so. I took the consequences. A battle, short, fierce, and decisive ensued. The consequences came into my face and all over me. The enemy held the battle ground. In a sadly demoralized condition, I fled. My enemy was a *pole-cat*.

Taking to the road again, I walked on very cautiously. Every few minutes, I stopped to listen. I was very anxious to know the character of the large body of horsemen that had so recently passed. No matter to which side they belonged, they were strong enough to be masters of the situation in that vicinity for the present. If they proved to be friends, I would be comparatively safe in following so closely in their rear. If they proved to be enemies, my danger would be greatly increased. Presently day began to dawn. I was debating whether to leave the road for greater safety, or to keep right on until I came to some house at which I could procure food, when I met a Union soldier. He was bare-head, was without a coat, and wore only one boot. He was a German and spoke English very badly. With his little knowledge of English, however, and my little knowledge of German, he made me understand that he was a teamster belonging to a provision train that had camped, on the preceding night, only one or two miles from where we then were; that, just before day-break, a large body of rebel cavalry had attacked their train; that, when he was only half-dressed, he had been captured and left in the care of a single guard; that, while the guard was watching the fighting that was going on at another point, he had knocked the guard down with a neck-yoke that belonged to his wagon, and had made his escape in the dark. He said that, before he was out of sight, the train was being burned.[1] I advised him to leave

---

1. On Feb. 25, a detached force of five hundred Texas Rangers attacked the Federals' supply line near Keetsville, Barry County, Mo., a few miles north of the Arkansas line, "killing 2 men, taking 60 or 70 horses, and burning some 5 sutler wagons" (Gen. Samuel R. Curtis, Report, Feb. 27, 1862, *OR*, ser. 1, vol. 8, 74; and see 74–76). See also Shea and Hess, *Pea Ridge*, 54.

the road and take to the hills to avoid recapture. He said that he would get lost, if he did this; that he must keep the road, even if he were recaptured.

I now left the road, but kept near enough to it to see any thing that might be upon it. Presently I perceived the smoke of the nearly consumed train. Under cover of a large thicket of under-brush, I approached to within about thirty yards of the nearest portions of the burned train. Not a living being was to be seen. I could see many boxes of goods of some kind that had been removed from the fire. Hoping that they might contain food of some kind, I ventured out and examined them. To my great joy, I did find them filled with food;—butter, sweet butter-crackers, and bologna sausages. Being ravenously hungry, and not knowing when I should have another opportunity to procure food, I supplied myself according to my appetite. Besides filling my haver-sack and all my pockets with butter-crackers, I loosed my blouse above my belt, and, inside if this, around my body stuffed nearly half a bushel more of butter-crackers and oyster cans filled with butter. Being thus, as steam-boat men would express it, "loaded down to the guards," I began to look about me to see in what direction to "navigate." Just then, I perceived a party of about fifteen rebel horsemen approaching. They were about three hundred yards off, but they had evidently seen me. I moved quietly toward the brush. At this, they all put spurs to their horses and came dashing after me at full speed, waving their revolvers in the air. I broke to run, then, as fast as I could; but the great weight and bulk of the cargo around my body made it as inconvenient to me in running as Parson Bullen's great belly was to him when he ran naked out of church to escape from Sut Lovegood's lizards. I reached the brush, however, a good deal in advance of my pursuers; and, finding two large fallen trees that lay close together, I tumbled in between them and lay down. I soon heard my pursuers tearing through the brush around the end of these trees. In about an hour, they passed back, only one of them coming near me. Knowing that they had given up the chase, I now felt safe enough. While lying here waiting, I had literally crammed myself with sweet butter-crackers. These made me feel as stupid as an anaconda after he has bolted a calf. The sun, too, had arisen, and was now shining down upon me with a warmth so agreeable that an irresistible sleepiness came over me. I concluded, therefore, to lie there and sleep.

When I awaked, the shadows of evening were gathering about me in the silent forest. I left my hiding place, and started on, coming out into the road as soon as darkness came on. My stomach was sick, and I spit up whole mouthfuls of butter, the undigested remains of my over-gorge of butter-crackers in the morning. I have never since liked this kind of cracker. About midnight, I reached Cassville and found the troops there greatly excited over the prospect of an attack by the body of rebel cavalry of whom I have already spoken, and who were still hovering in the neighborhood. In anticipation of this attack, I remained there until the next evening. Then, the enemy having left the neighborhood, I departed, and traveled slowly and cautiously all night. When morning came I was weary, hungry, and sleepy. I therefore sought a country house at which I might warm myself and obtain food. I presently found an old house which seemed to be vacant. The door was closed but the door knob was gone. Wishing to see what might be inside, I gave the door a violent kick or push with the bottom of my foot. The latch gave way, and the door flew open. I entered, holding my revolver in my hand, ready for any danger that might present itself. In a poor bed, on the opposite side of the room, lay a consumptive looking young man and his wife. He jumped out of bed and fell upon his knees, begging me piteously to spare his life; that he was a sick man unable to fight on either side; that he had never hurt any body, &c. &c. His wife, too, rather a pretty woman, joined him in pleading for his life. I felt amused at their fright, and ashamed at the thought of having so rudely broken in upon their virtuous slumbers. I told them to close up their whinings as soon as they conveniently could; that I did not want any body's life; that I wanted a fire to warm by and some breakfast. In a remarkably short time, these were prepared.

Greatly refreshed, I now started on again. I left the road, however, and turned to the westward several miles to a place called King's Prairie. Here were a number of Union men who had organized themselves into a kind of independent military company, and who, in their own way, were defending themselves and their homes against the various bands of rebel guerillas that were infesting the whole country.[2] The wild deeds of daring performed by some of these independent warriors would furnish good material for a thrilling romance. With these men, I remained three days. During this time, we made one scout, capturing a few prisoners, whom we sent to Springfield,

---

2. King's Prairie was a township, and then a precinct of McDonald Township, in Barry County, Missouri. An 1888 county history describes a state militia of ninety-two men being formed sometime in 1862 before fall consisting of Unionists who apparently had not been persuaded by Kelso's spring recruitment effort. See *History of Newton, Lawrence, Barry, and McDonald Counties, Missouri* (Chicago: Goodspeed, 1888), 639.

and a few guns and horses, which we kept for our own use. I kept a fine, intelligent, clay-bank horse, which I trained very carefully, and which, on more than one future occasion, saved me from capture if not from death. I named him Hawk Eye. At the end of three days, I left for Springfield which place I reached in two days. I left an appointment, however, at King's Prairie, to speak on the 15th of March, when I expected to receive most of these independent warriors as recruits.[3]

While at Springfield, I heard the news of the terrible battle of Pea Ridge, in which most of my comrades were engaged. I greatly regretted not having been present in this engagement. It was fought on the 5th of March, 1882 [*sic;* March 6–8, 1862]. I made a trip into Christian County and obtained several recruits. Col. S. H. Boyd, who was a great liar, however, had informed me that he had made arrangements to have two companies of mounted scouts attached to his regiment; and that I was to command the first one formed of these companies.[4] My recruits, therefore, volunteered under the expectation that they were to be mounted men, to be commanded by myself, and to belong to that regiment in which most of them had friends. Under these expectations, recruiting progressed rapidly. I soon had over fifty men enrolled.

On the 15th of March, I filled my appointment at King's Prairie, in Barry County, and enrolled over thirty recruits. These, added to those I had at Springfield would form my company, and a day was already appointed, near the close of the month, to muster them all in at Springfield. Having a few days to spare before that time arrived, I concluded to go upon a scout with my recruits, who were armed with shot-guns and common old-style rifles. This did not prove to be a very glorious expedition. On the evening of the first day,

3. Many years later, Dr. Beverly A. Barrett recalled meeting Kelso at a farm on Wilson's Creek, a few miles from Springfield. Barrett (b. 1826) had practiced medicine in Kelso's Dallas County until 1858, when he moved to Springfield (Holcombe, *History of Greene County*, 603–4). He was a Confederate sympathizer who was aiding the wounded after the Battle of Pea Ridge. He considered Kelso a "villainous" character with a great amount of "low down cunning." According to Barrett, Kelso "was in command of a squad of federal troops"—perhaps, rather, his "independent warriors?"—"most of them as unprincipled as their commander. He and his men raided Mr. Sharps' home, carried away everything eatable from his place, made threats of murder to us and our wounded men, and may have carried [out] his murderous intentions had not a gentlemanly Col. of Gen. Curtis' [staff] arrived with an escort bringing some prisoners from Pea Ridge to Springfield. Everything became instantly quiet and Kelso and his men left in a hurry. We had no further trouble. . . . John R. Kelso had mean qualifications[;] during their stay around them that dark night, [he] unscrewed a nut off one wheel of our wagon wheels, which instantly [was] discovered by one of the federal guard, and another supplied by them as soon as could be" (Beverly A. Barrett to unknown, Feb. 22, 1897, typescript, Bradbury Collection).
4. On Boyd, see chap. 2, note 16, above.

before we had gained any victories calculated to immortalize our names, we
met a forage train from our army which, after the battle of Pea Ridge, though
victorious in that engagement, had fallen back into Missouri, and now lay at
Keitsville.⁵ My recruits, being dressed in citizen's clothes, and armed with citizen's weapons, could not, of course, be distinguished from the rebel guerillas
who were dressed and armed in the same way. As soon, therefore, as the
commander of this train saw us, across a large corn-field, he turned his wagons
and began a disorderly retreat. Not wishing him to return with empty wagons
and to send out troops after us, we unfurled a Union flag which we carried with
us. This did no good. I then started across the field alone to where they were.
Seeing me coming thus alone, they halted and waited my coming. I explained
to them who we were, and handed to the commander some papers that would
confirm all I said. He was a lieutenant belonging to the 4th Iowa Infantry. He
replied that he did not doubt the truth of all I said, but that he did not then have
time to examine my papers, and would be glad if I and my men would go by
his camp, which was near at hand, and stop while he examined these papers. To
this I agreed. He then said that of course I would have no objection to giving
up my arms and having my men give up theirs, for a few minutes, to be all
given back just as soon as my papers were examined. I thought that, in this, he
was expecting a little too much, but, wishing to avoid all trouble, and not
suspecting any treachery on his part, I agreed to this also.

When we reached his camp, I requested him to look over my papers as
quickly as possible, as we were on an important scout and did not wish to be
delayed. He then very coolly informed me that I could not leave till morning;
that my papers might be forged, and that he should not pay any attention to
them. In vain, I remonstrated against this vile act of cowardice and treachery.
I asked him if he thought that enemies would have come as we had across a
large field to surrender to an inferior force which was already in disorderly
retreat? I asked him if he did not know that we could have captured his whole

5. Gen. Samuel R. Curtis to Capt. N. H. McClean, March 18, 1862: "The enemy again approaching in
force. We will have to fall back to near Keetsville; otherwise my supplies will be in danger" (*OR*, ser. 1,
vol. 8, 624). Capt. William P. Black of the 37th Illinois Infantry, in a letter on March 26, 1862, thought
that his camp had been changed "for the purpose of getting forage for the teams. The greater part of our
army is between us [in northern Arkansas] & Keetsville, but our division still upholds our flag in
Arkansas" (Michael E. Banasik, ed., *Duty, Honor, and Country: The Civil War Experiences of Captain
William P. Black, Thirty-Seventh Illinois Infantry* [Iowa City: Camp Pope Bookshop, 2006], 88). This
pullback was temporary. Curtis's army, including the 4th Iowa Infantry, which had had a prominent role
in the Battle of Pea Ridge, would soon push further south to Helena, Arkansas.

train, and that, if we had been enemies, we would have captured it. In reply to these questions, he simply said: "You've got to stay." Being in the treacherous brute's power, we did have to stay. He promised, however, to give up our guns and let us off in the morning as soon as his train started. This promise, he also broke. Instead of letting us off in the morning, he said we must go to Keitsville; and that, if we did not go peaceably, he would use force. I let him know that I had an appointment that day to meet another lot of recruits, and that, after meeting them, we had to go on to Springfield to be mustered into the U. S. service. I let him know that his taking us to Keitsville would render us unable to meet these appointments, although we would at once be released when we reached that place. All in vain. We had to go. Then I exhausted all the adjectives in Webster's Unabridged Dictionary. Liar, coward, traitor, thief, son of a _____, were among the mildest epithets I applied to him. His men expressed themselves ashamed of his conduct. I told him, that, if ever we met after I was free, we would settle the matter,—not in words.

When we reached Keitsville, it was evening. The first guard that we passed was a particular friend of mine. I told him that, by the basest of treachery, the cowardly villain by my side had taken us prisoners, and that I wished him to convey word at once to Major Weston of this fact.[6] Moving on, we soon found ourselves in the midst of my regiment. The men and officers were out on the parade ground playing ball. Seeing where we were, I assumed command, and ordered a halt, saying that we would go no farther. The men and officers crowded around us, glad to see us. I then commenced explaining the treacherous and cowardly manner in which we had been taken prisoners. I intended, as soon as I had explained these things, to pull the cowardly Lieutenant off his horse and give him a good beating. While I was speaking, he ordered his command to move on to the camp of the Fourth Iowa. I ordered them not to move, and they obeyed me. My friends of the Twenty Fourth Missouri, men and officers, began to run for their arms, saying that, if the Fourth Iowa got us, they would get us after they had destroyed the Twenty Fourth Missouri. Not thinking that he would desert his command, I had not yet seized the cowardly villain at my side. Seeing how affairs stood, however, he did put spurs to his horse and, deserting his command, did make his escape. I have never seen him since. Were I to meet him, even yet, I would punish him. He is doubtless still living. Such men

6. Maj. Eli W. Weston, 24th Regt., Infantry Volunteers ("Soldiers' Records," MDH).

never get killed, and rarely die. When they do die, they always enter heaven,—get in by treachery. This one is doubtless now a member of some church,—such men usually are—, a teacher in some Sunday school, and a member of the Young Men's Christian Association. Through the influence of these societies, he may even have attained the distinction of a defaulting cashier of a bank, or at least to that of a merchant's clerk who has robbed the till of his employers. In any event, he has doubtless seduced several weak women, young girls and silly wives, his sisters in the Lord.

Having taken our guns from the wagons, we let our late guards pass on. They expressed a good deal of indignation at the manner in which their commander had acted. I then called upon Major Weston who informed me that they were on short rations, and that he could not furnish either food for ourselves or forage for our horses;—that the best he could do for us was to pass us out, and let us supply ourselves off the country. At the close of my conversation with the major, a musician, who had heard all that passed between us, took me aside and gave me five dollars with which to buy food for my men. He said that he would gladly give me more if he had it. I have never seen him since; but he was a hero. He probably fell in battle or died. Such men do frequently perish thus. He also probably went to hell. Such men do usually go there. In order to enter heaven they have to play the sneak, entering upon a borrowed ticket, and this these men will not do. It was now dark. We left Keitsville, hungry, weary, and ill-tempered. About ten o'clock, we came to the farm of a wealthy old secessionist. Passing ourselves for rebels, we were bountifully provided for. Leaving this place about midnight, we sent a messenger to notify the rest of the recruits, and then moved on to Springfield, at which place we arrived on the next evening.

In all, I now had over a hundred recruits, all first-class men. To my great disappointment, however, I now learned that Boyd had misled me and caused me to mislead these men; that he had not obtained permission to have mounted men joined to his regiment; and that all those who entered that regiment at all, would have to enter as infantry. When the men learned the true state of affairs, they were all greatly disappointed and dissatisfied. About half of them, mostly Christian County men, having friends and relations in the Twenty Fourth Missouri, determined to join that regiment any way. The other half, mostly Barry County men, determined to join none but a cavalry regiment. No matter, then, with which division I remained, I was bound to lose the other division. I fell more under obligation to the Barry County men, because my personal influence had been more used in bringing them out. I wrote to Lieut. Col. James K. Mills, who was then in command of my regiment, asking what to do in the dilemma in which I was placed.[7] He replied by directing me to take my cavalry recruits and enter the Fourteenth M. S. M. Cavalry, which was then being formed by Col. John M. Richardson.[8] I did this, Col. Mills assuring me that he would have me properly discharged from the Twenty Fourth Missouri Infantry. This promise was not kept. My name disappeared from the rolls of that regiment without a word of explanation, leaving several months' pay still due me.[9]

The M. S. M. Cavalry was a special military organization which never existed anywhere else or on any other occasion. It consisted of 10,000 men that Missouri raised above her quota. These troops were, in all respects, the same as any other U. S. Volunteers, except that being in excess of Missouri's quota, they were, by special contract between Missouri and the United States, to be retained within Missouri or near her borders for her especial protection.[10] I was now a member of this organization, and had men enough to make me certain of a First Lieutenant's commission. I was now very glad to be assured of even this office. My family sorely needed the fair pay I would now receive, and my social position would be greatly elevated. I had now learned that a pair of officer's straps alone outweighed the highest degree of

---

7. Lt. Col. James K. Mills (1830–74), a lawyer before the war, enlisted first as a private in the 3rd U.S. Reserve Corps. in St. Louis in April 1861. In Aug. 1861, he was appointed lieutenant colonel of the 24th Missouri Infantry. He would serve as post commander at Springfield, provost marshal for southwest Missouri, and colonel of his regiment before resigning for health reasons (tuberculosis) in 1864 ("Soldiers' Records," MDH; Banasik, ed., *Duty, Honor, and Country*, 98–99n22).

8. Col. John M. Richardson (1820–89) had been a lawyer, a state representative for Jasper and Newton Counties, a Greene County attorney, a newspaper editor, a prominent politician in the faction of the Missouri Democratic Party led by Thomas Hart Benton, a candidate for Congress, and Missouri's secretary of state under Gov. Sterling Price (1853–56). He was a strong Unionist and voted for Lincoln in 1860. He enlisted as a captain in Dallas County on Jan. 24, 1862. After the war he became a conservative and supported President Andrew Johnson. See Holcombe, *History of Greene County*, 217, 248, 252, 257–59, 271–73, 410, 503–6; Malcolm G. McGregor, *The Biographical Record of Jasper County, Missouri* (Chicago: Lewis, 1901), 67–68; and "Soldiers' Records," MDH.

9. On Kelso's back pay, see chap. 2, note 23, above.

10. U.S. Pension and Record Office, *Organization and Status of Missouri Troops*, 21: "The Missouri State Militia was a peculiar force, entirely separate and distinct from all other militia organizations in the State, and its status in the service was the subject of considerable controversy during the period of its existence. Its organization was the result of a desire on the part of the officials of the State to place in the field a force of State militia at the expense of the General Government." Perplexing questions arose as to whether the MSM was a state force under the governor or U.S. troops commanded by the president (see pp. 21–47). Federal district commanders had the authority to move troops in Missouri; when not needed for federal operations they followed a chain of command that led to the state's governor.

valor, patriotism, intelligence, and moral worth without them. I expected soon, however, to raise enough more recruits to fill my company and to entitle me to a Captain's commission; but, in this expectation, I was sorely disappointed. I learned that the ten thousand men required for this organization were already enrolled and that I would have to unite my part of a company with about the same number of men raised by my friend Burch of Dallas County. Since I had to unite with some one, I was glad to unite with him. He was an excellent man [in] every way, and most of his men were old friends of mine. When the day came for electing officers, several of my men were sick of measles, and could not attend. Had all been present, I would have been elected Captain by three majority. As it was, Burch was elected by a majority of two. I was, of course, elected First Lieutenant. Amos Norton, one of Burch's men, of whom I have already spoken, was elected Second Lieutenant. My division was allowed four Sergeants and four Corporals; Burch's division, one Sergeant and four Corporals. The arrangement was as good as could well have been made. It was now about the last of March, 1862.

When our company was thus organized, we went into training, till about the 20th of April. Then we were ordered to Linn Creek, about eighty miles North of Springfield. Of the march to Linn Creek I remember scarcely any thing at all. I will therefore simply give a part of a letter written from Linn Creek to my wife, who was still in Collinsville, Illinois:

> My Dearest Susie:—Seated by the side of the beautiful little stream called Linn Creek, I proceed to inform you why I am here. . . ."[11] We left Springfield on Monday. Tuesday night, we spent in Buffalo; and had you been there, I should have considered it one of the happiest occasions of my life. I visited Mr. Norton's family, and had a very pleasant talk with old Anthony Lindsay. I next called to see Marshall McConnell and Smantha. Next, Mrs. Hovey and family. Eva ran to meet me, and all appeared very glad to see me. I next called to see John McConnell's wife. She and her little boy were well, but were having a rather lonely time. Smantha will have a lonely time also, as Marshall has enlisted in our company. I next called to see Mr. Lovan and family. Tilman and I stayed over night with them. I next called to see Mrs. Boothe and Mrs. Burch, who are both living at Boothe's place. Mrs. Burch's little boy is a fine child. I next visited Augustine

11. Kelso's ellipses.

and the Humphrey girls. Augustine seemed rejoiced to see me, but said she "was about to count me out" for not coming to see her till the very last. As I passed, I called to see Mrs. Morrow and family. Like all the rest, they greeted me with joy. In fact, the joy that was manifested on every hand at meeting me, made me feel that though my loyalty has lost to me all my kindred, it has filled their places with many devoted friends. Mrs. Hovey is eager to hear from the Doctor. She requested me to say that she and the children were well. I visited Mrs. Langston the night before we left Springfield. She will hardly live long. Aggie, too, is sick. I guess West is responsible for her condition. Ellen was happy to see me. She looks younger and healthier than she did. Mandyvil was there, and you better believe she is pretty. I did not know her at first, but had quite a chat with her when I found her out. She is really an interesting lady. Walter is at home, a more noble man than ever. Annie West was there, and was glad to see me. She has a bouncing big boy for a baby.

Your Loving Husband, John R. Kelso

Linn Creek, Apr. 25th 1862[12]

How long we remained at Linn Creek I do not now remember but I think we returned to Springfield about the 20th of May, having been gone about

---

12. At the time of the 1860 census, Amos Norton (b. 1822) and his wife, Elizabeth (b. 1823), had five children. "Old" Anthony Lindsay was forty-three and living alone. (Joseph) Marshall McConnell (b. 1839) and John N. McConnell (b. 1837) were born in Tennessee. John's wife was Sarah London. (John served in the Home Guard and the 24th Missouri Infantry and Marshall in the 14th MSM Cavalry.) Samantha Williams was thirteen in 1860 and lived in the Hovey household. Dr. Hovey's wife, Caroline, had three small children and two adult daughters in the household as of 1860. William Loven (b. 1810) lived with his six children. Tillman H. Barnes was born in Indiana in 1839. He was in the 8th Regt., MSM Cavalry, and in 1870 would be living with the Kelsos and working as a farmhand. Hannah Booth (b. 1828), the wife of Robert C. Booth (b. 1822), had four children. Milton Burch's wife, Mary (b. 1836), had three children: William (age three), Robert (one), and Cordelia (seven months). The Humphrey girls—Mary (b. 1839), Ruth (b. 1842), and Catharine (b. 1853)—lived with their parents, John (b. 1805) and Ruth (b. 1807), very near the Hoveys and the Burches. It is not clear to which of three Augustines in Benton Township Kelso was referring. Sarah Morrow (b. 1823) lived with her husband and nine children. Mrs. Merivale Langston (b. 1816) was a widow running a sizeable farm outside of Springfield. Walter is probably Merivale's son Walter W. Langston (b. 1839). Aggie, Ellen, Mandyvil, and Annie West have not been identified (1860 U.S. Census: Benton Township, Dallas County, Missouri, family nos. 4 [Norton], 240 [Lindsay], 230 [John McConnell], 236 [Loven], 222 [Boothe], 244 [Burch], 1 [Morrow], and 242 [Humphrey]; Campbell Township, Greene County, Missouri, family no. 245 [Walter Langston]; Taylor Township, Greene County, Missouri, family no. 750 [Merivale Langston]; 1870 U.S. Census: Benton Township, Dallas County, Missouri, family no. 188 [Joseph Marshall McConnell]; Campbell Township, Greene County, Missouri, family no. 1086 [Kelso with Barnes]; "Soldiers' Records," MDH; NPS Soldiers' Database).

one month.[13] Soon after our return, I think it was, an election was held for the two Majors to which our regiment was entitled. By an almost unanimous vote, I was elected First Major and Captain Stephen A. Julian Second Major.[14] Col. Richardson, however, not wishing these offices filled with honest men, suppressed the returns of this election, and had his son-in-law, J. C. Wilbur, a bold and skillful villain, appointed in my place, and a man of similar character in place of Captain Julian.[15] With such field officers, he expected to make his office of Colonel a very lucrative one. The injustice done to me in this case came very near creating a mutiny among the men.

Of the events that occurred while we were at Linn Creek, and while we were on our return to Springfield, I remember but little. I will, therefore, give another letter which covers a portion, at least of that period, and shows what my feelings then were. This letter was written to my wife from Springfield May 25th 1862.

> My Dearest Susie:—Since returning to this place, I found your kind letter of April 20th and concluded to reply, although I had already replied to one of a later date. I went to Linn Creek, after I wrote to you, returned to Buffalo, had another pleasant time visiting, then came to this place. As soon as I arrived, I visited Jack McElhany and family. I found them all well, and all glad to see me. Mabe Anderson was here. He has changed a good deal since I saw him last. He says that your relatives are all well except your father, who has long been

13. Kelso's Co. H of the 14th MSM Cavalry was stationed at Linn Creek, May 1–4, 1862; May 5–21, "Marched to Buffalo, to Springfield May 20 and 21"; May 26–27, "Marched to Mount Vernon"; May 28–29, "Marched to Neosho" (Janet B. Hewett, ed., *Supplement to the Official Records of the Union and Confederate Armies, Part II, Record of Events*, vol. 35 [hereafter *OR, Supplement*] [Wilmington, N.C.: Broadfoot, 1996], 771).

14. Capt. Stephen H. Julian (b. 1822) of the 14th MSM Cavalry had lived before the war in Greene County with his wife, Sarah, and their four children ("Soldiers' Records," MDH; 1860 U.S. Census, Cass Township, Greene County, Missouri, family no. 606).

15. Maj. John C. Wilbur (or Wilber; b. 1817), Cos. F and S, 14th MSM Cavalry, was promoted from adjutant in July 1862. He was not yet Colonel Richardson's son-in-law: Wilbur and Kenyon Richardson married in Feb. 1865 (*Missouri Marriage Records*); they divorced by 1880 (1880 U.S. Census, Carthage Township, Jasper County, Missouri, family no. 131). Wilbur left the army in July 1863. He was practicing law with Richardson by the end of 1863 (see a note about a prison escape on "Richardson & Wilber, Attorneys & Counsellors at Law" letterhead, May 4, 1864, MDH Provost Marshal Papers, reel F1648, file 18940). By 1864 he was acting as an attorney and soldiers' claims agent (Advertising Card, c. 1864–65, Old State House Museum Collection, Little Rock, Ark.). See also *Journal of the Senate of the State of Missouri at the Adjourned Session of the 22nd General Assembly* (Jefferson City, Mo.: J. P. Amet, 1863), 335 (his promotion); and "Soldiers' Records," MDH.

lingering on the brink of the grave. I fear that we shall never see him again. I have heard nothing of Matthie's family on my return. I have seen Walter Langston. He says his mother is still lingering about as she was. Ellen has gone home. She has written to Tilman since she reached home.[16] She is strong Union as ever. There has been some skirmishing in the country since I wrote last. On one of these skirmishes, one of our Dallas County Boys was killed. Another, Willoughby Hoover, was severely wounded.[17] A plot, in which some seven or eight rebels were concerned, was formed for the purpose of shooting myself and Captain Burch from the bush. The plot was discovered, however, and no harm happened to us. One of the villains concerned is in prison here now. The rebels have offered a reward for my head. I think, however, that their money is safe. Some of their scalps may not be safe.

A very sad event occurred here a few days ago. A widow lady by the name of Willis fled from Arkansas last fall, on account of the Union sentiments of herself and sons, and settled in this city. Before coming, however, one of her sons was butchered in her own yard, before her eyes, another was murdered in the field where he was at work, and still another scarce escaped, amid a shower of bullets, by running to the bush. This was all done by the rebels, from whom but little better treatment could have been expected. The hardest part of all, however, is that which I commenced to tell. Her house is near some of our camps. Some of the soldiers, having become trouble-some, a guard was placed at her door. A Captain Clark and one of his men came to the door drunk, and demanded supper, which Mrs. Willis declared that she was not able to prepare for them. They grew furious, swore that they *would* come in, and then made an attack upon the guard. The Captain drew his revolver, but was himself shot dead by the guard. The Captain's comrade then fired, but, missing the guard, shot Miss Mary Willis dead. The guard then shot him, wounding him, I think, mortally. I was well acquainted

16. John McElhany (b. 1823 in Tenn.) lived in 1860 in Greene County near Wilson's Creek with his wife, Margaret, and their nine children (1860 U.S. Census, Wilson Township, Greene County, Missouri, family no. 108). Walter W. Langston (b. 1839) was a son of Merivale (1860 U.S. Census, Campbell Township, Greene County, Missouri, family no. 245, and see chap. 6, note 12, above). Mabe Anderson, Matthie, and Ellen have not been identified.

17. Pvt. James W. Hoover, Co. A, 14th MSM Calvary, was discharged with a disability on July 20, 1862 ("Soldiers' Records," MDH).

with Mrs. Willis and her daughter, and esteemed them as friends and as worthy ladies. Some time ago, they showed me the clothes of the two murdered boys, pierced in many places with the instruments of death. My heart bled for the sorrow of those two desolate mourners. But who can speak the woe of the *one* that *now* remains! What can earth ever be to her again![18]

Whitson is here in prison. Thief Green was taken, but has made his escape.[19] We do not trouble head-quarters much with prisoners. We prefer patronizing the *brimstone* head-quarters. I understand that I am appointed Quartermaster of our regiment, but I expect to decline accepting that office. I would receive ten dollars more a month, but the place does not, by any means, suit me. It grieves me, Susie, to know that you are in want, and I not able to assist you. I have received only one payment since I entered the service. There is, no doubt, money ready for me in the Lyon Legion (24th Mo. Inf.), but *where* is that now, and *when* shall I see it again? We have no idea when we shall receive pay for our present service. I have never spent one dime foolishly. I am not dressed as my rank requires, but still I do not complain. I mean to be such a man as you will be proud of, if you *can* be proud of one who seems born for misfortune only, and who has, unintentionally, been the cause of so much sorrow and suffering to yourself. O Susie! how much I wish to be worthy of your admiration! Then you would *love* me with that devotion with which I have *so long clung to you*. I dreamed of you again last night. I thought we were in a beautiful place, and that I was resting by your side, with your arm for my pillow. As I looked into your eyes, I thought I could read in their depths so deep a love and so great a joy as filled my heart with unspeakable gladness. The only thing that hinders me from coming after you is want of money. I think it will be better to sell the wagon at any price. We can come on the cars to Rolla, and, from that place, Jack McElhany will bring

18. Capt. John R. Clark, Co. B of the 5th Kansas Cavalry, was a veteran of the Mexican War and had been Mercer County sheriff and a delegate to the Democratic State Convention in 1856. His companion, Pvt. Andrew J. Rice, Co. B, 5th Kansas Cavalry, eventually died from his wound. The incident was reported in an Ohio newspaper because Clark had lived there until moving to Missouri in 1836; see "Federal Officer and Young Lady Killed," Columbus, Ohio, *The Crisis*, June 18, 1862, 165. See also Holcombe, *History of Greene County*, 417–18, and NPS Soldiers' Database.
19. B. S. Whitson is on the list of prisoners released on oath and bond, Aug. 4, 1862, MDH Provost Marshal Papers, reel F1587, file 1918. Thief Green has not been identified.

us in his wagon either to Buffalo or to Springfield. Under all these circumstances that surround us, I think it will be better to come here. While the war lasts, it will make but little difference at which place you stop. After the war, however, I could do much better business here than I could in Buffalo. But, notwithstanding all this, I wish you to decide for yourself at which place you will stop. You could get a small school at either place; perhaps a very good one here, if you could manage to teach in one room and to keep house in another. Goods, also, are cheaper here than they are in Buffalo. Just so soon as I get money, I expect to come for you or to send in case I can not come myself. I wish to get you away from that unhealthy place before the sickly season comes on. Prepare your mind, however, to bear even the disappointment of not coming at all. You would hardly find so generous friends here as you find there; and, should any new disappointment fall upon me, you would be better off where you are. You are going to be disappointed, I fear, in regard to visiting your people. I see no prospect now of your being able soon to make that visit. I hope you will be able to bear this disappointment bravely. You have borne all your trials, Susie, with so much of noble philosophy that I admire and love you more than ever. How much I long for the time to come when we shall have even the most humble little home in which we may enjoy each other's society. Should this ever be our lot, let us not forget to appreciate the blessings we may enjoy. Let us not complain any more; but striving to be noble and good, let us find the *true wealth* in each other's love, and in the confidence of those around us. We are passing away, Susie, and it becomes us to prepare the immortal part of our being for those glorious abodes,— "those fields of light, celestial plains," toward which we are tending.——Your Johny.[20]

I did not soon get my family away from Collinsville. They remained there during the dreaded sickly season, and our youngest child, our sweet little Ianthus, who still suffered from the exposure of our dreadful retreat from Missouri, fell a victim to the malarial diseases of the place, and there, in an unknown grave, his dust yet reposes.[21]

---

20. "Ye fields of light, celestial plains" is from a Protestant hymn based on Psalm 148 (see *Hymns of the Protestant Episcopal Church in the United States of America* [Philadelphia: S. F. Bradford, 1827], 8).
21. On Ianthus, see chap. 8, note 9, below.

Besides my desire to have my family nearer me and in a more healthy place, there was another reason, not even hinted at in these letters, why I wished them to leave Collinsville. I wished to get my wife, who was now the idol of my soul, away from the influence of Doctor Hovey, the Chesterfield of whom I have already often spoken. Having sent his family back to Missouri, he was himself still lingering in Collinsville, ostensibly finishing up his business there. Almost blindly unsuspicious, though I am by nature, and never inclined to be jealous, my intuitions, sharpened by my great love, now told me that the indefinite lingering of this fascinating but unscrupulous man near my lovely and unsuspecting young wife, after the departure of his own family, boded no good to my domestic happiness. While his good wife was there, I felt sure that she would be a great protection to my wife against his seductive wiles. Now, that her protecting influence was gone, I suffered a constant agonizing dread of what the consequences might be. And the future proved that my fears were well founded. He did succeed in winning my darling and beautiful wife's love from me. He did succeed in blighting her life and mine! Whether he ever won more than her *love*, I never knew and never wished to know. I still try to believe that he did not.

7. A Defeat and a Victory

May to July 1862

After our return from Linn Creek, we again remained in camp training. We were then ordered to Neosho, a large town about eighty miles distant in a south-westerly direction.[1] The men were armed with old style muzzle-loading muskets, totally unfit for the use of cavalry men. Our horse equipments were such old saddles, bridles, &c. as we had been able to bring from home for our own use. Armed and equipped thus, even veterans would have labored under fearful disadvantages in a battle. Raw recruits, like our men, armed and equipped thus, and commanded, as we were, by an officer in whose skill no one had any faith; and who, many believed, was even capable of selling us to the enemy,—raw recruits, I repeat, thus situated were simply doomed to defeat and demoralization, if they met any enemy at all. Our Colonel, however, had just received his commission, and had just donned a pair of straps that had eagles on them. And now, like Don Quixote when he attacked the windmills, our doughty Colonel was burning to win for his own brows the laurels of the conqueror. He said: "The *name* of my Mountain Rangers will be sufficient to scare Col. Coffee and Gen. Standwaite out of the country."[2] And yet, as I have just shown, his "Mountain Rangers," as he

Source: Kelso, "Auto-Biography," chap. 15, 760–67.

1. Kelso's Co. H of the 14th MSM Cavalry, "Marched to Neosho," May 28–29, 1862 (*OR, Supplement,* 771).

2. Col. John Trousdale Coffee (1816–90) commanded the 6th Missouri Cavalry of the Missouri State Guard ("Soldiers' Records," MDH), but he operated independently of Sterling Price's forces and from the Confederate Army. A lawyer before the war, he had also served in the Missouri Assembly and Senate

called his men, were as yet, little more than a mob. No matter how brave they were, they were not in a condition to fight.

In a letter written to my wife on the 6th of June, after our return to Springfield, I briefly described the principal events of this expedition. I will, therefore, give the letter:

My Dear Susie:—Once more at Springfield, I find your kind letters of the 26th ult. and the 1st inst. waiting me. I am very glad to hear that you are doing so well as you are. I approve of all you have done, and I approve of your wish to visit your people. I do not as yet, however, see how you can make that visit. It seems almost useless for you to come back to a country in which men are almost daily shot down at their plows or in their own yards. Refugee families are passing daily on the roads, from the counties below this, and serious alarms occur even here. So soon as I receive any money, I will come to see you, and then we will conclude what to do. Try to bear all your trials like a little philosopher as you really are. I am at Jack McElhany's now. Himself and family are all well, and all rejoiced to see me again.

On last Monday we marched to Mount Vernon. There we met some other forces, and, with them, marched to Neosho.[3] While on our way, I was sent out in command of a scouting party of the men and had some interesting adventures which I will relate when I see you. We took several prisoners, horses, and guns. When we reached Neosho, I found the camp pitched in a very bad place and badly guarded.[4] This was on Thursday. On one side of the camp, partially surrounding it in the form of a semi-circle, was a high bluff, so steep

---

and was briefly a captain in the U.S. Army. See John N. Edwards, *Noted Guerrillas; or, The Warfare on the Border* (St. Louis: Bryan, Brand, 1877), 93, 100, 105; Nichols, *Guerrilla Warfare in Civil War Missouri*, 1:37, 43, 81–82; and Gerteis, *Civil War in Missouri*, 145–46. See also Emmett MacDonald to Thomas C. Hindman, Sept. 1, 1862 (attempts to recruit Coffee for the Confederacy), Peter Wellington Alexander Papers, Box 2, and Charges Filed against John T. Coffee, c. Oct. 1862 (on his drunkenness and dereliction of duty), Wellington Papers, Box 10, Rare Book and Manuscript Library, Columbia University, New York, MDH. Stand Watie (1806–71) was a leader of the Cherokee Nation and became a colonel of the 1st Regt., Cherokee Mounted Volunteers (CSA), principal chief of the Confederate Cherokees, and then a brigadier general for the Confederacy. See Kenny A. Franks, *Stand Watie and the Agony of the Cherokee Nation* (Memphis: Memphis State University Press, 1979), and Franks, "Watie, Stand," *ANB*.

3. Cos. A, C, E, G, and Kelso's H, numbering 220 men, marched from Mt. Vernon to Neosho (forty miles), May 28–29, 1862 (*OR, Supplement*, 771, 785). The force also included one company of the 10th Illinois Cavalry (*OR*, ser. 1, vol. 13, 92).

4. "Report of Col. John M. Richardson, Fourteenth Regiment Missouri Militia," June 11, 1862, *OR*, ser. 1, vol. 13, 91–92: "I was careful in selecting the camp. The ground was first chosen by General [Franz]

that cavalry could not climb it and thickly covered with under-
brush. This was on the side toward the enemy; and, as I knew that
they could not fail to know all about our numbers, our position, our
pickets, &c. I felt sure that, if they attacked us, as I believed they
would, the advantage of ground was so entirely in their favor that
they would be sure to defeat us. At first I thought that our Colonel
had made only a temporary stop upon this ground, and that he surely
would not place us at the mercy of the enemy by having us encamp
for the night in so extremely unfavorable a position. To my surprise
and dismay, however, the men were soon commanded to put up their
tents upon this ground—the very ground that the enemy would
have selected for us, had the selection been left to them, as it probably was. The Colonel had chosen for his head-quarters a house in
the vicinity, and there, with his staff, and with such other officers as
felt convivially inclined, he was having a good time over his wine,
his oysters, &c. The delightfulness of this convivial scene was
greatly heightened, too, by the smiles and the wit of a bevy of rebel
women—beautiful and bright, old friends of the Colonel who used
to live in this town. Everything went "merry as a marriage bell."
The men in all the companies but my own were fiddling, dancing,
singing songs, playing cards, and enjoying themselves generally. In
my own company, when night came on, all was silent, the tents dark,
the men lying with their clothes on, their guns in their hands, and
their cartridge boxes under their heads. They had orders, in case of
an alarm, to spring at once into line in front of our row of tents. This
was all my work. Captain Burch having been placed in command of

Sigel, and in this last instance by Captain Wilson, of Company K, Tenth Illinois, and myself, as being
the best in the vicinity of Neosho. I saw to placing the pickets [guards] in person." "Report of Lieut.
Col. James K. Mills, Twenty-fourth Missouri Infantry" (investigation after the battle), June 13, 1862,
OR, ser. 1, vol. 13, 93–94: "Neither were any of the ordinary precautions in the way of guards and
scouts omitted, save the unaccountable neglect to post a picket upon the hill to the southwest of the
camp, over and down which, under the cover of the brush, the enemy approached. . . . Whether good
judgment was displayed in the selection of the camp ground so near the brush—60 yards—instead of
placing it farther to the eastward and out of gun-shot distance, cannot fairly be determined without an
inspection of the ground." "Report of Brig. Gen. Egbert B. Brown, Missouri Militia," June 17, 1862,
OR, ser. 1, vol. 13, 90: "From [the reports of Col. J. M. Richardson and Lieut. Col. James K. Mills] I
learn that the location of the camp was so that the foe approached it unseen from two directions. A want
of proper precaution against surprise and foolhardiness in not taking a defensive position when it was
known by the commander that a force of about 600 men was near him, the want of discipline, and doubt
of the men in their arms were the causes of Colonel Richardson's defeat."

the guard, I was, of course, left in command of the company.[5] When I lay down in my tent, I could not sleep. Lieutenant Norton, also who lay by my side, appeared restless and uneasy.[6] I asked him what he thought of our situation. He said he did not like it. I replied that I did not like it either, and that twenty five resolute rebels could throw our whole command into confusion, and stampede them like so many cattle. I told him that I would get up and go to see Colonel Richardson. He said he would go with me. On our way we met Captain Julian and a few other prudent officers who, like ourselves, did not like the existing state of affairs. These officers went with us. Before this occurred, indeed, just as daylight was fading, the firing of three guns had been heard somewhere on the wooded hill which I have just described. Some of the prisoners that I had taken declared that Standwaite's whole army was only a few miles away in that direction. A negro had brought us word that an attack upon us was about to be made. A Union woman, also, had sent us word that the college grounds, near her house, and *within rifle-range of our camps,* were full of men and horses. No guards were placed on that hill, and no one was permitted to ascend it to ascertain what might be there.[7] Had that hill been reconnoitered, our Colonel's old law partner, Rick Johnson, a prominent rebel officer, would have been found there with his command.[8] When darkness set in, the dogs still barked

---

5. Richardson's report also mentions that Burch was in command of the guard that evening (*OR*, ser. 1, vol. 13, 92).

6. Lt. Amos Norton (see chap. 4, note 20, above).

7. Report of Lieutenant Colonel Mills after the battle (*OR*, ser. 1, vol. 13, 93): "In the evening of the 30th, after nightfall, a rumor was brought into camp that a force of men were in the college yard (some half a mile from camp), and the woods full of horses. A council of war was held, the rumor traced to its source, and scouts sent out to examine the facts, but the rumor was not verified. The camp guard was doubled."

8. A Capt. Rick Johnson did command a company of Confederate irregulars in Missouri ("Soldiers' Records," MDH) but no ties to Neosho, Richardson, or this battle have been established. Milton Burch, writing from Neosho two years later on Aug. 5, 1864, identified the rebel Col. Rector Johnson as "formerly a citizen of this place" (*OR*, ser. 1, vol. 41, part 1, 194). A Capt. M. R. Johnson, who operated in southwestern Missouri and was killed by federal troops in 1863 (Nichols, *Guerrilla Warfare in Civil War Missouri*, 2:280), might have been the M. R. Johnson listed in Neosho in the 1860 census, but, again, no link of either Rector or M. R. to the Neosho skirmish or to Richardson has been established. Confederate Col. Stand Watie's June 1, 1862, report on the skirmish mentions only officers Col. John T. Coffee, Capt. Robert C. Parks, and Capt. Thomas R. Livingston (*OR*, ser. 1, vol. 13, 94–95). None is linked to Neosho or Richardson. Robert C. Parks became a lieutenant colonel in the 1st Regt., Cherokee Mounted Volunteers, CSA (NPS Soldiers' Database). Livingston had been a miner and brawler before the war (Nichols, *Guerrilla Warfare in Civil War Missouri*, 1:37).

upon the hill, and the citizens all around us seemed in confusion. Indeed, after lying down, by placing my ear to the ground, I could hear a low rumbling as of the distant trampling of many horses. It was then that I spoke to Lieutenant Norton, and that we arose to go see the Colonel.

When we reached the Colonel's head-quarters, he and the other "gay and festive" officers hastily gathered about us to learn our business. I briefly told them what I thought of our situation, and asked permission to go out alone and reconnoiter the dark woods on the hill, and also to learn what was moving upon the roads beyond our pickets. This very proper and very reasonable request was refused, and some insinuations of cowardice were made by some of the principal festive officers in regard to those who exhibited, as I did, some anxiety. Even the Colonel, with a very brave look, said: "It is very natural for some men to be chicken-hearted." He assured us that these reports were rebel lies fabricated by persons who wished to scare us away. He seemed to think that the enemy was a long way off and that he was very timid and inoffensive. "Why," said he, "even if Gen. Standwaite and Col. Coffee should conclude to attack *me*, it would be impossible for them, under a day yet, to hear of *my* arrival, and then it would take them at least two more days to reach this place. But they'll never attack *me*."[9] I returned to my tent grieved. I once thought of going out between the pickets without permission, but this, I knew, was not the way for a soldier to do. I therefore went around and saw that all my men were sleeping with their guns in their arms according to my orders. I found everything all right among them. I expected the attack at the dawning of the day; and, as I afterwards learned, this was the time at first fixed upon by the enemy. This time was changed by them, however, for a later hour,—the hour at which the men, by orders issued on the previous evening, were to *lead their horses to water without bridles or saddles.* When the enemy were duly notified, as they soon were, of

9. In his report after the battle, Colonel Richardson claimed that on that night, he "called a council of my captains" and furthermore that "they were all of the opinion there was no danger and no necessity of moving camp." He also said that "at a late hour of the night I went with the officer of the day (Captain Burch) to examine the position of the camp guard, to determine for myself if it was far enough off to warn us in time to be ready in case of an attack" (*OR*, ser. 1, vol. 13, 92). Wiley Britton, in *Civil War on the Border*, 1:283–86, follows Richardson's account.

these orders, they knew that the best time of all to make their attack would be while the men were thus watering their horses.

The night passed, the morning dawned, and yet no attack. Breakfast was eaten, and even I had come to the conclusion that no real danger had threatened us at present. Leaving my arms in my tent, I took a short stroll to a little creek that skirted one side of our camping ground. While here, I was met by Captain Julian, Lieutenant Worley, and several other officers who said they had orders to take me with them to break open certain cells in the jail in which rebel ammunition was supposed to be stored. I went on with them, without returning for my arms. At the same time, another party, composed almost entirely of prominent officers, was sent to put up a flag in town.[10] This was done at the request of our Col's. rebel ladies who said that they had not seen a Union flag for so long a time that they would like to see one now. As I have since learned, the flag business was merely a stratagem to get as many of our officers as possible out of our camp, at the time the attack was to be made. Whether our Colonel weakly permitted his fair rebel charmers to make all these plans for him, or whether, for a consideration, he deliberately contracted with the enemy to surrender us into their power, I do not know. Certain it is, however, that all the efficient officers were sent out in these two parties, and that, too, at the very time fixed upon by the enemy for their attack,—the very time at which the men would be leading their horses to water and would be at some distance from their guns and their horse equipments. These were certainly strange coincidences.

While I and my party were busy in the jail, we heard some small boys, who had gathered at the door, exclaiming: "They're shoot'n! They're run'n!" Going to the door to learn what they meant, we heard brisk firing in the direction of our camps. Running out, we saw the citizens scampering in all directions,—the soldiers scattered about the town running toward the camps. We joined in the headlong race. The distance was about 300 yards. As we ran, Worley who, like myself, was doubtless thinking of the unfortunate absence

10. In a supplement to his June 1 report on the Neosho skirmish, Confederate Col. Stand Watie noted that "our boys captured two Federal flags, one being allowed to wave only about a quarter of an hour on the steeple of the court-house at Neosho" (*OR*, ser. 1, vol. 13, 95). Watie, who had not been at the scene of the battle, said nothing about any coordinated signal from the townspeople or from Richardson.

at that particular moment of all the efficient officers, exclaimed: "If our men will only stand till we get there!"[11] I replied: "I hope they will." Just then, Burch, who had been visiting his guards on the other side of the town, passed us on horse-back. This was joy to us. He was one of our best officers, and he would soon be with the men. I and Worley were soon among the very foremost in the race. As we came from behind all intervening houses, and were streaking it down an open street, the bullets began to whistle uncomfortably thick and close about our ears. We were running straight toward the enemy who were concealed in the bushes on a hill close to our camps. As we came nearer, the bullets flew thicker about us. One of our men cried out that he was shot. At this, several other men ducked their heads and dived in behind any object that could conceal them. The rest of us kept right on. As we neared the hill, we heard a rebel officer command: "Fire on that squad coming in!" Till now, the firing had been irregular. At this command, however, a hundred guns thundered out at once, and the bullets pattered like hail around us in the dust, or screamed through the air around our heads. How so many of us escaped, I can not understand.[12] By this time, the men had bridled and saddled their horses, and, mounting with their long infantry guns, had formed into an irregular line partially protected by the foliage of an open grove.[13] We quickly passed behind this line. Then, however, the storm that had broken upon us, burst with double fury upon the whole line. The terrific crash of bullets among the foliage around us seemed sufficient to wither every-thing before it. The roar of the guns, the fearful yelling of the indians and other rebels, the rearing the plunging of our frightened horses made a scene dreadful almost beyond description. My own company was at

11. Capt. Abraham Worley, Co. A, 14th MSM Cavalry.
12. Colonel Richardson's report: "Four of my best officers—Captains Julian and Burch and Lieutenants Worley and Kelso—were unfortunately absent, the three former on duty. They made a desperate effort to get into the action. These gallant officers in their effort to get by my side subjected themselves to the fire of one whole company of rebels. It was a terrible gauntlet to run, but they came through unharmed; too late, however, to aid in saving the day. They proved themselves entirely worthy of my confidence and are entitled to that of the Government" (*OR*, ser. 1, vol. 13, 91).
13. Colonel Richardson's report: "I ordered Lieutenant Wilson to take a position with Company A on the south side of the camp, facing the right of the enemy's center. Lieutenant Norton had formed Company H facing the left of the enemy's center. Captains Breeden's, Julian's, and Hargrove's companies in good time formed in the center and to the north of the camp" (*OR*, ser. 1, vol. 13, 91).

the farther end of this line. Could I reach them in time, I would dismount them, and, taking shelter behind the low, steep bank of the creek, behind which the whole command might have been sheltered, I would still hold the field. The men were now doing nothing at all except trying to manage their frightened horses. Just then I heard our Colonel command: "Mountain Rangers, charge that hill!" I knew that this was the command of an idiot, a madman, or a traitor. The men could not charge the hill. Only one moved forward. This was Wesley Rice a former student of mine. He darted forward, two or three rods, but finding himself all alone, he turned quietly around and came back to his place in the line.[14] I looked but a moment, and knew all was lost. I would not be able to even reach my own company. First a few men at a time turned and fled. Others cursed them for cowards, but quickly turned and followed. The Colonel's horse now fell dead. The Colonel was down, supposed to be killed. He was held down by one of his legs upon which his horse had fallen.[15] In a moment, *all* the men, like frightened sheep, crowded pell mell, thundered from the ground. I was now about the middle of the line opposite the opening in the corral of wagons that had been thrown around our camps on that side. Converging to this point from all parts of the line, the horses became fearfully jammed in front of this opening. They ran over me, knocked me down, knocked my hat off; bruised my right knee and skimmed my right hand. I tried to rise, but could not. There was no room for me between the closely packed bodies of the horses. My head was jarred by the knees and hoofs of the terrified animals, and I was again knocked down and rolled forward in the dust among their frantically trampling feet. A second attempt to rise resulted in the same way. To keep my hands and arms from being broken, I now drew them under my body, and lay still with my face to the ground till the whole command had passed over me. By a

14. Colonel Richardson reported that he ordered Lieutenant Wilson's company on the other end of the line to charge, and that it did so, causing the enemy to fall "back in haste and confusion into the brush" (*OR*, ser. 1, vol. 13, 91). Sgt. Wesley S. Rice (b. 1834), Co. A, 14th MSM Cavalry ("Soldiers' Records," MDH; 1860 U.S. Census, Green Township, Dallas County, Missouri, family no. 167).
15. Col. Richardson's report: "I was wounded in the right arm, my horse shot, and in falling fell on my left leg, the fall at the same time dislocating my shoulder and spraining my wrist. In this condition I was unable to rise. My troops, supposing their commander killed, and no other field officer being present to take command, became discouraged, confused, and began to leave" (*OR*, ser. 1, vol. 13, 91). Richardson was initially reported dead or mortally wounded; see *OR*, ser. 1, vol. 13, 90, 409.

strange kind of instinct, the horses, though they could not see me, all avoided stepping directly upon me. Some of them, however, not lifting their feet quite high enough, bruised the back of my head with the corks of their shoes.

When the whole command had passed over me, I arose, my eyes, nose, mouth, hair and neck filled with dust. Clearing my eyes a little, I thought for a moment of turning and going with the tide, as I saw the others were doing who had come in with me on foot from the town. This thought, however, was only for a moment. The shooting had nearly ceased. The enemy, I suppose, were mostly mounting to chase. My revolvers, my horse were thirty yards nearer the enemy. I sprang forward. Several bullets screamed passed me as I entered my tent. Several more passed through it while I was inside. Snatching up my revolvers, but leaving my saber, I ran to my horse a few yards away. He was tied to a large apple-tree, the low thick top of which greatly sheltered him from the shots of the enemy. He was rearing and trying to break away. He was firmly tied with a strong new rope, and it took me several seconds to untie the knot. When I had succeeded in this, and had bridled him, I found the storm of bullets growing heavier, I being now the only object left to shoot at. The enemy lay to the west of me. To the north, I saw a body of cavalry crossing a cornfield not far away. This, I mistook for a scouting party of our own men that had been sent out a short time before in that direction. I supposed that they had just returned, and that, seeing how our affairs stood, they had turned to follow our routed command. I started toward them at full speed. The dust they raised prevented my seeing their dress, and I discovered my mistake only when I was almost among them. I then perceived that there were too many of them to be any part of our own force. I perceived, too, that they were mostly indians dressed in fantastic hunting shirts.[16] They seemed to mistake me for one of their own party. At any rate, no one attempted to molest me in any way. They were standing up in their stirrups, looking straight to the front, and holding their guns ready to shoot. In his fright, my horse was almost

16. Col. Stand Watie sent two hundred men of the 1st Regt., Cherokee Cavalry, under the command of Capt. R. C. Parks. They joined Colonel Coffee's "something more than 200" and Captain Livingston's group (number unknown). See Watie's report, *OR*, ser. 1, vol. 13, 94.

unmanageable. Before I could check and turn him, he had carried me almost into the midst of these enemies. When I did get him turned, I struck back toward the camp, intending to take the route my comrades had taken.

I reached the camp. I glanced over it. Many horses and mules were still standing hitched. Many others were galloping about loose. Many others still were scattered around dead or dying. Strange to say, I could see *only two dead men.*[17] This was but a momentary glance. Again the bullets began to scream through and around me, and my horse was slightly wounded in his right shoulder. The enemy's infantry had come down from the hill and were now just entering the farther side of our camps. A body of cavalry had also come down on the south side of the camp and cut of[f] my intended retreat in that direction. Again I turned toward the field in the direction I had first taken. That field was still full of enemies. I was now surrounded on three sides by enemy and on the fourth side by the two strong and high fences of a door yard around a house. My scalp began to feel loose upon my head. I turned my horse to the first fence. Would he leap it? He *did* leap it, bounding over like a deer. Turning quickly around the house so as to have it between me and the enemy who were still firing upon me, I charged the other fence. My horse leaped that also in fine style. I now fled at full speed, keeping the house directly behind me until I was beyond gun-shot from that direction. Then, to avoid some high rail fences which no horse could have leaped, I turned to the left and came into contact with the rear of the body of cavalry that had been crossing the field. Not suspecting that an enemy would be thus in their rear on such an occasion, none of them paid any attention to me. All these things occurred in much less time than it takes to describe them.

As soon as the high fences just mentioned would permit, I turned square to the right and saw no more of the enemy. I had been within twenty yards of some of them. The first one of our own men that I saw was Col. Richardson himself, alone, on foot, and wounded. Badly as he had managed, I wished to save him. I tried to reach him to let him have my horse. He reached the brush, however, and

17. It was originally reported (June 2, 1862) that Richardson's command lost ten men killed, wounded, and missing; the next day the casualties were lowered to five (*OR*, ser. 1, vol. 13, 409, 412).

disappeared before I could overtake him.[18] I saw the brave old Captain Julian also reach the brush on foot at a speed rather remarkable for a man of his age and his weight.[19] Next, I found James Brewer, one of my own company, lying with his thighs broken partly in the water of a little creek.[20] I could do nothing for him. He was too badly hurt. Leaving him, I soon fell in with an old man, badly wounded, and a sick boy. I staid with them awhile, dismounting and putting the boy on my horse. A loose horse, which I had captured a few days before, now came up, and the old wounded man escaped upon him. I took the sick boy into the woods where I found some ten other men all on foot. One of these, being a friend to the sick boy, took charge of him. Few of these men had any guns. I advised them to scatter and wait till the pursuit was over.[21] I went off by myself, but had not gotten out of sight of the others when I fell in with Marion Glaspy and a man by the name of Greene, Captain Burch's brother-in-law.[22] Greene was severely wounded, having twelve buck-shots in him. I dismounted and put him upon my horse. We tried to make our way through the hills to Mount Vernon. The day being cloudy, however, we became bewildered, and, in a few hours, came back to the very spot at which I had taken Greene up. Near this place, we found twelve other footmen, one of whom was also badly wounded. I put him upon my horse behind Greene. We then all proceeded together, but after wandering about a long time, we came in sight of the *battleground*. Our tents, our wagons, everything was gone.[23] We had now traveled at least thirty miles over rough hills and were nearly tired out. It was very discouraging to know that we had not gained any thing at all. Our wounded men were not able to go any further. We must leave them and we must have a guide. We sought

---

18. According to the 1888 *History of Newton . . . Counties, Missouri*, when Richardson met a civilian (who was also fleeing) in the bush north of town, the colonel, mistaking the man for one of the enemy, "offered to surrender to him" (312).

19. Captain Julian was forty (1860 U.S. Census, Cass Township, Greene County, Missouri, family no. 606).

20. Pvt. Samuel T. Brewer, Co. H, 14th MSM Cavalry ("Soldiers' Records," MDH).

21. Colonel Watie's report: "Col. Coffee's cavalry . . . kept up the pursuit [of the retreating Federals] for miles" (*OR*, ser. 1, vol. 13, 95).

22. Pvt. Marion Galaspie (also spelled Gillespie) and Corp. William M. Green, Co. H, 14th MSM Cavalry. Green is listed as deserting on Nov. 20, 1863, at Springfield.

23. Colonel Watie's report: "Fourteen tents, 5 wagons and teams, arms, horses, some commissary stores and ammunition, and, in fact, the enemy's baggage, fell into the hands of the Confederates" (*OR*, ser. 1, vol. 13, 95).

the house of a man by the name of Powers.[24] He was a rebel, but was an honorable man. We found him at home and took him prisoner. He knew the country, and could guide us to Mount Vernon. We left our wounded men at his house. I feared that they would be murdered by the Indians or by the bush-whackers. I therefore told Mrs. Powers that her husband would be treated just as these were treated. If they were treated kindly, he would be treated in the same way and would be released and permitted to come home. If they were murdered in her house, he would be put to death. I was sure this would save them. With our new guide, we now again proceeded on our way. No guide could have done better. He soon made friends of us all. We suffered a good deal from thirst, but, having found a mining shaft that contained water, we pulled off our boots and drew up water in them to drink. The water was pretty strongly flavored with dead rabbits and with our sweaty boots, but it quenched our thirst all the same. About sun-set, we fell in with Worley and about a dozen more men all on foot. We all kept together. We travelled all night and till noon the next day to reach Mt. Vernon. The report of my death, and that of several others who did not die, had preceded us.

Great alarm prevails among the Union people here. The Secessionists are full of joy. Their women boast to our faces that we will be driven entirely out of South West Missouri in a few weeks. Soon after my arrival at Mt. Vernon, we started back to try it again in company with some Illinois troops under the command of Major Stephenson.[25] At Sarcoxie, we were ordered back. Why, I do not know. I was then ordered to this place to give my views in regard to the conduct of Col. Richardson. He is also ordered to this place to be tried for neglect of duty in suffering himself to be surprised and routed in the way he was. In the whole affair, he showed a total want of military judgment, if he did not show something much worse. We lost all our camp equipage, clothing, wagons, teams, &c. worth in all $50,000 or more. I lost some $30 worth of private property including all my books. Most of the other officers lost more than I did, from the fact that they had more to lose. Much excitement prevails. Many

24. David Powers (b. 1814 in S.C.) and his wife, Larisa, lived with their seven children on their farm in Neosho (1860 U.S. Census, Neosho Township, Newton County, Missouri, family no. 371).
25. Maj. Marshall L. Stephenson, Cos. F and S, 10th Regt., Illinois Cavalry (NPS Soldiers' Database).

returned "good Secessionists," who had taken the oath of allegiance to our government, hastened to way-lay the roads, as soon as they heard of our defeat, and to gather up our demoralized stragglers and take them back as prisoners to the enemy. In this way, we lost several men. Many of these oath-taking and oath-breaking rebels have already gone to join Coffee. Hell itself, I believe, is too good a place for some of these wretches. I have ceased to send prisoners to these head-quarters. I patronize the *brimstone head-quarters*. Tilman and Mattie were not in the battle. Bob was. They are all well. Dr. Barrett sends his respects to you.[26] I have just been sent for to go to head-quarters. I must close. Be my own dear Susie yet.

     Your Johny

(As given here, this letter, in some of its parts, is a considerable enlargement upon the original.)

     Col. Richardson was not tried. So soon as he had a talk with the commanding officer at Springfield, the matter was strangely hushed. How much it cost the Colonel to have it hushed, I never knew. It would have been madness, however, for him to again attempt to command his own regiment in the field. He was, therefore, made quarter-master, or something of that kind, at Rolla, where he would be at a safe distance both from the enemy and from his own men.[27] Coffee sent us a kind letter thanking us for bringing him so great an abundance of the very supplies he most needed, and for placing them where he could get them without any trouble and without any danger. What could be more galling than such a letter? Thus closed one of the most disgraceful military affairs in which I was ever involved. I took none of the disgrace, however, to myself. Our Colonel alone was to blame for it all.[28]

---

26. Dr. Beverly A. Barrett. There is no indication here of the hostile encounter between Barrett and Kelso that had occurred three months earlier, according to Barrett's 1897 recollection (see chap. 6, note 3, above).

27. *History of Newton . . . Counties, Missouri*, 311: "Richardson was not allowed to command again." But in fact he was commanding the post at Cassville by Nov. 1862 and led troops in battle again on Dec. 7, 1862 (*OR*, ser. 1, vol. 13, 360; vol. 22, part 1, 86–88).

28. Richardson blamed the defeat on his being shot off his horse and the lack of another field officer to take the command. He reported that four of his best officers were absent from the battle until too late: three of them, he conceded, were doing their duty elsewhere according to his orders, but one of them—Kelso—had not been ordered away. In Kelso's account, the other officers said that he was included in their orders, and the fact that all the field officers were sent away for one reason or another he took as support for his conspiracy theory. Col. James K. Mills, commander of the army post at Springfield, received special orders to conduct an inquiry on June 4, 1862. He reported that he conducted "the most

For several weeks after this affair we lay in camp at Springfield, training our horses and learning to use guns and sabers and to play cards. Being now properly armed and equipped, we were soon prepared to do efficient service in the field. While our regiment was lying here, I was sent out in command of 125 men to make a scout through the counties of Polk and Dallas. On this scout, I was absent several days and had some fine adventures which, however, I will not stop to describe. We killed several bush-whackers and took some sixty prisoners. Among the bush-whackers killed was Rude Arnold, who had been concerned in the burning of my house. Twenty eight of the prisoners, I carried to Springfield. The balance, I released on parole.[29]

Upon my return to Springfield, I learned that the battalion to which I belonged had gone to Ozark, where they were expected to remain for some time.[30] Ozark is the county town of Christian County, and is about fifteen miles from Springfield in a south-easterly direction. It then contained about

thorough investigation which the circumstances have permitted me to make" but noted that "there is scarcely a point upon which the testimony is not contradictory." Mills waved off criticism of the camp-site and the guards. He thought Richardson more vulnerable to criticism for ordering or permitting his officers to be away from their companies, but even on this point he thought that a commander needed to be able to exercise his own judgment on such matters. "I am not of the opinion," Mills concluded, "that charges should be preferred against Colonel Richardson." He then seemed to shift the blame to the junior officers: "Further investigation, however, is required to show why, upon the fall of Colonel Richardson, the next ranking officer did not assume command; why certain officers were absent from camp at the time of the attack, and why no effort, as it now appears, was made by the officers to rally their men after they first broke." Brig. Gen. E. B. Brown, commanding the Southwestern Division and also headquartered at Springfield, placed the blame squarely with Richardson (OR, ser. 1, vol. 13, 90–94).

29. In his official report, dated July 25, 1862, Kelso wrote that he led a detachment of fifty men on the evening of June 19 in the direction of Buffalo. By 10:00 p.m. they had reached Pomme de Terre, seventeen miles north of Springfield. There he divided his command into three groups and sent each to the houses of known rebels in different neighborhoods. The three groups met the next morning eight miles south of Buffalo, having captured a total of thirty-seven prisoners. He released seventeen on parole and had a detachment march the others to Springfield. The remainder of the command rested in Buffalo until the morning of June 23. They captured "a number of prisoners," paroling all but five. Back at Pomme de Terre, they found a large stash of concealed corn. He sent Sergeant Baxter and a small party after "Capt. Thomas Lofton and his gang." In the resulting skirmish, Rude Arnold was killed. Four more prisoners were taken, but Isham Case escaped and a horse thief named Greene (probably "Thief Green"), who had previously escaped from prison twice, escaped again but was badly wounded (OR, ser. 1, vol. 13, 164–66). Jonas Rudisill ("Rude") Arnold, Jr. (b. 1829, d. July 24, 1862), had lived in Benton Township, Dallas County, Mo., with his wife, Mary, and their year-old baby in 1860. His father, Jonas Rudsill Arnold, Sr., was on the Sept. 1862 list of Dallas County rebels or rebel sympathizers. See 1860 U.S. Census, Benton Township, Dallas County, Missouri, family nos. 46 and 47; MDH Provost Marshal Papers, reel F1588, files 2133, 1236; and www.findagrave.com, nos. 75652033, 37707799.

30. Co. H, 14th MSM Cavalry, marched from Springfield to Ozark (fifteen miles) on July 19, 1862, where they would be stationed until the end of the year (OR, Supplement, 785).

600 inhabitants, most of them disloyal. Immediately upon my arrival, I was put in command as Provost Marshall. I did not like the position at all.[31] I desired active service in the field, and from this service I would be debarred while acting as Provost Marshall.[32] I chafed, too, under the knowledge that the appointment was made by Major Wilbur for the express purpose of rendering me unable to win any more laurels in the field. I was becoming entirely too popular with the men to suit him. He was regarded as the usurper of my place, and, being a tyrannical man any way, was universally hated by the men. I appealed, but appealed in vain, to the commanding officer at Springfield to be relieved from this appointment. Being compelled to serve in this capacity, I went to work in earnest and was soon the most popular Provost Marshall on the whole frontier. My office was a very dignified court-room in which I presided as judge, jury, attorney, and every thing else that chanced to be necessary. Some of my modes of trial were entirely original. I made most of my own laws, and had them strictly executed. I was just, but I was severe. A few cases were appealed to my superior at Springfield, but he uniformly confirmed my action. Bribes were offered more than once. Men offered me money, and beautiful women offered me something that was much more tempting to me than the money was. I managed, however, to withstand all these temptations.

Toward the latter part of August, I think it was, Major Wilber went out on a scout of several days taking all the men except about 75, most of whom were sick men, nurses, teamsters, cooks, &c. He left Capt. Burch in command

31. On Aug. 4, 1862, Kelso wrote to Maj. James H. Steger, asking to be relieved of his duty as provost marshal and sent back to the field. After eight days he could tell that the sedentary desk job was bad for his health, he wrote. He was eager to serve his country in combat and make a reputation for himself as a soldier. Furthermore, he argued, his captain (Burch) needed a lieutenant (John R. Kelso, Provost Marshal's Office, Ozark, Mo., to Maj. James H. Steger, Aug. 4, 1862, photocopy, Bradbury Collection).
32. The provost marshal system enforced martial law. "History of the Provost Marshal," MDH Provost Marshal Papers: "In districts with active fighting, the provost marshal's primary duty was to limit marauding against citizens, prevent stragglers on long marches, and generally suppress gambling or other vices not conducive to good order and discipline. However, in many districts, the war's fighting was somewhat removed and the area did not see battles. In these areas, the provost marshal's duties were more magisterial. The provost marshal had the power to administer and enforce the law when it came to regulating public places; conduct searches, seizures, and arrests; issue passes to citizens for movement in and out of Union lines; and record and investigate citizen complaints. It was not uncommon for the law to be suspended in many cases and for the provost marshal, mostly independent of any real supervision, to dispense with the rules of civil procedure." On the operation of the provost marshal system in Missouri during the Civil War, see esp. Boman, *Lincoln and Citizens' Rights*.

of these men.[33] At this place, we had a considerable amount of government property which we knew the rebels would like to possess. We knew, too, that the rebel Col. Lawthers, with 400 fine cavalry men, was hovering about the country only one day's march away.[34] We feared that, during Major Wilber's absence, he would undertake to capture our station. We therefore sent out small parties of well mounted and reliable men to watch his movements. In this way, we soon learned that he was coming sure enough. Our parties of look-outs retired quietly in front of him without being discovered. From time to time, they gave us notice of his progress. At dusk, he stopped to feed only three miles away. He seemed confident of success. He expected to completely surprise us. He did not hurry. Had a Richardson been in command, he would have been all right. But he had now to deal with a Burch and a Kelso. As he soon learned, this made a great difference. Every rod of his further progress was watched by our men. We were encamped on the lower side of a large open wheat field. About midnight, he crept silently out of the forest on the opposite side of this field, and formed his men into line in the dark shade of the tall trees. To our great joy, we learned that he was going to charge our camps on horse-back. We had expected this, hoped for it, and prepared for it. We placed lights in our tents and hung up coats and hats so that they might cast shadows upon the sides of the tents, resembling the shadows of men. We meant for them to charge through our camps and empty their guns upon our coats and hats. We then had hung ropes stretched across the way to throw their horses just as they would be leaving our camp after charging through. Having hidden our horses in a suitable place, still farther back, we concealed ourselves near these ropes. We drew in our guards silently and waited. It was a still clear summer night. Presently the most profound silence was broken by the most terrific yells. A dark mass moved out from the shade of the forest, and swept down upon us with a noise that resembled thunder. Like a tornado, they swept into our camps. They raised still more

33. According to Burch's Aug. 5, 1862, report, Major Wilber left him in command of about eighty men on July 23 (OR, ser. 1, vol. 13, 196).

34. In his report to the Confederate command, filed from Springfield, Mo., Aug. 2, 1862, Col. Robert R. Lawther, Missouri Partisan Rangers, wrote that he marched his men (an effective fighting force of only fifty-five, others being unarmed or not suitably armed) to within two and a half miles of Ozark on July 31 (OR, ser. 1, vol. 13, 199–200). Lawther (1836–1911) had been a grocer in Jefferson City, Mo., before the war. He enlisted in the State Guard, was elected major of the 3rd Missouri Cavalry, and was promoted to colonel after the Battle of Pea Ridge. See Memorial and Biographical History of Dallas County, Texas (Chicago: Lewis, 1892), 754–65, and NPS Soldiers' Database.

terrific yells. They poured their harmless shots into our empty tents. On they rushed. Their horses struck our cable ropes and down they tumbled, those behind tumbling upon those in front, pell mell, the men, many of them being thrown, and many losing guns, pistols, hats, blankets, saddlebags, &c., while all rent the air with their yells and their curses. Then was our time. Like young devils let loose, our boys raised their battle cry and lit up the darkness of night with the livid flashings of their fire arms. For a few moments, all was terrible confusion, friends and foes all mingled together, all yelling and shouting,—the horses rearing and plunging, some tumbling into ditches, others shot down and struggling upon the ground; while the hills, reëchoing all these confused sounds, still brightened the terrors of the scene.[35]

Quick as the storm had come, it passed. The rebels fled in confusion. Most of them dashed into a dense grove of black jacks, through which even in the day time, a man could scarce ride with safety. Soon all was still again. Then we came out and captured a few dismounted stragglers who had become too much confused to escape. We had none killed and only two wounded. We also lost four horses. We could not ascertain the exact loss of the enemy, as several of them died after they left the ground. A dozen would probably cover their entire loss in killed. Their wounded were quite numerous; more of them having been hurt by the low snaggy limbs of the black jacks, among which they dashed, than were hurt by our bullets.[36] Considering our advantages, we did poor shooting. The men nearly all

35. Kelso is probably using a later account from Burch in which Burch drew language from his Aug. 5, 1862, report, for the report too described the enemy coming "like a tornado" and used the phrase "then was our time." Kelso did not apparently have a full copy of the report itself because he got the date wrong and gave a different estimate of enemy troop strength and casualties. Burch in the report added, "Lieutenants Kelso and [Cleon M.] Etter seemed to really enjoy the scene, and their men partook of their spirit" (OR, ser. 1, vol. 13, 197).

36. Burch estimated that the enemy attacked with 120 men. He reported "that our loss was 2 men wounded, 1 only slightly, and 2 horses killed. The enemy lost 1 man, taken prisoner, and, as we have since learned from Union men who were taken prisoners, they lost 9 wounded, 3 of whom died before reaching Forsyth. They also lost 2 horses, killed on the ground, and several severely wounded, which had to be left behind in their flight. We captured 2 horses, 8 guns, 2 holsters, 2 revolvers, 3 saddles, and other articles, such as saddle bags, blankets, hats, &c." (OR, ser. 1, vol. 13, 197). Lawther described the battle very differently: "On arriving on the sight of their camp I found that they had been advised of our approach, and were prepared to defend themselves, having all of their tents lighted up." He mentioned nothing about his men firing into empty tents or being unhorsed by the picket ropes. Instead, he wrote that his men attacked the Federals on the streets of Ozark and drove them into the surrounding brush (where Burch and Kelso said they were waiting from the beginning). A second charge drove other Union soldiers to take shelter in houses and stables, in Lawther's version: "I then drew off my men and formed them in line of battle on the enemy's camp ground, expecting them to come out of the houses and give us a fair fight; but we soon found that it was impossible to draw them out, and as they had 8 men

over-shot the enemy. This we learned from the marks of our bullets on objects beyond. This is nearly always the fault of new soldiers. We captured a good many horses whose riders had been killed or thrown. We also captured many guns, revolvers, and other articles. Next morning we gathered up nearly a mule load of hats, blankets, guns, &c. in the black jack grove above mentioned. This victory put our men in fine spirits and made them eager for another fight. It also placed Burch and myself still higher in favor with the men and with the loyal people generally. It made us dreaded by the enemy. Most of our men behaved remarkably well. We had, however, a few cowards among us. One ran entirely away and went to Springfield. A few others concealed themselves in some large sycamore gums that happened to be not far away.

After this defeat by one seventh of his own numbers, the redoubtable Col. Lawthers retired to the south side of White River fifty miles away. In a few days, Major Wilber returned with the balance of our forces, and then, after they had rested a little, the men began to clamor to be allowed to return Lawther's call, under the command of Captain Burch or myself. The result was that an expedition was resolved upon to be commanded by Captain Burch, I cursing the hateful office that prevented me from accompanying him. His force consisted of 100 good men, just a fourth the number of the force he was going to attack. The account of this expedition as given by Captain Burch will be found in the next chapter. I will say, however, that the Captain was better at fighting than at writing. Though good, his description of that truly brilliant affair hardly does himself and his brave men justice. I awaited his return with much impatience. Knowing his skill and his desperate bravery, I expected a good result.

---

to our 1 I concluded that it would not be prudent to attempt to drive them out of the houses." Lawther claimed he had only two men slightly wounded and estimated that the Federals had three to ten killed and ten to twenty wounded. See Lawther's report, *OR*, ser. 1, vol. 13, 199–200.

8. The Battle of Forsyth, and a Raid on Thieves and Cut-Throats

July to August 1862

(Major Burch's account of the Battle of Forsythe.)

You know, Captain, that, after our fight at Ozark, I was ordered by Brig. Gen. Brown to take command of 100 men of our battalion, and to proceed to Forsythe and, if possible, ascertain what number of the enemy were in that vicinity. In obedience to this order, I started with Mr. Phenix (afterwards Captain) as guide.[1] After a march of some 15 miles, night overtook us and the darkness became intense. I then ordered Sergt. Baxter to proceed with an advance guard of 10 men. I instructed him to be very careful in approaching houses, and, if possible, to capture every man that might be at home, and thus to prevent them from carrying to the enemy intelligence of our approach. Having advanced about two miles, he captured and sent back to me an ex-rebel Captain by the name of Jackson, and a spy that major Wilber had sent down to White River a few days before.[2] This spy had been captured by Col. Lawther and kept as a prisoner

Source: Kelso, "Auto-Biography," chap. 16, 768–75.

1. The Captain Phenix (or Phoenix) has not been identified. Forsyth was strategically important: the White River was navigable to that point and could serve the Confederates as a supply route to the Mississippi.

2. Probably Capt. D. F. Jackson, 1st Regt., Missouri Infantry, who enlisted in early July 1861; took an active part in the Battle of Forsyth on July 22, 1861; was wounded (initially reported killed); and resigned

three days. Having satisfied Lawther that he was a good rebel, he was then released, and was now trying to work his way back to Ozark. From him I learned that Lawther was encamped near Sharp's farm, two miles from Forsythe, on the south side of White River.[3] I then questioned the ex-rebel Captain and learned that he was well acquainted with that part of the country. I learned that, by going ten miles down White River, to a point near the mouth of Big Beaver, I could cross the river, and then, by passing through a gap in the mountains, could approach the enemy's camp without coming in contact with his pickets. I then told Jackson that, if he failed to lead me through all right, he would go up the spout.[4]

When we arrived within a half mile of Phenix's Mill, I halted the command and sent Baxter forward with eight men to reconnoiter the mill. If he found only a few rebels there, he was to take them in himself; if he found many, he was to inform me and I was to move on to his assistance. He found only two rebels who were running the mill. One of these was the noted Bob Wiseman who had acted as a spy for the rebels on many occasions. Baxter quickly took these two men in out of the wet and turned them over to me. I questioned them, but could not get any information out of them. They feigned to be two ignorant farmers who wished to stay at home. Again we moved on and, without the occurrence of any incident worth mentioning, reached a point within two miles of the enemy's camp. Here Wiseman, putting spurs to his horse, attempted to escape. He was shot by his guard, however, and so severely wounded that he could not manage his horse. I then ran upon him and dispatched him at once.[5] Moving on again, we soon discovered, near the dim path

---

by the end of the month (*OR*, ser. 1, vol. 3, 44; "Soldiers' Records," MDH; Holcombe, *History of Greene County*, 295). In his Aug. 5, 1862, report, Milton Burch added that "Jackson had been a rebel captain, but had taken the oath of allegiance to the United States. He informed me that he was an old settler, and knew every hog path in that part of the country" (*OR*, ser. 1, vol. 13, 198).

3. Burch's Aug. 5, 1862, report referred to "Snapp's," not Sharp's, farm in Taney County, owned by Harrison Snapp (b. 1813) (*OR*, ser. 1, vol. 13, 198; 1860 U.S. Census, Swan Township, Taney County, Missouri, family no. 235).

4. Burch's 1862 report: "I gave him to understand that if he in any way proved false I would put him to instant death" (*OR*, ser. 1, vol. 13, 198).

5. Burch's 1862 report only said, "we found Bob Wisener [not Wiseman], whom we killed," but then added that Wisener "was a man of considerable influence, and his death has created quite a sensation among the rebel sympathizers about Ozark" (*OR*, ser. 1, vol. 13, 198). Four Wissner (or Wisner)

which we were following, some twenty horses in an old field. I was now confident that the enemy was close at hand, but I did not know his exact position. I then ordered Jackson to guide me to within a half mile of Sharp's. Baxter was still in command of the advance guard. Jackson did not do as I ordered him. He led us to the Yellville road a half mile beyond Sharp's. It was now growing light, and, as we were ascending a long slope, I saw the advance guard come to a halt. I galloped forward to see what was the matter, and there, directly in front of us, were two horsemen who did not seem at all surprised or alarmed at our appearance. I now supposed that Lawther had intelligence of our approach, and was prepared to give us a warm reception. Knowing that his force was several times greater than my own, and that he had the advantage in the ground, I knew that I must act with great prudence or there would be danger of my getting my command cut to pieces. I therefore dismounted sixty men who had infantry guns, and ordered them to advance to our aid as fast as they could. With the remaining 40 men, who were armed with sabers and revolvers, I then moved forward. As soon as the two horsemen of whom I have spoken saw us advancing, they put spurs to their horses and fled as if the devil was after them. We pursued them at full speed. They ran directly to their camps, which were only a half mile distant, but ran right through it and away without stopping to help their companions in arms, or to even tell them what the danger was. We charged into their camps like a tornado. They were completely surprised and panic stricken. About half of them, who were camped outside of Sharp's field, being the first that we came upon, did not make any attempt to fight at all. Springing from their beds, they left their guns, their clothing,—every thing they had and, with shirt tails fluttering in the morning breeze, fled like so many frightened sheep. The balance,—those who were camped in Sharp's field, fired one round upon us and then fled like the others. We would have killed a great many of them had it not been that a dense thicket was near into which they dived and into which we could not follow them. We took all their camp equipage and clothing, most of their

brothers lived with their mother in Christian County in 1860, but Robert S. was the youngest (only nineteen in 1862) and was not perhaps the man of considerable influence that Burch killed (1860 U.S. Census, Finley Township, Christian County, Missouri, family no. 252).

arms, and 75 of their horses.[6] Col. Lawther himself went off *en dishabille*. He left a full suit of rebel uniform, a sword, and a sash. The sash I still have. He left bare-footed and in his shirt and drawers. Most of his men went off in their shirt tails. A woman afterwards told me that she saw 15 of them all in one body with no clothing but their shirts, making their way to Yellville. Lawther's commission as Col. in the C. S. A. fell into my hands, as did also some 200 printed hand-bills in which he vauntingly declared that, within 60 days, he would rid Missouri of all the Yankee Hessians, and would also invade both Iowa and Illinois. He did, indeed, within 60 days, invade Illinois. Before the expiration of that time, he was taken prisoner and confined in the Alton penitentiary.[7]

Although, in his modest account of this really brilliant achievement, Major Burch does not so state, several of his own men were slightly wounded in these engagements, and some half dozen rebels were killed.[8] On this occasion, Burch captured the largest shot-gun that I ever saw. This gun he swapped to me for a smaller and finer shot-gun which I had captured on a former occasion. This enormous shot gun I carried till the close of the war, killing twelve rebels with it and rendering it almost as famous as I rendered myself. At the close of the war, I was offered many times its real worth for it, but I declined to sell it at all. I wished to keep it during my lifetime and then leave it to one of my sons. When I left Missouri, however, I left it in my wife's care, and she sold it together with many other things that I would like to have kept.

Soon after the return of this expedition, I was relieved from duty as Provost Marshall and sent on a scout with some 75 men among the mountains

6. Burch's 1862 report: "We captured 23 horses, 2 mules, 30 stand of small arms, 75 saddles and bridles, all their commissary stores, numbers of saddle bags full of clothing, all their camp equipage, numbers of blankets, hats, shoes, &c., as well as the colonel's trunk, containing all his documents, and many other articles" (*OR*, ser. 1, vol. 13, 199).

7. Col. Robert Lawther was captured in Osage County, Mo., on Sept. 1, 1862, and after spending time in the Gratiot Street Prison in St. Louis and the military prison at Alton, Ill., was exchanged at Camp Chase, Ohio, on Jan. 31, 1863. He subsequently commanded the 10th Missouri Cavalry for the Confederacy. See "Roll of Prisoners Received at Military Prison, Alton, Illinois," in "Civil War Prisoner of War Records, 1861–1865," www.ancestry.com, and *Memorial and Biographical History of Dallas County, Texas,* 754–55.

8. Burch's 1862 report: four Confederates "were left dead upon the field. Many others, from the way they ran, were thought to be severely wounded. . . . Two of my men were wounded, one seriously" (*OR*, ser. 1, vol. 13, 199).

to the south east of Ozark. On this scout, I captured several rebels with their guns and horses but had very little fighting. On my return, I wrote the following letter to my wife:

Camp at Ozark, Missouri,—Sept. 12, 1862.

My Dear Susie:—Having just returned from a toilsome scout of three days in the mountains south east of this place, I find your letter of the 31st ult. waiting me. I reply immediately, although this may even now be too late to reach you. You speak of merely coming to *visit* me. This would be pleasant, but I would rather you would come to share with me *permanently* my rude and ever-shifting soldier's home.

Visiting at so great a distance would be attended with expense beyond our means. Make your arrangements, therefore, to remain with me and dispose of your effects accordingly. As to the best mode of coming, I have already written all that I could write on the subject. Do not delay. Come the best way you can.

You speak of your devoted affection for me. I am happy to read such expressions, as *my heart* too has been yearning for a return of *its best affections*. If I did not love you, why did I use to be sad, when I missed your smile, long ago, when you were only a school girl, and when I was not your husband? Why should I have trusted my happiness in your hands after the sad experience I had had in married life? Why have I so often grieved bitterly in solitude when you have complained of me or spoken unkind words to me? My kindred have all forsaken me, and in the whole wide world there is but *one* to whom my heart may now cling, and that one is my *Susie*. Time and distance have not changed me. During the long months of toil and of danger that have elapsed since I saw you, I have *thought* of you *daily*, almost *hourly*,—have *dreamed* of you almost *nightly*. Last night, though I lay in the dark woods upon the wet earth, though the chilling rain poured down upon me until I was drenched to the skin, and though the water stood in puddles around me and under me, yet, wearied out, I slept. I was *happy*, for, in my dreams, you came to me again. Your smiling face, your earnest eye told me that you *loved* me. I folded you to my bosom, and, with tears of joy, I _____ *waked* to look into the black night and to hear the dreary sound of the rain as it fell in torrents through the wild forests of the mountain.

Your Johnny.

It was about this time that I heard of the death of my poor little Ianthus. I received the letter that contained the account of his death in the evening just as I was going on duty as officer of the guard. The night was stormy and I did not try to sleep. When not occupied with my guards, I walked back and forth in the dreary night and composed the poem, "Ianthus," which will be found among my miscellaneous writings. That was one of the sad nights of my life. When morning dawned, I committed the poem to writing and then slept. Poor little Ianthus! His sweet life went out in the dawning of his existence, and, for many long years, there has been no one to place flowers upon his unknown grave.[9]

After being relieved from duty as Provost Marshall, in which office I had gained a good deal of popularity, I was appointed Quartermaster, Ordnance-master, and commissary,—three offices in one. This was the work of Major Wilber, who seemed determined to break me down some way by putting upon me more than I could accomplish. I now had to perform the duties of three officers, and I was allowed only one clerk. Indeed, I might say that I had to perform the duties of six officers, since I had two distinct classes of troops to deal with, in the U. S. Volunteers and the Missouri Militia, and since this rendered it necessary for me to keep two entirely distinct sets of books. Besides all this, there being no other officer in my company who could well make out the pay rolls, and the muster rolls of the company, I did this in addition to all my other work. I often missed my meals, not having time to eat them, and I often worked all night, wetting my face in cold water every few minutes to keep myself awake. Most of the time, I had to rule my own blanks, and this greatly increased the amount of my labor. And yet so far from failing, as Wilber hoped and expected that I would, in any of my many duties,—instead of getting into trouble in any of the departments in which I was acting, I received letters of special commendation from those departments. Besides this, I still grew in favor with the men. Knowing that Wilber was determined to keep me out of the field by giving me so unreasonable an amount of official duty to perform, I was just as determined that I would not be kept out of the field. Whenever, therefore, an important scouting party

9. "Ianthus" is a poem of eight quatrains, the last of which reads: "And thou art gone, Ianthus, long years may pass away, / And yet I'll think of thee, my child, I'll think of thee each day; / Thy little image will remain, engraven on my heart, / Nor time, nor distance can efface, or cause it to depart" ("John R. Kelso's Complete Works," 43).

was sent out, I would accompany it, and then, by robbing myself of sleep, when I returned, catch up with the work of my various offices. On all these expeditions, I won fresh laurels and grew more in favor with the men. So far from breaking me down, Wilber's ill disguised malice toward me reacted upon himself, causing him to be intensely hated by the men as I was loved by them. Indeed, so very obnoxious did Wilber and the few officers who sustained him become that, at times, it required all the influence of myself, Burch, and the other popular officers to keep the men from open mutiny. On one occasion, when Burch and I were not present, they did mutiny. They appeared before the office of our regimental Adjutant, one of Wilber's creatures, and required him either to write out his resignation at once or take a ride on a rail which they brought with them. He wrote out his resignation, and, though some of the leaders of the mutiny received slight punishment, that resignation was accepted and he disappeared from among us.[10] Major Wilber himself and Capt. Flagg, another of his vile creatures, came very near being treated in the same manner. They richly deserved such treatment.

About this time, a scouting party of 60 men was sent out under the command of Capt. Masten Brieden, a good and brave officer, who resigned, however, and retired from the service a few months afterwards.[11] I accompanied this party as second in command. Our point of destination was a place in Arkansas, distant about 70 miles. This was called Medlock's, and was the lurking place of a large band of rebel thieves and cut-throats led by the two Medlock brothers, the one as Capt. the other as Lieut.[12] From a deserter, who

10. According to the *Official Register of Missouri Troops for 1862* (St. Louis: Adjutant General's Office, 1863), 101–2, and the *Annual Report of the Adjutant General of Missouri for 1863* (Jefferson City, Mo.: W. A. Curry, 1864), 207–8, it was the quartermaster, T. W. Moses (appointed Oct. 2, 1862), who resigned (Dec. 8, 1862), and not the adjutant, Roland P. Wilcox.

11. Capt. Mastin Breeden (b. 1830), Co. G, 14th MSM Cavalry, a farmer from Barton County, Mo., was not discharged for disability until March 10, 1863 (1860 U.S. Census, Golden Grove Township, Barton County, Missouri, family no. 5; "Soldiers' Records," MDH; *History of Hickory, Polk, Cedar, Dade, and Barton Counties, Missouri* [Chicago: Goodspeed, 1889], 859–60).

12. The Medlock brothers have not been positively identified. "Captain" and "Lieutenant" may have been unofficial honorifics in the rebel band and not formally recognized ranks; moreover, Medlock is a family name with many spelling variants in the records. An affidavit in the Provost Marshal Papers identifies David Medlock, Sr., as a rebel in Shannon County with three sons in the Confederate service; a son-in-law, Malachi Pewit (of Dent County, Mo.), as a "Bushwhacker" operating in Arkansas; and a fourth son, David, Jr., who was said to have "returned from the South at the latter end of October 1862 after an absence of two months," claiming "that he had been out giving the Black Republicans a round and doing his best against them." One of these Shannon County Medlocks, William H., enlisted in the 8th Regt., Missouri Infantry, in Aug. 1862—the same regiment joined by two other Medlocks, William

accompanied us as guide, we learned that these out-laws, some 40 in number, usually occupied four large hewed log houses, which were prepared with port-holes, and which stood out about half a mile apart near a large road. When such houses were well defended, it was almost impossible to take them without artillery, and this we did not have. Our only hope, therefore, was that we might be able to capture them by surprise.

We left Ozark early in the day and wound our way leisurely southward among the wild and picturesque scenes of the Ozark Mountains. The day was beautiful, and the merriment of the men made our party seem more like one of pleasure than of war. The country was sparsely inhabited and we had no adventures that day worth mentioning. By dusk, we had made about 35 miles. We then stopped to feed and to rest our horses for a few hours at a convenient cornfield. At about 10 o'clock at night, we moved forward very cautiously, and as day-light was approaching, found ourselves within about a dozen miles of our point of destination. Finding a cornfield, we loaded our horses as well as we could with corn, and then sought the shelter of a dense forest in which we proposed to lie concealed all day. Having fed our horses, we all slept as long as we pleased. In the afternoon, I wandered alone among the beautiful hills and valleys in the vicinity. For me, this wild life and these wild scenes had an indescribable charm, and I was as nearly happy, I suppose, as so restless a spirit can ever be. While rambling about on this occasion, I perceived a well-dressed and well-mounted woman who had evidently discovered our presence, and who seemed to be trying to get a view of our camps without exposing herself to view. Knowing that every body here was likely to be an enemy, I thought it would be better to capture her and not let her carry to the enemy any intelligence of our approach. This I did, taking her to Captain Brieden who detained her till night, although he was so gallant a man that he could not well resist the pleadings of a pretty woman.

When the shades of night began to gather about us, and the hooting of a solitary owl alone broke the silence that reigned in the forest, we released

---

and Pleasant, the first from Barry County, on the Arkansas border. None of these Medlocks, however, was killed in the fall of 1862, as in Kelso's account (Affidavit of Elizabeth Moore, Jan. 23, 1864, MDH Provost Marshal Papers, reel F1606, file 7618; "Soldiers' Records," MDH; NPS Soldiers' Database; 1850 U.S. Census, District 2, Hopkins County, Kentucky, family no. 713 [David Medlock]; 1860 U. S. Census: Jackson Township, Shannon County, Missouri, family no. 229 [David Medlock]; Texas Township, Dent County, Missouri, family no. 331 [Pewitt]; McDowell Township, Barry County, Missouri, family no. 876 [William Medlock]; "Matlock Civil War Records," http://matlocks.us/gen/civwar.htm).

our fair prisoner and then cautiously wound our way among the dark hills in the direction of Medlock's. We soon reached the house of the notorious Alf. Bolen, but did not find him at home. He was the leader of a small independent band of thieves and murderers and did not belong to the Medlock band.[13] At the next house, which was some five miles from Medlock's, we found one well armed man. He fought and we killed him. We then advanced, without further incident, to within half a mile of the first of the four houses which were usually occupied by the members of the Medlock band. Here we left our horses in the charge of 12 men. We then divided our attacking force into four parties of 12 men each. The first of these parties was to silently surround the first house but were not to make any attack until the other three parties had, in like manner, surrounded their respective houses. The firing was to begin at the last house and then, when this firing was heard, at all the others. The Captain and by far the largest body of the enemy being at the last house, I led in person the party that were to attack it. The first house was surrounded all right. This house contained only three men and they surrendered without firing a gun. At the second house, the enemy, some half dozen in number, were aroused by the fierce barking of a large dog. Breaking out of the house, they fled, and the firing began. They all escaped, but left several guns, revolvers, and horses. We were still about half a mile from the third house and about a mile from the fourth. The firing would almost certainly be heard at the third house, hardly at the fourth. We, therefore, who were to attack these houses, ran at full speed so as to reach the third house before its inmates could dress and give information to the party at the fourth house. Most of my party and of party No. 3 gave out before we reached the third house. When we did reach it, the enemy, commanded by Lieut. Medlock, began a brisk fire upon us from the windows and port-holes. Several of my party turned out here to help in this fight. With reckless speed, I hurried on, with only three comrades to reach the fourth house before its inmates could dress and be off

13. "Alfred Bolin robbed, raped and murdered persons from Union families over a wide area between Ozark, Mo., and Crooked Creek, Ark. . . . Many of Bolin's crimes were alleged to have occurred at Murder Rocks, an unusual geological formation located on the Carollton-Forsyth road, a few miles north of the Missouri-Arkansas state line" (Ingenthron, *Borderland Rebellion*, 285–89, 286 [quotation]). Maj. John C. Wilber of the 14th MSM Cavalry had encountered Bolin's gang in early Aug. 1862, killing two of them (*OR*, ser. 1, vol. 13, 222–23, though transcribed as "Boler"). Bolin was killed by a Union soldier in early Feb. 1863, and his head was allegedly displayed on a pole in Ozark. See Ingenthron, *Borderland Rebellion*, 288–89; Allen Wellington Reminiscence, 1885, C0692, State Historical Society of Missouri; and Larry Wood, "Alf Bolin: Just the Facts," parts 1–2, http://ozarks-history.blogspot.com.

or be ready to fight. Two of my comrades soon gave out, and, after a long race, the remaining one declared himself unable to run any farther. "Well," said I, "Come on as soon as you can, and I will go ahead and have the enemy stirred up by the time you get there." Alone, then, I hurried onward, feeling a kind of strange, wild delight in the very madness of my undertaking. This house was off the road, and I tried to reach it upon a dim pathway. I missed my way, however, and came out several hundred yards beyond the house. Perceiving that I was lost and that the day was dawning, I turned and took as nearly a direct course as I could back to my men. Presently I struck a hog path that led in the right direction through the thick underbrush with which the ground was covered. Following this path at full speed for a few minutes, I suddenly dashed out of the brush upon the very house that I had been looking for. The enemy, some 20 in number, were, most of them, sleeping around camp fires in the door yard. The balance, with Capt. Medlock who lived here, were sleeping in the house. They did not seem to have been aroused at all by the firing at the other houses. At any rate, but few of them were out of bed and none of these were fully dressed. The Captain, whom I knew from the description our guide had given of him, was just taking a seat on the outside of the house near the door to put on a pair of shoes which he held in his hands. Another man in his shirt only was just appearing in the open door with a pair of pantaloons in his hands. These men saw me and gazed at me as if they did not know what to make of me. With that perfect presence of mind which has never failed me in time of danger, I rushed right into the camp yelling at the top of my voice, "*Close in, boys, we'll get every one of them! Close in, boys, we'll get every one of them!*" The man in the door-way darted out and fled with his pantaloons in his hand. Those in the yard bounded up from their blankets and fled. A few snatched up their guns and fled with these. A few fled with boots or pantaloons in their hands. Most of them, however, left everything and fled as if in speed alone lay their only hope of salvation. Supposing that the brush that lay on three sides of the house was full of my men, they mostly fled on the fourth side which was comparatively open. I had never before seen such a fluttering of shirt tails in the morning twilight, and the scene delighted me. Just then, the naked breeches of the men themselves were far more pleasing in my eyes than would have been the naked muzzles of their guns. At first, Captain Medlock, who was a very large heavy man, started to run. Having reached the end of the house farthest from me, he stopped, looked about him a moment, and then turned back to get his gun which was in the house. By this time,—and only a few seconds had elapsed—, several large coarse-looking women had appeared in the doorway. Seeing that I would reach the door nearly as soon as he would, these women cried, "*Run, he'll get you! Run, he'll get you!*" When he reached the door, they tried to keep him from entering, still urging him to run. When I was at his back, they parted, and let him pass in between them. I followed through the same opening, and just as he placed his hand on his gun, at the further side of the room, I place my revolver—a Colt's dragoon—against his back and fired. He fell like an ox, the weight of his fall shaking the whole house. Rushing out, I charged in the direction taken by the balance of the band. The hindmost was some 60 yards away, running with a rifle in one hand and a pair of boots in the other. I called out, "*You infernal son of a _____, come back!*" He turned quickly around and fired at me, his shot grazing the left side of my neck. He then threw down his gun and ran. I took as good aim at him as I could and fired. He did not fall just then, though, as I afterwards learned, he did fall a little farther on and died of the wound I gave him. Just then, I saw, a little way off to my right, a long hungry looking fellow sitting down upon the ground, holding both of his legs up and putting on a pair of pantaloons just as fast as he could. "*Oh! you thief, here you are,*" I said, and went for him at full speed. Seeing that he could not get his pantaloons on in time, he pulled them off and threw them down. By this time, I was almost upon him. I took aim, and pulled trigger. The dew, however, had injured my caps and my revolver missed fire. I pursued him with all my might, still trying to fire, but a piece of broken cap had so caught in my revolver that it would not revolve. I still pursued, however, determined, if possible, to strike him down with the barrel of my revolver. His long, slender white legs fairly whizzed through the young hazels and briers that covered the ground. I wanted him very much. If I had had ten thousand dollars, I would, in my excitement just then, have given it for the ability to run just a little faster. In spite of my utmost efforts, however, he out-ran me and made his escape. I felt that in not letting me kill him, he had done me a great wrong.

Having given up the race, I went back to where this nimble fellow had thrown down his pantaloons. In the pockets of these I found a roll of Confederate bills. Taking the pantaloons with me to the house, I placed them on a log and cut them to pieces with an axe. This I did with all the balance of the captured clothing, first clearing the pockets of whatever they might contain of value. The revolvers, the ammunition, the Bowie knives, and the best of the guns I saved. The balance I destroyed. Besides this plunder, I had a fine lot of good horses. I felt jubilant. But why did not my men come on? Had they been beaten at the other house, or had they given me up for lost and departed? I was growing extremely anxious. The rebels that I had routed might learn that I was alone, and might return, several of them with guns. Presently I heard a single shot fired at the back of a little cornfield, nearly in the direction of my men, and soon afterwards I saw one of my men running with all his might in my direction. Drawing near and stopping to pant after nearly every word, he cried, "*Lieutenant———I met a fellow———down yonder by the creek———in his shirt-tail—-and I throwed him!*" And sure enough he had. The horses having been brought forward, the men soon all made their appearance. Several of them had been pretty severely wounded, but none of them fatally so, at the third house at which all the real fighting was done. Learning what I had accomplished alone, the men could hardly find language with which to express their admiration.

Leaving most of the command near this place to rest and to feed, I took a small party and went to a house some three miles away. Here we expected to find some half dozen armed rebels who constituted a little band of their own. Leaving our horses, we crept stealthily upon the house and surrounded it. Only two men were visible. These were sitting in the door yard paring peaches. Their guns were resting against the house near them. Putting a good shot-gun, which I had just captured, through a crack in the fence, with a good rest, I was just about to fire on them, when a large dog arose right in the way and began to bark. A pretty little child then came and joined the dog, placing itself in the way. The men did not still see us. A woman, however, who was standing in the door, did see us, and seizing the two guns from the side of the house, she ran to me with them, crying out, "*You can not hurt them now, they are disarmed, they surrender.*" Of course, we did not hurt them. We took them prisoners. One of them joined us soon afterwards. He became a good soldier and a firm friend of mine. How glad I am that I was prevented from killing him.

Returning to our comrades, I revisited the scene of conflict at the third house. Some half dozen dead rebels lay there stiff and cold. Lieutenant Medlock was laid out on a kind of cooling board and had a white cloth spread over him. I removed this cloth and discovered that he was alive and still conscious. His wife, a lovely woman, seeing the discovery I had made, seemed greatly alarmed. She did not speak, but with a look far more eloquent than words, she plead for the life of her wounded husband. I ordered the few men who were with me to mount and proceed on their way. When they were gone, I said in the Lieutenant's ear, "*You are not dead, and you know it; and you know that I know it. And now let me give you a little good advice. If you recover from your present wounds, quit this robbing business, go south and fight like a man for your cause. And when you are gone, remember that it was Kelso that saved you.*" He opened his eyes and gave me one look of real gratitude. I replaced the cloth over his face and departed. He did recover and did go south as I advised. My men never knew that he was knowingly spared by myself. He deserved to die, and my men would have blamed me for sparing him, as he had been guilty of several murders upon unarmed Union citizens, but his wounds, and the pleading eyes of his loving wife, were too much for me. I had to spare him.

Learning that a large force of the enemy were close upon us, we hastily collected a large number of cattle and horses which this band of robbers had brought from Missouri, and started on our return, reaching Ozark on the evening of the next day.

9. A Plundering Expedition

September to October 1862

It was now about the close of Sept. 1862. By pressing into our service a large number of disloyal citizens and their teams, we had completed a fine two story block house on Sugar Loaf Hill almost half a mile north of the town of Ozark. This block house had double walls of hewed logs and was impregnable against any force not supplied with artillery. Around this block house, we enclosed some two acres with a double log wall six feet in height and provided with port holes. Inside of this fortification, we were safe against the strongest guerilla band that ever infested that part of the country. Only an army with artillery could have dislodged us.

About this time my wife and children arrived from Collinsville Illinois. I placed them in a small and scantily furnished house in Ozark, and here, with them, I spent the few hours that I could spare from my duties. My wife was more cheerful and affectionate than I expected her to be. I was comparatively happy, and I came to love my wife more devotedly than ever. I was proud, too, of my three children.

About the 1st of October, Major Wilber concluded to make an expedition into Arkansas with our entire available force, over 200 men. At first, it was his intention to have no officers accompany this expedition except Captain Flagg and a few other creatures of his own. This fact created a suspicion that the expedition was meant to be one of disgraceful plunder and not one of honorable warfare. Had he meant warfare, he would have wanted officers to

Source: Kelso, "Auto-Biography," chap. 17, 775–80.

accompany him who were fighters and not those only who were thieves. This suspicion was increased when it was learned that this expedition was unauthorized by any higher authority. The men were angry and would have mutinied had the Major not at last consented to let me go as third in command. Though thus compelled to let me accompany the expedition, he did not consult me on any occasion or even make known to me his plans. He called into council only those officers who belonged to his own dishonorable set.[1]

Besides my own company, (H.), another company, (F.), which had no officers present, was placed under my command. Being the segnior [*sic*] company commander, Capt. Flagg, of course, had a right to march in front the first day. This he did. On the second day, according to custom if not according to law, he should have fallen to the rear and let the next company have the front. On the next day, however, he took the front again, the commander of the second company making but a feeble defense of his right. On the third day, it was my turn to march in front and, accordingly, I took my place in front. Capt. Flagg came up and ordered me back. I refused to go and let him know that he could not so easily usurp my place as he had that of the second company on the preceding day. We had some warm words, and would probably have come to something more, had not the Major appeared on the scene. He ordered me back. I replied: "*I will obey you, Major, but I do so because I am obliged to and not because I have any respect for such officers as you and Capt. Flagg. I respect my two horses, Hank and Sigel, far more than I do such miserable substitutes for officers.*"

On this day, our march lay through a well settled and comparatively wealthy portion of the country, known as Tolbert Barrens. At every house we stopped. Wilber, Flagg, and about a dozen of their creatures entered the house, drank the milk, ate the provisions, and seized upon such valuables, gold watches, &c. as they could find.[2] The balance of the command were forbidden to break ranks. I rode forward at one house, however, to watch the doings of Wilber, Flagg, and their set. Never was our flag more thoroughly

1. "Report of Maj. John C. Wilber," 14th MSM Cavalry, Oct. 20, 1862, *OR*, ser. 1, vol. 13, 317: "In accordance with instructions from Brigadier-General [Francis J.] Herron, I took up my line of march from this post in the direction of Yellville on October 12, at 6 p. m." He reported taking 125 men from the 14th MSM Cavalry and 100 men from the Enrolled Militia. Wilber's intention, he wrote, was to take the enemy force at Yellville, Ark.; capture supplies; and then pull back to Ozark.
2. Major Wilber's report, *OR*, ser. 1, vol. 13, 317: "On the morning of the 16th, I moved my force to Talbot's Barrens. 8 miles east of this [Talbot's] ferry [on the White River], to await the return of my spy from Yellville, before I dare cross the river with my small force." Talbot's (or Talbert's) Barrens, also called Rapp's Barrens, Marion County, Ark. (though a prominent citizen was S. H. Tolbert), was later called Mountain Home, which is in what is now Baxter County, Arkansas.

disgraced than on that expedition. From one house, Wilber and Flagg carried off a beautiful young married woman,—carried her away from her babe, only a few months old. She cried and begged to be permitted to go back to her babe. As the price of her liberty, they required her virtue. She appealed to the men and other officers for protection against these brutes. Her appeal was not in vain. The brutes were glad to release her.

About sun-set, we went into camp near a beautiful country mansion the proprietor of which, together with his wife, had died only a few months before. The mansion was now occupied by two beautiful, intelligent, and refined young ladies, daughters of the late proprietor. On the preceding evenings, Flagg had claimed for himself all the milk, the provisions, the beds, &c. of the houses at which we stopped. Being myself in advance, this time, I was the first to enter the house. I did not, however, claim any thing. In a moment, Flagg rushed in, crying: "This is *my* room, this is *my* cook-stove, these are *my* beds, all this milk is *mine*, &c." as he rushed from one room to another. I followed him every where to see what he would do, or, rather, to see what he would not do. When he reached the milk-house, he took out several pans of milk and placed them upon a table that stood near. He then left the room for a few moments. While he was out, but while I was still present, one of my men, who had had nothing to eat all day, came in, and, looking upon a pan of milk, walked off with it. Coming in a moment later and missing this pan of milk, Flagg asked me who had taken it. I replied that one of the men had taken it. He rushed out, overtook the man, and seizing the pan out of his hands, began cursing him as a _____ thief, and threaten to cut his throat. The man, a good and brave but half-witted soldier, did not dare open his mouth. I could bear no more. Springing to Flagg, I whirled my fist under his nose, saying: "*You infernal cowardly thief, talk to the one who is in a position to defend himself! Talk to* **me**, *you vile thief!*" As I continued to discourse to him thus, and to twist my fist close under his nose, he trembled with abject fear, set the pan of milk down, and, without replying a word, slunk around the house to where Major Wilber was, and actually got behind him for protection. I told the Major what the vile wretch had done, and added: "*Major, I look upon you as but little better than he is. You have encouraged him in all his disgraceful conduct. You have kept him in front, when he did not belong there, just to give him a chance to disgrace our flag and to rob and outrage unarmed citizens and women. I hold you responsible for his base conduct.*" Though Wilber was a thief, he was not a coward. He drew his revolver. I drew mine. All of three companies, and over half of Flagg's company, were instantly in line by my side, every one with a revolver in his hand. The balance of Flagg's men stood scattered about not taking either side. Wilber presented his revolver at the men and ordered them to disperse. Not a man moved except to cock his revolver. Wilber repeated his order. The men seemed to be statues. Seeing that he could accomplish nothing by bravado, he then turned to me and said that I should have my rights, that on the next day I should march in front, and that I should not any more have cause to complain. Turning to the men as I put up my revolver, I said, *"Boys, let's feed."* Every revolver went into its sheath, and the men quietly dispersed.

Half an hour later, while my blood was still hot, one of Flagg's men, a minister of the gospel who had formerly made the very house one of his preaching places, came to me and said that the two young ladies had appealed to him for protection against Wilber and Flagg who were robbing them of all their valuables,—even of their trunks of fine clothing, and agreeing to give them back only on condition that the young ladies would consent to share the foul beds of the vile wretches. I went to the house at once, and found that these villains had taken gold watches, a trunk, and a fine mare from the girls. I told them to bring to me whatever else that they had that they valued most, and that I would guard these things till morning, and then return them. They brought me a gold watch, a trunk, a fine mare, and $500.00 in money, all of which I returned safe next morning. As to the safety of their persons, I told the girls to have no fear about that. They seemed truly grateful for my protection, and, if they are still living, I feel sure that they sometimes think of me kindly. I am sorry that such wretches as Wilber and Flagg fought on our side. Such men sully whatever their vile hands touch.

On the next day, I led the advance through a fine, fertile, and well-cultivated country. Considerable bands sometimes 40 or more of mounted rebels now began to dispute our way, and skirmishing became the order of the day. Flagg was now very willing to march safely in the rear. As yet I did not know the point of our destination. Wilber himself or his guide directed my route. It afterwards appeared that our chief point of destination was the splendid mansion of a very wealthy man who was running a private bank, and who was said to have on hand several thousand dollars in coin. To rob this bank for their own benefit was the principle object of these two wretches, Wilber and Flagg. When we were about three miles from this place, Wilber sent me off with a small party on a side scout, so that I might not be present when the robbing was done. Contrary to his expectation, however, I arrived soon after he did. At the door, I found a guard who said that Major Wilber, Capt Flagg, and Lieut. Cross were inside, and that he had orders not to admit any others. "*But,*" said I, "*the Major surely did not mean you to exclude me, one of the principal officers.*" "*I suppose not, of course,*" said he, and let me pass. I knew very well, however, that I was the very man, above all others, that the Major did mean to exclude.

Having thus passed the guard, I found Lieut. Cross in the hall trying to persuade a handsome young colored woman to accompany him to Ozark.[3] As it afterwards proved, he persuaded her. Wilber and Flagg also each persuaded away a colored woman from this house. These women went ostensibly as cooks, but really as mistresses of these disgraceful officers. Proceeding to an inner room I found Wilber and Flagg in the presence of an aged banker who was lying upon a bed very ill, and who died a few days afterward. Flagg was searching the room. Wilber was holding a fine gold watch which he had just taken from a young daughter of the banker. She was pleading for her watch, saying that it was a present to her from her poor sick father. She plead in vain. When Wilber saw me, he looked surprised, frightened, and angry. "*Why Lieut.,*" said he, "*how did you get in?*" "*I came in,*" said I. He then stepped quickly to the guard and then reprimanded him severely for letting me in. Then he went out and ordered ten men to be detailed at once and mounted for a scout. Having done this, he reëntered the house and ordered me to take immediate command of these men and to proceed to a place, which he named, some ten miles south of our present position. I knew that this scout was a suddenly-thought-of affair designed to get rid of me while the robbing was being done. I knew, too, that I and my little party were being sent out to nearly certain destruction. I did not then know, however, that under the circumstances, that I would be justifiable in refusing to go. I simply asked the major what I was to go *for* and what I was to do when I reached the point named. When I asked these questions, he seemed confused, having evidently not thought of any object in connection with my scout except that of getting me out of his way. After some hesitating and stammering, he said that I was to take such property as we were in the habit of taking. I then asked where I should find him on my return. He replied that I should find him where he then was or a few hundred yards further out upon the road.

3. Lt. John Cross, Co. M, 4th Regt., Cavalry State Militia Volunteers ("Soldiers' Records," MDH).

When I was gone, as I afterwards learned, he finished robbing the house, taking several large bags of gold from under the head of the dying banker. This done, so far from waiting for me as he had promised, he ordered an immediate retreat, which was kept up all night, the teams being goaded with sabers to increase their speed. He evidently made this retreat on my account.[4] He wished me to be destroyed and my testimony against him thus forever hushed. He meant to be a murderer. To cover his retreat, he left a rear guard under the command of a good and brave officer, Lieut. Mooney, whose loss, next to mine, would have been very acceptable to the Major and his guilty partners. Mooney's guard consisted of only 30 men. Marching at a long distance to the rear of Wilber, this party chanced to be cut off by a large party of rebels who came in on another road and followed Wilber. Presently these rebels, who were now directly between Wilber and Mooney, went into camp, lighting some 15 large fires. When Mooney came up, he supposed these were Wilber's camp fires. The rebels, too, were just as badly deceived, supposing that Wilber's men were all in front, and mistaking Mooney and his party for friends. After a few moments conversation, both parties perceived their mistake. The rebels quickly seizing their guns began to fire. Unable to fight so large a party, Mooney of course fled. He was severely wounded himself, but made his escape. Several of his men were thrown from their horses. These men hid themselves in the forest and were picked up by my party, when we came on several two days later.[5]

4. Major Wilber's report, *OR*, ser. 1, vol. 13, 317–18: "Here [at Talbot's Barrens] I learned that Colonel [James R.] Shaler [27th Regt., Arkansas Infantry, CSA], with 2,000 infantry, 1,000 cavalry, and four pieces of artillery, was approaching Yellville by forced marches, and was then within one day's march of our camp. . . . On learning this information I concluded it would be imprudent to place the White River between me and this post [at Ozark], which was then impassable except by ferries and having an over-whelming force moving rapidly up to cut off our retreat. We collected about 50 head of horses, 5 wagons and teams, and a considerable amount of other property useful to the army, and commenced our retreat about 8 p. m. on the 16th instant. I placed our train of horses, mules, and wagons in the advance, with sufficient guard for its protection, and kept my main force between it and the advancing enemy. The most perfect order was maintained."

5. Major Wilber's report, *OR*, ser.1, vol. 13, 318: "About 2 o'clock in the morning our rear guard, consisting of 25 men, under the command of Lieutenant Mooney, Company D, Fourteenth Regiment Missouri State Militia, was attacked by a battalion of Colonel Shaler's command, who in the darkness had gained a position between the rear guard and our main force. Lieutenant Mooney, seeing he was cut off from the column, ordered a charge, which was made with such impetuosity and gallantry by his little band that he succeeded in carving his way through their lines without the loss of a man, though the lieu-tenant himself was severely wounded. In the *mélée* some of our men were dismounted, but all succeeded in riding out a horse; if not their own, an enemy's. . . . I think, from the reports of all, that not less than 10 [enemy] men were killed and double the number wounded."

Leaving Wilber at Tolbert Barrens, I proceeded southward according to his orders. Finding the road swarming with parties of rebels too strong for me to fight, I took to the forest and made my way as well as I could, by course alone, till night came on. Then I returned to the road. I soon learned that a large party had passed us going northward, and that they were now between us and Wilber. We still kept on however, southward, keeping one man in advance on foot to warn us of the approach of any parties of the enemy. When we met large parties, we retired from the road and kept silent till they had passed. When we met small parties, we fired into them by surprise, they not thinking of meeting enemies so close in the rear of their main body. We killed a good many and captured a good many fine horses and valuable arms without much real danger to ourselves.

About midnight, we reached the point of our destination. This was a small village, the name of which I do not now remember. Here was the residence of a rebel officer of some note. We surrounded his house and searched it, hoping that he might chance to be at home and that we might be able to take him alive. His life in our hands would greatly advance our own chances for life. We found no one. We then started on our return to Tolbert Barrens, which place, however, owing to the caution with which we had to move, we did not reach till after sunrise. Having learned of Wilber's disgraceful flight, and that the rebel forces were still between ourselves and him, we sought refuge as soon as we could in the wild recesses of a forest. When night came on we returned to the road and lay in ambush, killing a few more stragglers and adding enough to our livestock to make one extra horse a piece to my entire party. Having done so well, we were now very anxious to make our own escape. Early in the morning, the rebels that had been chasing Wilber passed back on their return. When they passed, we were concealed some 200 yards from the road. When they were at a safe distance, we came out, obtained breakfast at a farm house, and then boldly taking the open road, proceeded in the direction taken by Wilber in his cowardly flight two days before. Presently, we came to the rebel camping ground of which I have already spoken. Here we discovered unmistakable signs of a conflict. Following the trail made by Mooney's party into the forest, we found several hats which we knew to be those of our friends. We knew from the signs that a small party of our friends had been beaten and we had come to a correct conclusion in the way this had been done. Presently we were hailed by a man from a bluff a little way to our right. He was one of Mooney's men who had been thrown from his horse, and who had lain concealed ever since in the forest. He was greatly rejoiced to meet us, and to get something to eat. In a short time, we picked up two more stragglers who were in the same condition.

In the evening, we reached Beaver Station, and to my surprise, as well as my delight, we found Wilber still there.[6] He and Flagg were the first to greet me, and this they did, to my surprise, with marks of unfeigned joy. I soon learned the reason of all these things. On reaching this place, the men had sullenly refused to retreat any further until I rejoined them. They had also let Wilber know that his life and Flagg's must atone for mine, if, through their cowardly and treacherous desertion of me, myself and party were lost. Two days had been given in which for me to return. The time was nearly up. No wonder, then, that these treacherous villains were glad that they had failed in their attempt to have me destroyed. Next day we proceeded to Ozark, where I was received as a hero; Wilber and Flagg as cowards.

Soon after our return, I heard Wilber condemning Captain Burch, in very severe terms, for something he declared that Burch had done during our absence. I asked the Major whether he had or had not said all these things to Burch's face. He said that he had not. Then I replied that Burch was a judicious officer and had not, I was sure, been guilty of the conduct thus insultingly charged against him;—that he should, at any rate, have a hearing, and that I would go at once and inform him of the language that was being used against him. I did so inform him. Whirling round a time or two, as he always did when suddenly excited, he said: "*God damn! I will go and see him about it!*" he did go, and I followed. The Major cowered before him and made no reply. Turning to me, however, the major said that he could have me arrested for something I had done on our recent scout. Springing to him as quick as the night, I twisted my fist under his nose and said: "*You infernal son of a _____, just squirm, and I will tear you limb from limb! Just squirm, will you!*" He did not squirm. He simply turned pale and trembled. Thus ended this disgraceful expedition.

6. Beaver Station was a Union outpost on Beaver Creek in Taney County, Missouri.

10. Fighting Rebels in Arkansas

October to November 1862

It was now about the middle of October, 1862. During the balance of this year, Capt. Burch and I led many expeditions into various portions of Arkansas. On all of these expeditions, we were remarkably successful. Without losing any men at all ourselves, we killed a good many of the enemy, and brought in large numbers of prisoners, horses, arms, &c. We became the idols of the men, and won the emphatic praise of Major General S. R. Curtis, commanding our department, and of other officers of high rank.[1] Of some of these expeditions I will give an account, though I am by no means sure that I shall give them all in the order in which they occurred.

One of these expeditions,—the first one, I think,—was into a portion of Arkansas which had not, as yet, been visited by Federal troops, and which, as we had learned, was held by two companies of rebel militia. These bodies of militia, being destitute of tents, and the weather being now inclement, were occupying various farm houses in the vicinity of each other. We hoped to surprise some of these houses and capture them, but we did not propose to throw away the lives of our men by openly attacking them.

Leaving Ozark late in the day, we marched, with one halt to feed, till the next morning. Then we sought the shelter of a forest and lay concealed all day. At dusk, we moved out and marched all night. When morning dawned, we were within a few miles of our point of destination. As yet, our

Source: Kelso, "Auto-Biography," chap. 18, 780–84.
1. Maj. Gen. S. R. Curtis, in a letter to Maj. Gen. W. S. Rosecrans, Feb. 20, 1864, *OR*, ser. 1, vol. 34, part 2, 384, singled out Burch and Kelso as "good officers for the border service."

approach had not been discovered. But we were nearly sure to be discovered before the coming on of another night. It would not do for us to wait. We sought the shelter of a forest only one mile distant from the nearest house.[2] Here I dressed ten men like rebel bush-whackers, then taking four men in their proper uniforms, pretended that they were prisoners, the other ten men carrying their arms. Issuing from the forest, in which Burch remained with the balance of the men—about 50 in number—I boldly took the road to the nearest house. I was now playing the role of a rebel guerilla leader, Lieut. Russell. The four Federal prisoners were very obnoxious characters whom I proposed to hang on that day at two o'clock P. M.[3]

Without any incident worth mentioning, we reached the first house. Seeing us approach, some 8 or 10 men who were in the door-yard ran into the house and quickly appeared with their guns at the windows and the port-holes. We rode quietly up to the gate and called. A woman answered from one of the doors, and finally came out to the gate. I told her my story, and she being satisfied that we were all right, called out some of the men. To them I repeated my story, with which they, too, seemed satisfied. I told them—and this part of my story was true—that we had traveled all night, that we were very hungry, weary, and sleepy, and that we would like to stop with them till toward evening, to eat, rest, and sleep. Calling some of them aside, out of the hearing of the pretended prisoners, I told them also of the proposed hanging at two o'clock. They kindly gave us the use of the entire house, and the women[,] some of whom were good talkers, went to work with a will to get us some breakfast, their breakfast being already over. We entered at once, leaving the men to feed our horses.[4] We were playing a critical game. What if myself or some of my men should be recognized? Once in the house,

2. According to Capt. Milton Burch's report of Nov. 13, 1862, *OR*, ser. 1, vol. 13, 356–58, the command of eighty men left Ozark on Nov. 8 and at about 10:00 in the morning of Nov. 9 arrived at Lawrence Mills (Beaver Station) in Taney County, Mo., thirty-five miles south. Learning that there were rebels at Dubuque, thirty miles further south and just over the line into Arkansas, they marched at dusk on the evening of Nov. 10, "and during the greater part of the night traveled through the woods, sometimes on a dim road and sometimes without any road at all. Toward morning I ordered a halt, to rest and feed. At daylight the march was renewed, and about 10 a.m. on the 11th we arrived within three miles of Dubuque" (357).

3. Burch's report, *OR*, ser. 1, vol. 13, 357: "Here I concealed my men in the woods, and sent Lieut. John R. Kelso, with 10 Enrolled Militia, to play the part of rebels. They were to take 4 men of the Second Battalion, Fourteenth Regiment of Missouri State Militia, and conduct them as Federal prisoners into the vicinity of Dubuque, and assemble a sufficient number of the rebel provost guards to take charge of the prisoners."

4. Burch's report, *OR*, ser. 1, vol. 13, 357: "Lieutenant Kelso proceeded to the house of a man named Yandle, who was very willing to aid in assembling the provost guards." There were seven men named Yandle in the 19th Regt., Arkansas Infantry, CSA, none of them living in Carroll County at the time of the census two years earlier (NPS Soldiers' Database; 1860 U.S. Census, Carroll County, Arkansas).

we were all right. We could now, in case of discovery, defend ourselves against any probable attack until Burch could come to our assistance. The house was built in the form of an ell and contained only two large rooms. In one of these rooms, the ell, I placed the four prisoners together with their four guards and the four extra guns. With the remaining six men, I took possession of the other room.

It was understood between myself and Burch that he was not to come until I sent for him, unless he heard firing. I had also explained to the men of my party what I proposed doing. I thought they all understood me. I was to send back a man every hour, professedly to stand guard on our trail, but really, of course, to keep Burch posted in regard to the progress of my under-taking.[5] When I ordered the first man back, our new rebel friends told me that there was no need of such precaution, that no Federals were likely to ever venture in there, and that if they should do so, not one of them would ever get out alive. I replied—and truly, too,—that I never allowed a feeling of security to betray me into any neglect of precaution; and that, on this occasion, the Federals might pursue me in the hope of retaking the prisoners in my hands. Having sent back one guard, and made arrangements for an hourly relief, I ate my breakfast and then talked a long time with a pleasant and intelligent woman who was so enthusiastic a little rebel that she was eager to do a little fighting herself for the holy cause. At last, growing sleepy in spite of the musical clattering of this bright little rebeless' tongue, I lay down upon a bed and fell asleep.

I knew that curiosity to see us and witness the hanging would bring out many of the men from the other houses which were so near that their inmates would be sure very soon to hear of our arrival. I meant to wait till some 50 were present, then send for Burch. I thought that we could manage that number very easily having them, as we would, between two fires, and we having in all 65 men. As I expected, the men were flocking in from the other houses. Over 30 were in when I fell asleep. I was to be waked in one hour. I was scarcely asleep, however, when I was suddenly aroused by the women who seemed greatly alarmed about something. Springing up and running to

5. Burch's report, *OR*, ser. 1, vol. 13, 357: "In the mean time I was to be kept informed of the progress of the affair by a messenger sent out on a pretense of standing picket at a distance from the house at which the party should stop. At the proper time I was to surround the house and make prisoners of all the rebels who had assembled."

the door, I heard one or two shots fired, and saw our horses breaking loose and, in great fright, galloping about the yard. On the outside of the yard, dashing around it in two directions, and surrounding us as if by magic, I saw—as it just then appeared to me—a party of about 200 men, better handled than I had ever before seen men handled. "*Caught in my own trap,*" said I to myself. "*These rebels have me hemmed in. Burch will come, but he will come to perish at the hands of this overwhelming force of wonderfully disciplined men.*" I glanced at the rebels in the yard. I expected to see a look of triumph in their faces. I saw no such look. On the contrary, I saw a look of surprise and alarm. There was no understanding between these men and the new arrivals. Glancing again at the attacking party, I recognized Burch and his party. Two hundred men sunk to fifty. My new rebel friends were bravely forming a line in front of the house, not 30 yards from the enemy. They all seemed to look to me to lead them in the fight. I called out all my men, except two who remained with the prisoners, and formed them on the right of the rebel line. Then throwing up my hands, I called out, "*We surrender! we surrender!*" I ordered my men to lay down their arms, and this they promptly did. The rebels looked disappointed and displeased. They had not expected the brave Lieut. Russell to surrender to only slightly superior numbers without firing a gun. I ordered them to lay down their arms, and this they did in a very surly manner. Burch dismounted a number of men who took possession of these arms. The surrender being completed, and the prisoners placed under guard, we threw off our disguise and began to talk and jest with our pretended captors. Our poor betrayed rebel friends cast at us looks of inexpressible indignation. Replying to these looks, I said: "*Well, boys, it was a mean trick: But it was far better to deceive you and take you alive than to be obliged to kill you all, as we would have been, had we not deceived you. Besides this, you are now, for the first time in your lives, in good company, and since there are enough of you to elect a Lieutenant, you may proceed to do so, if you wish, and enter our service.*" Presently their anger subsided. They admitted that, in deceiving them as we had, we had done no more than they would have done to us. Won by our kind treatment of them, several of them did afterwards join our service.

But why had Burch come without being sent for? It seems that one of my men had either misunderstood my instructions or had become alarmed at my position. At any rate, when sent back as a guard, he urged Burch to hurry up as a large force of rebels were present, and that I was liable to be overpowered at any moment, should I chance to be recognized. Supposing that I had sent this word, Burch did hurry up with the result which I have already described.[6]

Being now encumbered with a large number of guns and with a considerable amount of plunder, and having half as many prisoners as we had men, Burch very correctly decided that it would not be wise for us to make any further aggressive movements. He determined, therefore, after giving the men and horses two hours in which to eat and rest, to start on our return march to Ozark. I asked permission, however, to cross White River with a small party, during these two hours, and attack the village of Dubuque at which one company of rebel militia were stationed.[7] Burch replied that he could not order men to go upon an expedition so full of danger. He said, however, that, if my heart was set upon undertaking this fool-hardy enterprise, I might explain the matter to the men, letting them fully understand the danger, and then, if ten of them would volunteer to accompany me, I might take that number and go; "*but,*" added he, "*be very cautious, for I can send no men to help you.*" I explained the matter to the men, and every man wanted to be one of the ten. I then selected ten who were splendidly mounted, promising the others, that, on my next scout, I would take some of them.[8]

Dashing off at a gallop, we were soon at the river, and there, coming up the bank on our side, we met three rebel soldiers. The nature of the ground had kept us from seeing them, and them from seeing us, until the two parties were within a few rods of each other. When they perceived us, they whirled about and dashed down the bank and splashed through the water which was not very deep. We dashed after them at full speed. Two of them were splendidly mounted, and would give us a close race to the village, a mile away, over good road. The third man was poorly mounted. To him, escape was

6. Burch's report, *OR*, ser. 1, vol. 13, 357: "By a mistake on the part of the man who was to report to me, I marched too soon, and the result was that I took only 2 rebels, with their horses and arms."

7. Larry Wood, "Ozarks History: Dubuque, Arkansas," http://ozarks-history.blogspot.com: Dubuque "was located on the south bank of the White River just below the Missouri-Arkansas line. . . . During the first half of the nineteenth century, Dubuque was the northern-most point for steamboat travel on the White river, and the town was a receiving point for merchandise headed to Forsyth and other places upstream via the old Dubuque-Forsyth road and a shipping point for furs and other goods headed downstream. . . . During the Civil War, Dubuque was a Confederate stronghold and the site of a lead smelter that supplied bullets for rebel forces." Today the site is under the waters of Bull Shoals Lake. See also Elmo Ingenthron, "The Dubuque-Forsyth Road," *White River Valley Historical Quarterly* 1, no. 6 (Winter 1962): 10.

8. Burch's report, *OR*, ser. 1, vol. 13, 357: "I remained a short time to feed and rest at Yandle's, while Lieutenant Kelso, with 12 men, went to Dubuque, the headquarters of Capt. Hudson's provost guards." Perhaps the reference is to Capt. A. L. Hudson, 14th Regt., Arkansas Infantry.

impossible. Darting past me on their magnificent chargers, Sergt. Smith and Sergt. Baxter,—two as brave men as ever fought upon earth—were soon raising a cloud of dust on the other side of the river.[9] I was not far behind, the third in the race, old Hawk-eye doing some wonderfully good running. Leaving the hindmost man to me, Smith and Baxter pressed the other two. Leaving this man to someone behind me, I dashed onward. In like manner, this poor rebel was passed back from man to man till he reached my hindmost man, who took him prisoner. The two foremost rebels and Smith and Baxter were now entering the village. They were all hidden in one cloud of dust out of which came the quick reports of the deadly revolvers. The two rebels had made a desperate race for life, but they had lost it. They fell at the entrance to the village. The soldiers were nearly all scattered about among the houses eating their dinners. Many of them did not even have their guns with them. Their surprise was complete, their panic uncontrollable. Without attempting any resistance, they fled like frightened sheep in all directions. Dashing up the streets after them, we cut them down like mullion stalks in an old meadow. I got two for my share. Smith and Baxter did better. All did well. How many were killed in all, I do not know.[10]

The fight, or, rather, the slaughter being over, we burned their barracks, plundered their suttler store and their post-office, and then departed as we had come in a cloud of dust. Burch and the rest of our comrades were highly pleased with our report. We had oysters and other luxuries enough for the whole command. I afterward returned all the letters and other documents which we had taken from the post-office, except such as were of some military value.

While the men were plundering and burning the barracks, I searched the house of an officer whom I had slain at the edge of the village. I found nothing that I wanted. A beautiful young woman, a governess, I believe, in the family, begged me not to burn the house. I saw that she was very much frightened, as she well might be. I spoke kindly to her, assuring her that nothing except the barracks would be burned, and that nothing would be taken except arms and such other things as pertain to war. My words seemed

9. Sgt. John T. Smith and Sgt. John M. Baxter would both be promoted to second lieutenants under Burch; Smith would be killed in battle on June 5, 1864, and Baxter would be killed in battle on Feb. 20, 1865 ("Soldiers' Records," MDH).

10. Burch's report, *OR*, ser. 1, vol. 13, 357: "[Capt. Hudson's] company, as we before learned, were not in camp. Three rebels only were found, all of whom fled on the approach of Lieutenant Kelso and party. They were all overtaken, however, and 2 killed and 1 taken prisoner." Burch identified one of the killed men as "a surgeon in a rebel regiment" and the other as Dubuque's postmaster. "They both had arms."

to do her good. That night, however, as I learned afterwards, she died,—died of heart disease brought on by excessive fright. Before breathing her last, she told her friends that she remembered nothing distinctly except the kind words which an officer spoke to her after the battle was over. This was one of the saddest episodes of my wild military career. Oh! war! war! why shouldst thou ever exist?

About two o'clock, we began our march toward Ozark, taking an entirely different route from the one on which we had come. In coming, we had avoided the settlements as much as possible. For our return route, we selected the most thickly settled portions of the country. When about five miles from the place at which we had captured our prisoners, we met a party of half dozen or more rebel militiamen who had not yet heard of our approach. They fired upon us and then fled, through an open wood. Several of them were overtaken and slain. I got one more here, making three for me that day. A little farther on, we met another party, who exchanged shots with us, but they all escaped. Next day we captured a little party, mostly officers, and killed one man who, refusing to surrender, attempted to escape by running through a field of corn. This man had a brother in our party. Two of the captured officers were brothers by the name of Herd.[11] They were thorough gentlemen, and I feel sure that, by our courteous treatment of them, Burch and I made them our warm personal friends.[12]

---

11. 1st Lt. W. J. Herd and Capt. J. B. Herd, both in Co. A, 2nd Regt., Missouri State Guard (NPS Soldiers' Database).

12. Burch's report, *OR*, ser. 1, vol. 13, 357: "After the return of Lieutenant Kelso I proceeded up White River, marching so rapidly that no information of my approach preceded me. At almost every house I surprised and took some of the provost guards of Captain Hudson's and Captain Crabtree's companies." This was probably Capt. Benjamin F. Crabtree, Co. F, 3rd Regt., Missouri Cavalry, CSA, which was "organized during the summer of 1862 with men from Springfield and Newtonia, and Polk County" (NPS Soldiers' Database). Burch: "Most of them surrendered without resistance. Some ran, and these, when overtaken, were shot. At dusk we arrived at Captain Crabtree's, who was at home but who escaped." They feasted and rested at Crabtree's until midnight, and then "marched to Clapp's Mills, where we surprised and took several rebels, among them a captain, an adjutant, and a lieutenant, of Colonel Hawthorne's regiment." Hawthorne was likely Col. A. T. Hawthorne of Cocke's Regt., Arkansas Infantry, also called the 39th Infantry, organized in the summer of 1862 (NPS Soldiers' Database). Burch tallied four killed in the four-day campaign but mentioned an indeterminate number who fled and were shot down. He reported that they took twenty-five prisoners but, contrary to Kelso's account, nearly all of these were taken in the houses they visited after Yandle's. He concluded his report with praise for his officers and men: "I must speak a word of praise for the noble manner in which Lieutenants Day and Kelso aided me in all my undertakings. They are both brave men and good officers. The men also deserve the highest praise. They bore the fatigue of the long night marches without a murmur and faced every danger with the utmost coolness. With such officers and men I shall always consider victory certain, even against great superiority of numbers."

11. Capturing and Destroying

November to December 1862

It was now about the close of November, 1862. Burch and I concluded to make another expedition to Arkansas. We had two objects in view; one of which was the capture of a rebel captain by the name of Mooney and his band; the other was the capture of the Salt-peter caves. This Captain Mooney was an uncle of the brave Lieut. Mooney of our battalion of whom I have spoken.[1] This rebel Captain had recently captured some of our Enrolled Militia and had treated them remarkably well. Returning to them their blankets and filling their haversacks with provisions, he escorted them in person beyond his lines, and then said to them: "*Go home and tell your friends that this is the way we treat our prisoners.*" When I heard of this I said: "*Boys, we must go ahead and capture that old Captain and repay him for the magnanimity with which he treated his prisoners.*" Unless we were obliged to do so, we did not propose to hurt him. We wished simply to capture him. He lived on our side of the White River. The Salt-peter caves were on the other side not many miles from Yellville, and about 100 miles, the way we had to go, from Ozark.

Source: Kelso, "Auto-Biography," chap. 19, 784–89.
1. Joseph Hale Mooney, Co. C, 8th Missouri Infantry, CSA, enlisted at Elma Springs, Ark.; served as a private from Feb. 4 to Aug. 4, 1862; and then was promoted to captain. 2nd Lt. Reuben P. Mooney, Co. D, 14th MSM Cavalry, enlisted at Springfield, Mo., on March 29, 1862, and was wounded in action on Oct. 17, 1862, but had returned to the field ("Soldiers' Records," MDH). Joseph Hale Mooney lived in Texas Co., Mo. (*History of Laclede . . . Counties, Missouri*, 461). On Captain Mooney, see also Nichols, *Guerilla Warfare in Civil War Missouri*, 1:118. Reuben (b. 1823 in Tenn.) in 1860 lived in Linden, Christian County, Mo., with his wife and nine children (1860 U.S. Census, Linden Township, Christian County, Missouri, family no. 888).

At these caves, the rebels had a considerable force at work manufacturing salt-peter for the Confederate powder factories. It was important that we destroy these salt-peter works.[2]

Taking about 50 men, we left Ozark in the morning and camped that night at Beaver Station, some 30 miles distant.[3] Our force was far too small to openly attack the parties against whom we were marching. As usual, however, we were depending upon surprising our enemies. Next day, we moved on very cautiously through a sparsely settled country. We met with no adventures that I now remember. We had an excellent guide;—a faithful man who had been, for 40 years, a hunter among those very hills. At night, we stopped a few hours to rest and to feed.[4] We then moved on, I leading the advance guard. Mooney kept most of his men at his own residence, he having an abundance of room for them. Since most of them belonged in the immediate neighborhood, however, they were wont, in times of supposed security, to scatter off to their own homes, leaving, sometimes, less than a dozen in camp with the Captain. We hoped to find him thus with only a few men enjoying fancied security. And we did so find him. Several miles from his residence, he kept a picket station. On these pickets, he depended for timely notice of the approach of an enemy. Our guide knew the exact location of this picket station. When we approached it we dismounted and, creeping as silently as serpents, surrounded the pickets, covering them at short range with our rifles as they sat between us and their camp fire. There were three of them. They

2. On the Confederate saltpeter mining operation near Yellville and its role in gunpowder production, see James J. Johnston, "Bullets for Johnny Reb: Confederate Nitre and Mining Bureau in Arkansas," *Arkansas Historical Quarterly* 49 (Summer 1990): 124–67.

3. Report of Capt. Milton Burch, Dec. 18, 1862, *OR*, ser. 1, vol. 22, part 1, 159–61: Burch left Ozark with forty men from Cos. D, F, G, and H of the 14th MSM Cavalry on the morning of Dec. 9, 1862, and marched thirty-five miles to Lawrence's Mill (Beaver Station). They arrived in the night and stayed until noon on the 10th. During that time he consulted with his own officers and others stationed at the fort: "Having received information that a rebel captain by the name of Mooney, with 75 men, were encamped at Tolbert's Ferry, on the White river, 60 miles from us, I resolved, with the advice of the other officers, to go and capture them" (160). He was reinforced by sixty militiamen from Beaver Station.

4. Burch's report, *OR*, ser. 1, vol. 22, part 1, 160: "The march continued on the morning of the 11th, but, instead of keeping the road, I bore eastward, and marched through the wood, under the guidance of an excellent woodman by the name of Willoughby Hall. I arrived within 8 miles of the ferry by dusk, and stopped to feed and rest in the dense forest, near an out of the way corn-field." According to an oral history recorded by Silas Claiborne Turnbo later in the nineteenth century, Hugh McClure, a southern sympathizer, holding Hall partly responsible for the murder of his son, was with a company of men who shot down Hall. As Hall lay dying, McClure took a knife and scalped him. See Turnbo, *The Evil That Men Do: Guerrilla and Civil War Stories of the Ozarks*, ed. Bill Dwayne Blevins (Mountain Home, Ark.: Infodatatech.net, 2002), 105.

were hopelessly in our power. They were talking and laughing. I called to them in a low voice so as not to be heard by their comrades who were sleeping in a house not far away. They instantly became as silent as death. They did not move. I let them know that the least noise or movement on their part would be instant death to them all. I meant what I said, and they so understood it. A silent surrender was the result. We then silently approached the house. This was a small log structure with only two rooms. We burst in the door with a single blow and sprang inside. The guards, being in bed, had no chance to resist. There were three of these. A large, coarse young woman, however, who was sitting by the nearly burned down fire, caught up an axe and charged upon us with a fury far more wonderful than womanly. Not knowing but that we might have a hand to hand fight in the house, several of us entered with drawn sabers. These we instantly placed at the breast of this formidable Amazon, threatening to run her through at once unless she dropped the ax. She did drop it, but I suspect that we would have fared badly, had we not greatly outnumbered her. I feared that this family would send word ahead of us to Captain Mooney. To prevent this, I called a Sergeant and, in the presence of the family, ordered him to remain with a party of men on the outside of the house, and, if any light was lit, any noise was made, or any door or window was opened before full day light next morning, to fire the house and report to me and I would kill all the prisoners. One of the prisoners was a brother of the fighting young woman. Some of the others were her near friends. I knew that she would not endanger their lives by opening the doors after I left. Of course, all I said was only a ruse. I had no thought of really leaving any guard at the house.

The most difficult part of our present undertaking was now accomplished. The prisoners informed us that Captain Mooney was depending upon them and that he was not likely to have any guards at all at his residence.[5] This information proved to be correct. We concluded to defer the attack till day began to dawn. In the meantime, however, an officer, whose name I do not now remember, was sent with a small party to take possession

5. Burch's report, *OR*, ser. 1, vol. 22, part 1, 160: "I sent Lieut. John R. Kelso, with 8 men, to capture some rebel pickets that I supposed would be found at the house of a rebel by the name of Brixy. Lieutenant Kelso soon returned, having found and captured 2 rebels, with their guns, and one horse. From these prisoners I learned that Captain Mooney's men had temporarily disbanded, and were not to assemble again for two days." Brixy was Pvt. Clark Brixy, Co. F, 34th Regt., Arkansas Infantry, CSA (NPS Soldiers' Database).

of a ferry across White River and to capture such parties as might come there to cross. In the morning, this officer brought in some 25 prisoners, twice as many as he had of men.[6] When morning dawned, we made the attack upon Mooney's house. Approaching unobserved, we burst in all the doors at once, and sprang inside. Three or four men were taken in their night clothes. No resistance was attempted. Rushing up the stairway, I called out that, if any one upstairs fired a shot, the house would be burned with all of them in it. At the head of the stairs, the Captain himself met me. "*I'm here,*" he said. From these words, and the tone in which they were spoken, I thought he meant to stay there,—in other words to fight. I brought my big shot-gun to bear upon him, but did not fire. He caught the gun and tried to wrest it from me. He was a powerful man, above my size, and I do not know how the struggle would have terminated had not one of my men, Sergt. Anderson, come to assist me. When Anderson seized him, he cried out: "*I surrender! I surrender!*" "*Why did you not say that a good while ago?*" said I. "*Because I did not think it necessary,*" replied he. Then, in my excitement, to my great shame, I called the old Captain several ugly names. For this, I made due apologies to him afterwards. He gave me a fine revolver, requesting me not to part with it till the close of the war or till he retook it by capturing me.[7] I promised to do this, and I kept my promise. I carried it till the close of the war. He said that none but a brave man had ever carried it, and that he did not want it to be ever carried by any but a brave man. He gave his rifle to Burch with the same remarks. He then invited us all to take breakfast with him. This we did, and he entertained us with that noble hospitality for which the planters of the south are so noted. After breakfast, we sent him and the other prisoners off under a sufficient guard to be kept at a designated point until our return.[8] The withdrawing of

6. Burch's report, *OR*, ser. 1, vol. 22, part 1, 160: "I remained here [at Mooney's] to feed and await the arrival of a party that I had sent out, with orders to meet at this point. They soon came in, bringing several prisoners."

7. Burch's report, *OR*, ser. 1, vol. 22, part 1, 160: "At midnight my little band emerged from the dark wood, where we had been resting, and silently wound along the hills in the direction of Captain Mooney's. Lieutenant Kelso led the advance, and, by the most excellent management, succeeded in capturing 7 or 8 rebels, who lived near the road, without giving any alarm to the country around. Just before day we captured a rebel recruiting officer by the name of Mings, formerly a lieutenant-colonel. At the break of day we reached Captain Mooney's residence. We took him, with one other man, together with 15 stand of small arms, most of which we destroyed, not being able to carry them." A William Mings is listed as a captain in the Missouri State Guard and in Wood's Regt., Missouri Cavalry ("Soldiers' Records," MDH; NPS Soldiers' Database).

8. Burch's report, *OR*, ser. 1, vol. 22, part 1, 160: "I then sent Captain [P. T.] Green, of the enrolled militia, back with the prisoners, 17 in number, and 25 men as an escort."

this guard left our party only 36 strong all told. A fearfully weak force with which to attempt the taking of the Salt-peter Caves, at which two companies of rebels were said to be stationed. We very well knew that a fair open fight was entirely out of the question. We were not the men, however, to abandon even a desperate undertaking without making a desperate effort for its achievement. We would trust to chance and skillful management.

Crossing the river, we marched by a circuitous route so as to approach the Salt-peter Caves from the south. By good management, we struck the Yellville road some three miles from the Caves. Here a remarkable chance favored us;—a chance which might have alarmed and disconcerted men less cool and determined than we were. We learned that a rebel force, some 2000 strong, were only a few miles behind us, marching, like ourselves, to the Salt-peter Caves at which place they were expected on that very day.[9] At this place, they expected to remain for some time, large quantities of provisions being already prepared for their use. We were now, as the boys expressed it, in a "*d——d tight place,*" with twice our number of enemies directly in front of us and fifty times our number close behind us. Those in front of us must be removed before we could cross the river and escape from the over-whelming force behind us.[10]

Never at a loss what to do, we quickly donned a number of Confederate uniforms, bush-whacker suits, &c. of which we usually carried a supply for such emergencies. Having made ourselves sufficiently motley to resemble the rebels of that section, we assumed to be the advance guard of the approaching rebel army. We were challenged by one guard, as a matter of form, but, since he "*was expecting*" us, we easily satisfied him that we were "*all right.*" He let us pass. We marched up to the barracks, which faced from us, and filed round on the other side in front of the doors. It was noon, and the men were all in at their dinner. Seeing us at their doors, they came pouring out with pleased looks upon their faces, leaving their guns inside. A few of them carried pistols in their belts. Burch called out: "*How are you, boys? Have you any fires for us*

9. Burch's report, *OR*, ser. 1, vol. 22, part 1, 161: "Learning that a party of Burbridge's command was hourly expected, I thought it better to retire." Col. John Q. (Jack) Burbridge, Missouri State Guard and 2nd Regt., Infantry Volunteers, CSA, was from Pike County in northeastern Missouri but was at the time leading irregulars in the Ozarks (Nichols, *Guerilla Warfare in Civil War Missouri,* 1:169, 180–81; "Soldiers' Records," MDH; NPS Soldiers' Database).

10. Burch divided his command of seventy-five remaining men into two divisions, sending one to hide on the other side of the river. So he approached the salt works with about thirty-five to forty men, and faced twenty-three working at the cave (Burch's report, *OR*, ser. 1, vol. 22, part 1, 160).

to warm by, and any thing for us to eat?" " *Yes,* " replied they, " *we have a plenty, dismount and go right in.*" About half of our party dismounted and went in, taking possession of all the doors, and cutting these poor deceived rebels off from their guns. When all this was accomplished, Burch, in tones of thunder, called out: "*Now, G-d d—n you, give up your arms and fall into line, and be d——d quick about it!*" They seemed paralyzed with astonishment. No one moved. I then called out: "*We are Federals; if you surrender without firing, you will be treated kindly, as prisoners of war. If a single shot is fired, every man of you dies. Now fall into line quickly.*" They did fall into line, but did it in a very surly manner.[11] One officer, Captain McNamara, bitterly cursed his own stupidity in suffering himself to be thus entrapped.[12] To comfort himself, however, he informed us that, within two hours, he and the other prisoners would be guarding us; that the river was not fordable at any point nearer than six miles, and that we could not possibly cross in time to escape the large force now close at hand. Our guide, however, knew of a ford close to this place.

These barracks and the village surrounding them stood on the top of a bluff bank several hundred feet above the river. The salt-peter works were at the bottom of this bank, near the water, and were reached by long flights of very good steps. Leaving Burch to secure the prisoners, collect the arms, &c. I dismounted and hastened down these steps to see what was going on below. The distance down was far greater than I had supposed it was, and, when I found myself so far separated from the men, I began to regret that I had thus ventured down alone. There might be a large party of the enemy down there. I kept right on, however, hoping that some of the men would soon follow me. Reaching the bottom, I found the works far more extensive and valuable than I had expected. I found but one man, the engineer, present. He did not see me till I was close upon him. When he did see me, he made a motion as if to

---

11. Burch's report, *OR*, ser. 1, vol. 22, part 1, 160: "It was just before noon when we reached the cave. The rebels were at their dinner, all unconscious of our approach. When at last they discovered us, they mistook us for a company of their own men which they were expecting, and they did not discover their error until we were in half pistol shot of them. I ordered them to surrender, which they did, without firing a gun." In an oral history recorded later in the nineteenth century by Silas Turnbo, "Mun" or "Mum" Treat, who was working at the caves that day, thought that Burch had attacked with 150 troops (Turnbo, *The Evil That Men Do*, 90).
12. Capt. Patrick S. McNamara, Nitre and Mining Bureau, War Department, CSA (NPS Soldiers' Database; see also Johnston, "Bullets for Johnny Reb," 133, 143).

reach a shot gun that stood at the side of the engine house. Having him covered with my formidable shot gun, I cried out: "*Move, and you die! Stand right still!*" He stood still. I had asked him only a few questions when Burch appeared followed by a large number of prisoners under guard. The prisoners were put to work with sledge hammers, axes, &c. to break and destroy the kettles and such of the machinery as could not be destroyed by fire. At first Captain McNamara refused to work, declaring that he had worked almost day and night for six months to get the works started, and now, having them in perfect order,—capable of supplying the whole Confederacy with salt-peter for powder—, he'd be d——d if he would help destroy them. I replied that I had been whipped many a time for refusing to do disagreeable things, and that, although this might be disagreeable to him, he'd have it to do. He went to work at last, but cursed bitterly all the time.

Having completed the destruction of some $80000.00 worth of machinery, we fired the buildings, and then hastily reascended the hill.[13] We might be a few moments too late. We had not near so many prisoners as we had hoped to capture, many of the rebels being scattered about in the neighborhood. We had only 42 that were fit to carry away,—only 6 more than there were of ourselves. Besides these, there were some half dozen sick men whom we had to leave.[14] Most of these requested me to put them on parole so they would not have to serve anymore till they were exchanged. This I did. Leaving myself and one man to fire the barracks and the block-house, which was filled with provisions, Burch and the balance of the men with the prisoners began to slide their horses down the long and steep bank into the river nearly in front of the block-house. It required a good many minutes to make this really hazardous descent, and one man and several horses were hurt in

13. Burch's report, *OR*, ser. 1, vol. 22, part 1, 160–61: "I ordered the salt-peter works to be destroyed, which was effectually done. These are gigantic works, having cost the rebel Government $30,000. Captain McNamar[a], who was in command, stated that in three days they could have had $6,000 worth of saltpeter ready for use." The report of Brig. Gen. Egbert B. Brown to Maj. Gen. Samuel R. Curtis, Dec. 18, 1862, *OR*, ser. 1, vol. 22, part 1, 159, praised Burch and his men for "burning and destroying 5 buildings, 1 engine, 26 large kettles, 6 tanks, blacksmiths' and carpenters' shops and tools; $6,000 worth of saltpeter, packed, which was to have been moved in two days; capturing 500 barrels of jerked beef, together with a full supply of other provisions for the winter, and returning, without a casualty, with 42 prisoners, their arms, horses, and equipments."
14. Burch reported twenty-three prisoners taken at the cave with three too sick to travel, but General Brown, apparently working from a separate itemized list, reported forty-two (*OR*, ser. 1, vol. 22, part 1, 159, 160).

making it. They all reached the bottom at last, however, forded the river, which was quite deep, and disappeared into the dense forest beyond.

While this descent was being made, I was sitting in my saddle, holding the bridle of my comrade's horse, and watching the road upon which the rebel army was advancing. My comrade soon had the barracks in flames. Many guns that had been overlooked in the search were heard firing in the flames. My comrade was now firing the block house. Many women came and begged me to permit them to save from the flames, for their own use, as much as they could of flour, salt, bacon, &c. I gave them permission, and if ever women worked in earnest they did. My comrade helped them roll out some barrels of salt and some sugar. The flames were now mounting upward in grand style, and at a distance of less than a mile, I could see clouds of dust rising among the trees. I called my comrade and had him descend the hill, I remaining at the top till he was at the bottom. When he was safely down, I began the descent. My horse, being left alone, was impatient and made all the haste he could in such a place. It was well for me that he did. I was growing a little anxious myself. I did not take time to look behind me, but my comrade, who was watching me from the other shore, began to signal for me to make all the haste possible. I had crossed the deepest part of the river and was splashing out through shallow water on the other side when a shower of spent bullets began to patter like hail all around me. Reaching my comrade, we crossed a sandy beach and took shelter among trees where only a very few shots could reach us at all.

Reaching the edges of the forest, we turned about to take a last look at the scene behind us, and that scene was of weird and wonderful grandeur;— one that can never fade from memory. The weather had long been remarkably dry for that season of the year. Now, however, intensely black thunder clouds were darkening the sky. Not a breath of air seemed to be stirring. Before us rolled the clear peaceful waters of the river. Beyond the river was the high hill surmounted by the burning block-house. The flames were rising perpendicularly to a height of 100 feet or more. The smoke arose a mile or more and there reaching a rarer atmosphere spread out like a vast umbrella in all directions, a grand dark canopy under the grander and darker canopy of the thunder clouds. On the brow of the hill, distinctly outlined upon the strange dark background of flames, of smoke, and of clouds, were a hundred or more horsemen drawn up in line. Unmindful of the wonderful grandeur and beauty of the scene of which they constituted an important element, these unappreciative men were trying to reach us with their rifles, and were, indeed, sending some of their naughty bullets uncomfortably near our position. How much I wish I could have made a painting of that wonderfully beautiful picture.

After viewing this scene for a few moments, my comrade and I turned and took the trail of our command[,] overtaking them about two miles farther on. Satisfied that we would have to run for our own lives as well as for our prisoners and our plunder, we now stopped a few minutes to prepare for the race. Wishing to have a few men unencumbered with prisoners, we dismounted about a dozen of the youngest of the prisoners and made them march on foot about the middle of the line. From the horses of the other prisoners, we took off the bridles, the horses being led by the guards. I then warned the prisoners that they must give us no trouble whatever,—that we were in a tight place, as they well knew, running for our lives,—and that their lives would not be worth much, if they attempted to escape or to retard our flight. I told them to each keep his eye to the front, and ordered the guards, within their hearing, to shoot dead every prisoner that looked around, or that tried in any way to communicate with other prisoners. I feared that Captain McNamara who was undoubtedly a man of desperate courage, and who, if any chance had offered, would doubtless have caused us a good deal of trouble. Besides him, we had 7 other commissioned officers, a Captain, four Lieutenants, a Lieut. Colonel, and a quartermaster. Of none of these, however, had I any fear. McNamara was more than all of these put together.

Having completed these arrangements, we pressed on as fast as we could. It would take the enemy some time to descend the hill and cross the river. We would have several miles the start. We could hold out till night, then the darkness would serve us. The prisoners gave us no trouble. Soon the storm of the elements burst upon us. The lightning flashed, the thunder roared, and the rain poured down in torrents. We were soon all wet to the skin. We still hurried on. At last darkness was beginning to come on. We left the road and took a shorter way by a dim trail through the forest. The darkness became so dense that we could not see our comrades, our prisoners, or our horses. I feared our prisoners would escape, but they did not. Sometimes our guide would stop and feel for marks on trees,—marks that he had made on former occasions to enable him to follow the trail on dark nights. A new danger now threatened us and made haste necessary. This was the rising of a large creek in advance of us. Should we be unable to cross it, we were still liable to be hemmed in next day and killed or captured. About midnight we reached the creek. It was barely fordable and was rapidly rising. A delay of half an hour would have made us too late. We stopped awhile on the other bank. Our pursuers were too late. The creek was no longer fordable. We had escaped. We were again on the main road. We found an unoccupied cabin with a single room in an old field. In this cabin, we built a fire and placed the prisoners and a few guards. The balance of us lay on the ground outside. The rain still poured down. The water covered the ground around us and under us. Being very weary, however, we drew our blankets over our heads, made pillows of our saddles, and slept. Soon the wind changed to the north and became very cold. The rain changed to sleet, then to snow. The cold increased. Morning came. Our clothes froze stiff upon our bodies and rattled and creaked as we moved about. We soon rejoined our other party with their prisoners, and all made a forced march to Ozark.[15] We arrived in the morning, weary, hungry, and almost frozen. As we were entering the town with our long line of prisoners, our load of guns, &c. our friends cheered us on every hand. As we were passing the house in which my family resided, my wife and three little children came out and hurrahed "for our side." The rebel families gazed upon us in sullen silence.

On this expedition, we had marched a long distance into the enemy's country, taken more than our own number of prisoners, more than our own number of horses, and more than our own number of guns. Besides this, the rebel property that we had destroyed was about $5000.00 to each man of our party. And all this we had accomplished without the firing of a gun. Major Gen. S. R. Curtis pronounced this one of the most brilliant achievements of the war. He placed an account of it in his battle book and said it should appear in history. Burch and myself became still more popular with the men who had now come to think that they could not be beaten when either of us was in command. And we never undeceived them. In dozens of future engagements, we never suffered them, in a single instance, to be beaten. They did become apparently invincible.

15. In praising his men, Burch mentioned marching "often without any food, except parched corn, and no shelter from the chilling rains." He noted the good work of his officers, singling out Kelso: "As to Lieutenant Kelso, his reputation as an intrepid soldier and skillful officer is too well known to require any comment at this time" (*OR*, ser. 1, vol. 22, part 1, 161).

And thus, in honor and glory to ourselves, closed the eventful year of 1862. Recognizing in Captain Mooney one of nature's true noblemen, I took him into my house and made him my honored guest, until he had to go to be exchanged. After being exchanged, he fought us bravely and honorably, and was promoted to the rank of Major. Toward the close of the war, he was again captured, and never again returned to the rebel services.[16]

16. The records list Captain Mooney as having been captured on Feb. 27, 1863, at Tolbert's Ferry, Ark. ("Soldiers' Records," MDH).

12. The Battle of Springfield

January 1863

On the morning of the 5th of January, 1863, Burch and I started in command of 200 men intending to make a more extensive expedition than usual into Arkansas.[1] On that day, without any incident worth mentioning, we reached Beaver Station.[2] The next evening found us some 30 miles south of that place. As daylight was fading, I stopped all alone to shoot some wild turkeys that I saw going to roost on some trees not far from the road. When I overtook the command, some two miles further on, they had stopped, and were anxiously awaiting me. They had captured a small party of rebels who claimed to be the advance look-outs of Marmaduke's army. This army consisted of 6000 fine cavalry and a pack of good artillery.[3] Burch threatened to kill the men

Source: Kelso, "Auto-Biography," chap. 20, 790–800.

1. "Report of Capt. Milton Burch, Fourteenth Missouri State Militia Cavalry, of Skirmish at Fort Lawrence, Beaver Station, Mo.," Jan. 16, 1863, *OR*, ser. 1, vol. 22, part 1, 193: "I started from Ozark on the morning of the 4th of January with 100 men."

2. Ingenthron, *Borderland Rebellion*, 258: "The Beaver Station post protected a water-powered mill built by William Lawrence prior to the war. In the winter of 1862–63, the mill was employed in grinding breadstuff for the Union army and the people living in the surrounding countryside. Usually the military installation was manned by about 100 militiamen from Douglas and Taney Counties, and also served as a base for scouting expeditions and guerilla activities. The fort was a two-story brick building, 150 feet long and 40 feet wide, constructed of logs 12 inches thick, dovetailed and closely fitted. The second story projected outward over the first story. Portholes for musketry lined the walls around the entire building and were mortised on the inside to enable turning muskets to almost any direction. Eight or ten log buildings adjacent to the fort were used as barracks."

3. The Union Army believed that the Confederate forces led by Brig. Gen. John S. Marmaduke did have as many as 6,000 troops, but actually the number was about 2,300, and he planned to rendezvous with a separate column of 850 under the command of Col. Joseph C. Porter. On Marmaduke's 1863 expedition

instantly if he caught them in a lie. They stuck to what they had said. He was satisfied of the truth of their story, and wished to turn back at once. I was not satisfied. What could Marmaduke be doing there in the rear of our army under Gen. Steele? The prisoners said that I could easily satisfy myself of the truth of their story by advancing half a mile further, or by remaining where we were half an hour longer. I requested Burch to have all things ready for a hasty retreat, if necessary, and I would, in person, ascertain the facts of the case. I had not gone more than two hundred yards, when, sure enough, I met a large body of men advancing, and could hear that peculiar rumbling which is produced by the trampling of many thousands of horses. I was satisfied. I hurried back. We began our retreat. We were fired upon from the rear. We did not return the fire. We only retreated a little faster.

Several times that night our rear was fired upon by the advance guard of the enemy. Although our horses were very weary, we were obliged to keep moving. A little while before daylight, we reached Beaver Station, which was held by a company of Enrolled Militia. The commander, either a traitor or an imbecile, would make no preparations for either a defense or an evacuation of the place. He professed to disbelieve our report of the approach of Marmaduke's army.[4] While we were parleying with him, firing was heard in the direction of the enemy. Leaving this wretch to his fate, we resumed our retreat. When we reached the ford of the creek below the mill dam, the enemy were almost upon us. I crossed in the rear which received a brisk but harmless fire from the enemy. After crossing the creek, we passed up a little on the right bank. This threw the mill pond between us and our pursuers.

---

into Missouri and the Battle of Springfield, see the dispatches and official reports of the Union and Confederate officers involved in *OR*, ser. 1, vol. 22, part 1, 178–211; "The Battle of Springfield, Mo.," *New York Times*, Jan. 26, 1863, by a reporter signing as "Kickapoo" who was at Fort No. 4 during the attack; John N. Edwards, *Shelby and His Men; or, The War in the West* (Cincinnati: Miami Printing, 1867), chaps. 8–9, by a Confederate major who was Col. Joseph Shelby's adjutant; and Holcombe, *History of Greene County*, 424–56, an excellent local history informed by interviews with some of the participants. See also Robinett, "Marmaduke's Expedition"; Ingenthron, *Borderland Rebellion*, chap. 25; Goman, *Up from Arkansas;* and Wood, *Civil War Springfield*, chaps. 10–11.

4. The Beaver Station commander was Maj. William Turner of the 73rd Enrolled Missouri Militia. Burch's report, Jan. 16, 1863, *OR*, ser. 1, vol. 22, part 1, 194: "I immediately [upon detecting Marmaduke] dispatched a messenger back to the Beaver Station, with instructions to dispatch forthwith to Ozark.... I arrived at Beaver Station at 4 o'clock in the morning of the 6th. I then asked the major if he was in a condition to fall back; he replied that he had no transportation." Holcombe, *History of Greene County*, 437: "Turner was an old man who had been long in the service, and had heard a great deal more of the Confederates than he had ever seen of them, and was incredulous about there being any more of them in the country than a squad of bushwhackers."

They were trying to fire across the pond at us, but their shots, falling short, only came rattling and skipping along on the smooth surface of the ice. We returned their fire and then continued our retreat.[5] We had already sent a messenger with orders to change horses at every opportunity and to warn Ozark and Springfield just as soon as possible. The advance of so large a force of the enemy could not mean anything else than the capture of Springfield, at which place were vast army stores, and, for the defense of which, only a very small force had been assigned.[6]

After leaving Beaver Station, we were not pressed any more by the enemy. We wondered at this and asked the prisoners the reason of it. One of the prisoners replied: *"Since I have commenced telling you the truth, I will continue to do so. There is a large division of this army marching by another road which unites with this road a few miles this side of Ozark. Your danger is not from those behind you. They will not be likely to crowd you. They will wish you to move slowly so as to give the other division time to reach the junction of the roads before you do. If you do not wish to be cut off by that division, you'd better crowd for Ozark, with all speed."* We did crowd, thanks to this truthful rebel, and it is well that we did so. We were only a few hundred yards in advance of the enemy approaching on the other road. They crowded us into Ozark. Orders were awaiting us there to continue our retreat right into Springfield. The balance of our battalion were all ready to retreat with us, abandoning

5. Beaver Station was attacked by 270 Confederate cavalry under the command of Col. Emmett MacDonald. Robinett, "Marmaduke's Expedition," 157: "The Confederates rushed the fort. Surprised, the Federal garrison fled leaving some 100 horses, five wagons, and 300 stands of arms. The fort and all supplies that could not be carried away were burned. The arms were buried." Ingenthron, *Borderland Rebellion*, 260: "Major Turner, the Union commander, was wounded in the attack, and some half dozen Federal soldiers were killed."

6. Holcombe, *History of Greene County*, 430: "Springfield was now the great military depot for the Federal 'Army of the Frontier.' . . . There were forts and cannon and muskets and powder and shot and shells and provisions and quartermaster's stores in great abundance,—but few soldiers. Nearly all the available troops had gone to the front." Gen. Egbert B. Brown, Enrolled Missouri Militia commander of the Southwest District, counted 453 men of the 3rd MSM Cavalry, 289 from the 4th MSM Cavalry, and 378 from the 18th Iowa Infantry. Kelso's 14th Cavalry, under Lt. Col. John Pound, would arrive with 223. An urgent call would go out to militia men in the surrounding counties, and a few hundred would arrive through the night of Jan. 7–8. A few hundred convalescents who had been recently discharged from medical care were in town or camp, and some of the sick or wounded men still in the buildings and tents serving as hospitals had to be well enough to prop themselves up and fire a gun. Civilian men and older boys willing to fight were issued arms. Altogether Brown estimated that he had a fighting force of about 2,000 men (General Brown's reports to Gen. Samuel R. Curtis, Jan. 8, 1863, 10:00 a.m. and 11:50 p.m., *OR*, ser. 1, vol. 22, part 1, 179–81). The 250 men from the Enrolled Missouri Militia would raise the total to over 2,300 (Goman, *Up from Arkansas*, 123n26).

whatever could not be carried away.[7] I called a few moments at my own door to speak to my wife and children. I had to leave them behind. Our troops were now pouring across the Finley bridge. While our rear was leaving the bridge at one end, the enemy was entering it at the other. It was now dark. For a time the enemy pressed us very closely, sometimes calling upon us to stop and give up our *overcoats,* declaring that they were very cold and that they wanted "*them overcoats d——d bad.*"

When within about five miles from Springfield, the pursuit ceased. About midnight, we reached Springfield. We got no sleep; no rest. All was bustle and preparation. Old dismounted cannons were being mounted on draymens' trucks, loyal citizens were being armed, and even the convalescent sick in the hospitals were being brought out and put on duty. After all, we had a heterogeneous force of only 800 men with which to resist a force of 6000 as fine cavalry as ever fought in a bad cause. We were pretty well fortified, however, with earth-works and rifle pits, and our men were eager to fight.[8]

I expected that, when daylight came on, a feint would be made in the south by the enemy's artillery, while the real attack would be made by a charge of the main body down Wilson Creek from the east. This was certainly the proper thing for the enemy to do, and, had he done it, the result of the battle could hardly have been otherwise than in his favor. He missed his chance, however, made his real attack on the south upon our strong earth-works, and, as a result of this mistake, gave us a glorious victory. I wondered that so able a warrior as was Gen. Marmaduke should have committed so

7. Burch's report, Jan. 16, 1863, *OR,* ser. 1, vol. 22, part 1, 194: "I started for Ozark, leaving the main road and taking a right-hand road. Hearing that a portion of the enemy had gone up Little Beaver with the intention of cutting us off from Ozark, I travelled slowly, using precaution against surprise, and arrived at Ozark about 10 o'clock of the night of the 6th. I then ordered all the baggage to be conveyed across the river on the road to Springfield, which was promptly complied with, and waited for further orders, which orders I received for us to fall back to Springfield."

8. Five forts and earthworks had been planned, but only two of the forts were finished and usable and only Fort No. 1 had any artillery (two brass cannons that fired six pound shells); see "The Battle of Springfield, Mo." On the artillery, see General Brown's dispatch, Jan. 8 [1863], 10:00 a.m., *OR,* ser. 1, vol. 22, part 1, 179–80: "I have our iron 6 and 12 pounder guns and howitzers, which I mounted last night, in addition to two brass 6-pounders at Fort No. 1." The iron cannon, as Wood describes in *Civil War Springfield,* 100, were "old guns . . . which were lying virtually abandoned on the grounds of the Calvary Presbyterian Church," and "were mounted on wagon wheels as temporary carriages, taken to the blacksmith shop for repair, and then rolled to Fort No. 4 and placed in position." Brown also reported that "the convalescents in hospitals, employees of quartermaster, commissary, and ordinance, and citizens of all ages are being armed. . . . The brick buildings are being pierced for musketry" (180). The *New York Times* reporter thought that the general feeling among the soldiers was, "We *may* hold the town, and we will not give it up without a fight; but we shall probably be whipped."

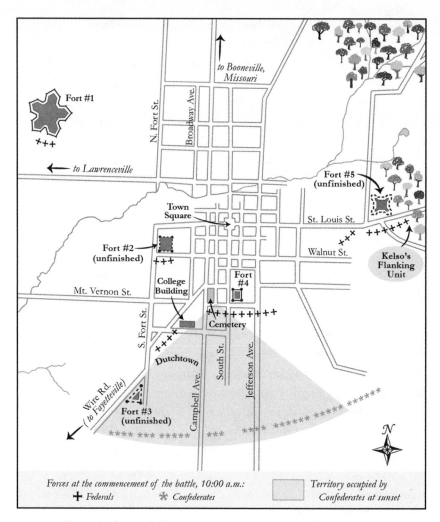

Figure 4. The Battle of Springfield, Missouri, January 8, 1863. Drawn by Rebecca Wrenn.
Map sources: Based on "Plan of Springfield, Mo., Showing the Location of the Forts," Record
Group 77, National Archives and Records Administration, Washington, D.C., in Frederick W.
Goman, *Up from Arkansas: Marmaduke's First Missouri Raid, Including the Battles of Springfield
and Hartville* (Springfield, Mo.: Privately printed, 1999); Elmo Ingenthron, *Borderland Rebellion:
A History of the Civil War on the Missouri-Arkansas Border* (Branson, Mo.: Ozarks Mountaineer,
[1989]), 262; and Larry Wood, *Civil War Springfield* (Charleston: The History Press, 2011), 106.

grave an error. I understand, however, that he afterwards explained the matter by saying that he was to act in concert with another force which was to attack on the east while he held us engaged on the south, and that his failure was due to the non-arrival of this other force. This gives a complexion to the affair more favorable to Marmaduke.[9]

I expected that the attack would be made as soon as daylight appeared. I also expected that, before opening fire upon the town, a notice would be given by the enemy to remove the women and children. It was ten o'clock, however, before we heard from the enemy, and then his first notice was in the form of several heavy shots sent crashing through our churches, our dwelling houses, our printing offices, &c. Several women and children were wounded by this barbarous fire. This fire was replied to from our earthworks, "Fort No. 4," at the outlet of South Street. Opened thus, the battle now raged, with varying success, till the darkness of the succeeding night compelled the combatants to cease their fearful work of mutual destruction.[10]

Brig. Gen. E. B. Brown was in command of our forces. Believing that I was correct in my views as to the point at which the real attack was to be made, he at first sent my entire battalion to defend the rifle pits on the east; and, seeming to think that the success on that side greatly depended upon me, he advised me how to act, and how to cou[n]sel my superiors in office.[11] Lieut.

9. "The Battle of Springfield, Mo.": "The city thus fortified lies half in the prairie and half in the timber. Upon the north and east all is forest; upon the south and west the country is entirely open. The rebels chose to make their attack from the south, which was an error, for two reasons. First, because they were more exposed to our view, in their advance from the south, than they would have been from the east; secondly, because the north and east side of the town were not defended by forts." See also Holcombe, *History of Greene County*, 438–39. General Marmaduke had hoped to be joined by Colonel Porter's brigade, but in his reports he did not mention Porter's absence as the explanation for his battlefield tactics or his ultimate retreat (*OR*, ser. 1, vol. 22, part 1, 194–98), though he may have done so later.

10. "The Battle of Springfield, Mo.": "Without one word of notice to remove the women and children, they opened fire upon the town, with solid shot, though they knew that scores of their own friends, both women and prisoners, were exposed to the same danger as our loyal citizens. . . . 'Gentlemen,' said Gen. Brown, who stood on the southwest bastion of Fort No. 4, 'this is unprecedented; it is barbarous!'" See also Holcombe, *History of Greene County*, 440: "It is not certain that Hoffman [the Union gunner at Fort No. 4] did not open the fight, by shelling Marmaduke's advance," but both Brown and the *New York Times* reporter were right with Hoffman at the fort and would have known. There were no official reports of injuries of women and children, although the *Times* article did note that one shell "exploded in a room where there were four women and two children lying upon the floor, covered with feather-beds."

11. "Report of Brig. Gen. Colly B. Holland, Missouri Militia, of Engagement at Springfield, Mo.," Jan. 11, 1863, *OR*, ser. 1, vol. 22, part 1, 182, describes the deployment of Union troops. Facing the enemy in the south, "General Brown formed his line of battle, with detachments of cavalry [including nearly all of Kelso's brigade] on the left, southeast of town, a detachment of the Eighteenth Iowa on their right."

Col. John A. Pound commanded our battalion. I commanded an advanced flanking party of 20 mounted men. Presently, all except my little party were with-drawn from that part of the town to aid in resisting the attack, on the south, upon Fort No. 4 and upon the stockade around the college building.[12] From my position on the extreme left, I could see but little of the real battle. Against me were matched 50 well-mounted rebels. With this party I skirmished all day, neither party accomplishing much except fine feats of horsemanship.[13] Sometimes, the rebel party would retire to a distance of a mile from our position, conceal themselves in a depression of ground, then send half a dozen of their number close to our position to call us out. We would chase them for some distance, then, when their whole party came after us, we would turn and get away as fast as our horses could carry us. They would chase us as close as they dared to our defenses, then stop, order us to give up our "*over-coats,*" our "*Lincoln coffee,* &c." They would also make obscene gestures, turning up their buttocks toward us and patting them with their hands.

Sometimes this party and my party would stop not far from each other and, from the higher ground which we occupied, watch the conflict that was raging a mile to the south west of us. The roar of artillery was incessant as was the rattle of musketry. We could see every movement,—the charges and

---

Fort No. 4, with two mounted guns, was in the center, with the 74th Enrolled Missouri Militia and the convalescent soldiers, dubbed the "Quinine Brigade" after their bitter fever medicine. About 250 yards further forward and to the right (west) there was an empty two-story brick college building, surrounded on three sides by a palisade, and a bit beyond that a regiment of 72nd Enrolled Missouri Militia with a few detachments of cavalry flanked further on the right. "Fort No. 1 about one-half mile to the rear, being the extreme right, . . . was garrisoned by the Eighteenth Iowa and citizens."

12. Holcombe, *History of Greene County*, 442: "At about 2 in the afternoon the Confederates, dismounted, began moving around toward the southwest part of town. . . . The Confederates advanced from the south towards the north and northwest, coming up the little valley at the foot of South and Campbell streets, and sweeping over the ground to the westward. On they came, through 'Dutchtown,' as a collection of houses at the foot of Campbell street was called, taking the houses and their outbuildings for shelter as they advanced—forward to the stockade college building, *which had been left unguarded, and captured it without losing a man.*" "Report of Col. Benjamin Crabb, Nineteenth Iowa Infantry, of Engagement at Springfield, Mo.," Jan. 10, 1863, *OR*, ser. 1, vol. 22, part 1, 185: By 3:00, the Confederates "were making strong efforts to turn our right, and, after being driven from our center, threw their main force forward for that purpose, when they were met by" the 72nd Enrolled Missouri Militia, the "Quinine Brigade," the 3rd and 4th MSM Cavalry, five companies of the 18th Iowa, and the 2nd Battalion 14th MSM Cavalry (Kelso's battalion, excluding his twenty men).

13. "The Battle of Springfield, Mo." described the cavalry charges: "My blood quickened its flow, as I watched our brave boys gallop forward to the charge, then saw the enemy galloping in a long line to meet them, and heard the sharp, rapid firing of carbines, on both sides. After each charge and fire both sides would turn and gallop back, with small loss on either side."

the counter-charges, the shells bursting in air, the actual intermingling of the ranks at one point in a deadly struggle for a field piece. The piece belonged to us; it soon belonged to the enemy.[14] Our men were driven from the Stockade and, by night, about one third of the town was in the hands of the enemy. The stockade and many buildings were burned.

During the whole action, a reserve force of the enemy 500 strong had stood holding their horses a short distance to the right of the ground upon which my party and our opposing party were practicing our feats of horsemanship. These reserves had paid so little attention to us that we began to have but little fear of them. When day-light began to fade, however, we were drawn out, nearer to them than usual by four rebels who really did almost let us run upon them, and whom we did, for once, try in earnest to catch or to kill. When we had thus been drawn out farther than on any previous occasion, the whole party came thundering out of a depression after us, crowding us more closely than ever before. To our dismay, the 500 reserves now mounted hastily and moved to cut off our retreat to town. With us, it was now a desperate race for life. We passed a few yards ahead of the intercepting party. I was in the rear. Sergt. McElhaney was next.[15] As we passed close in front of the head of the intercepting column, their yells and their shots were so terrific that they frightened my horse. He shied from the road, sprang into a pile of stones, and fell throwing me over his head and hurting me quite severely. As he arose, I sprang upon him, threw my arms around his neck, and, with my face to his mane, let him dart into the thick cluster of hawthorns that fortunately lined that side of the road. Thus I escaped, with the enemy in 20 yards of me. When he saw me fall, Sergt. McElhaney reigned up his horse to save me or share my fate, but I instantly cried out: "*Leave me! Save yourself!*"

As usual, my men halted near the rifle pits at the edge of the town. They thought that I was lost. They were greatly delighted, therefore, when,

14. A detachment from the 18th Iowa led by Capts. John A. Landis, William R. Blue, and Joseph Van Meter came down from Fort No. 1 to help fend off the attack with a fieldpiece—one of the brass six-pounders—but they wound up beyond the federal line and exposed to the enemy. Twenty Confederates led by Maj. John Bowman dashed forward to capture the gun. All the Federals' horses pulling the gun were shot down. Holcombe, *History of Greene County*, 444: "In the fierce fighting that followed Captains Blue and Van Meter were mortally wounded, two or three of their men were killed, and Capt. Landis and a dozen more Hawkeyes were severely wounded, while the Confederates lost Capt. Titsworth, Lieut. Buffington, and Lieut. McCoy, and four or five men killed, and perhaps twenty . . . wounded." (Holcombe notes that "the particulars of the fight for the gun have been obtained from actual participants on both sides.")
15. Sgt. Robert McElhaney, Co. H, 14th Regt., MSM Cavalry (NPS Soldiers' Database).

a few minutes later, I came up bare-head and well-scratched by the thorns through which my brave old Hawk-Eye had carried me. The enemy had halted in line 200 yards away. Fearing that they would come in on a charge, I sent for reinforcements to be hurried to me at once. My messenger brought back word that not a man could be spared, and that I must hold my part of the town with my twenty men or all would be lost. Capt. Bob. Matthews, with 15 other wounded men from the hospital, came out to aid me.[16] Even these poor heroic skeletons did me much good. Calling tauntingly to the enemy from our sheltered position, and sending some effective shots, we made them believe that we were quite strong and that we were eager for them to attack us. They withdrew. Dense darkness and an oppressive silence reigned around us. There had been a terrible struggle between the main bodies just as daylight was departing. Of the result of that struggle, we knew nothing. We cautiously moved toward the public square. It might be in possession of the enemy. At last we were met by a small party of men. It proved to be Burch and a few comrades of our own company. From them we learned the result of the battle as given above. We also learned that several members of our company had fallen—all like heroes. Burch afterward gave me the following account of his part of this battle:

> Dear Captain:—At the Battle of Springfield, you were engaged, you know, in a different part of the field. At about three o'clock P.M. Marmaduke was forcing his way into Springfield down South Street. At that time, we were on the Buffalo Road at the end of Booneville Street. Being ordered up, we met the rebels 50 yards from the public square. Lieut. Col. Pound was in command of the battalion. Capt. Flagg was at the head of the column dog drunk. We were marched up to within 20 yards of the advance column of the rebels and ordered to fire. The battalion were marching by fours. The rebels opened a destructive fire upon the battalion, and this fire caused some disorder. I was in the rear. I saw the peril that we were in. I galloped up and said to Col. Pound: "Col. *What are you going to do*," and he replied, "*What had we better do?*" I said "*Dismount and charge.*" He assented. I threw the men into line and ordered a charge, ordering the men to fire their revolvers. Just at that moment, the

---

16. Capt. Robert P. Matthews, Co. D, 8th Regt., Missouri Cavalry (NPS Soldiers' Database).

rebels had captured two pieces of artillery that had been brought from Fort No. 1. They now turned these pieces upon us. The men faltered a little. Soon, however, order prevailed, and we made the charge notwithstanding the artillery fire and the galling fire of small arms. Our boys raised the Indian war whoop and we drove the rebels back into the Stockade. On the right, our forces had been driven into Fort No. 1. When, however, they saw the rebels falling back, they sallied forth from the Fort, and again fiercely renewed the engagement on that side. As if with solid walls, we now held the rebels on every side. For an hour, I was exposed to a galling fire, I being the only mounted man on that line. (Having been severely wounded in the foot while a soldier in Texas, Burch was quite lame. Hence on nearly all occasions, to the great exposure of his life, he remained mounted.) My horse was shot in the head, and falling upon my left leg mashed it severely. I did not then know, however, that I was much hurt. As soon as I got loose from my horse, I went back, got my other horse, and returned to the front. You know Capt. how the other field officers acted. We held the rebels there till dark. Then, by Col. Pound's order we mounted and moved to the left to feel of the enemy. They threw a shell very near us. Then Col. Pound had us fall back 200 yards and dismount. When I dismounted, I could not stand, my leg had swollen so much.[17]

When I reached the public square, I found our battalion drawn up there awaiting orders. A few hard tacks were issued to the men where they stood, and a little feed to the horses. Every few moments, a flash of light would be seen, a heavy shot would crash through the houses or scream through the air over our heads, and the thunders of a cannon would burst forth on the silence of night. What was the enemy doing? Gen. Brown having been wounded,

17. Colonel Crabb's report, Jan. 10, 1863, *OR*, ser. 1, vol. 22, part 1, 186, gave a dimmer view of the 14th's performance: "At this critical time, an officer commanding a company in the Second Battalion Fourteenth Missouri State Militia, ordered his men to horse (as I was afterward informed), and the whole battalion came running in great confusion to the rear and took to horse. I tried in vain to rally them; they seemed panic-stricken. This caused a partial giving way among the other troops. I had no difficulty in rallying them, and they went again into the fight. It was now near dark, and the enemy an additional demonstration on our left. By this time, Lieutenant Colonel Pound, commanding, had succeeded in reforming the Second Battalion Fourteenth Missouri State Militia. I ordered him to advance on the enemy's right, which order he promptly executed. The enemy fired but a few rounds, and again retired, leaving us in full possession of this part of the field."

Col. Crabb of Iowa, a brave and efficient officer, was now in command.[18] I went to his office and found him trying to find out what the enemy was doing. The reports of his messengers were very unsatisfactory. At last, I told him that I could obtain for him the information he wanted. He said he wished that I would do so, and that he would have called upon me to do this only that he knew that I had had no sleep or rest for three days and two nights. He said he knew that I must now be nearly exhausted.

Leaving Col. Crabb's office, I passed up South Street to Fort No. 4.[19] Entering the fort a moment, I informed the officers that I was going out in front of their position to ascertain the movements of the enemy. I let them know this lest I might be shot by mistake from the fort. Leaving the fort, I passed out into the darkness on the Fayetteville road. When about a hundred yards from the fort, I got down and crept upon my hands and knees. I could hear the rebels coughing not far from me. They seemed to all have severe colds. The nearest coughing was in a blacksmith's shop that stood at the forks of the Fayetteville and the Ozark roads.[20] Creeping nearer, I learned that the coughing was done by guards stationed in the shop. Creeping around the shop at a little distance, I soon found myself upon the ground upon which the fiercest fighting had been done. I began to come upon dead men scattered

18. Wood, *Civil War Springfield*, 110–11: "As the fighting shifted westward, General Brown rode forward along South Street with his body guard to near the corner of State to oversee the battle and encourage his men. While there, consulting with some of his officers, he was shot from his horse by a Rebel sharp-shooter concealed in a house or other nearby hiding place. Brown was taken to the rear with a severely wounded arm, the bone having been broken above the left elbow, and he officially turned over command of the Union troops engaged in the battle to Colonel Crabb." On the Confederate side, Major Edwards admired Brown's courage: "General Brown made a splendid fight for his town, and exhibited conspic-uous courage and ability. . . . He rode [the] entire length [of Confederate Col. Joseph Shelby's brigade] under a severe fire, clad in bold regimentals, elegantly mounted and ahead of all so that the fire might be concentrated upon him. It was reckless bravado, and General Brown gained by one bold dash the admiration and respect of Shelby's soldiers" (Edwards, *Shelby and His Men*, 139). The *New York Times* reporter wrote in his Jan. 26, 1863, article "The Battle of Springfield, Mo." that "too much praise cannot be awarded Gen. Brown. . . . He has been much overlooked by higher authorities, much maligned by some of those under him, and even accused of cowardice. But his men now regard him with universal confidence and affection."

19. Fort No. 4 was a square about 160 feet long and wide with gun emplacements on its southeast and northwest corners (Goman, *Up from Arkansas*, 27, 40).

20. Holcombe, *History of Greene County*, 445–46: "The lines of the two forces after nightfall seem to have been as follows: The Confederates were in two wings, which formed a very obtuse angle or letter V with the arms much extended. The point of this angle rested on the stockade [college], and the right arm (or the Confederate left), extended in a southwesterly direction along the Fayetteville road. The left arm (the Confederate right), ran in a southeasterly course across State street, through 'Dutchtown,' and past a blacksmith shop, out into the open prairie."

about upon the ground. There was a flash of light and the thunder of cannon in front of me. The enemy was again firing upon the town. There was another flash and another burst of thunder, this time behind me. The fort was replying to the enemy's fire,—replying with shells that passed uncomfortably near my back as they went screaming over me. I felt the wind that they made, and saw the burning fuse pass like a faint streak of lightning. Many shells thus passed over me from the fort, and several heavy shots in the opposite direction from the rebel batteries. Whenever I saw a flash of light, I flattened myself against the ground till the messenger of death passed over me. Then I crept to one side to get out of the line of these messengers.[21]

The firing soon ceased on both sides. The rebel batteries were moving. I heard a good deal of coughing near the smoldering ruins of several houses that had been burned. Creeping nearer, I found the beds of coals that remained of these houses surrounded by men sleeping upon the ground.[22] Creeping around these sleepers without disturbing them, I crept farther out upon the battle ground. I found more dead men. Besides these, I found myself surrounded by several wounded men. Some of these were calling for help and for water. After calling awhile in vain, some of them would curse; others would pray. Some were delirious, talking, as they supposed, to their mothers and other dear ones in their far away homes. After awhile, some of these ceased to speak. A rattling in their throats ensued. Then all was still. And there they lay alone in the dark night stiffening upon the frozen ground of the battle-field. They never again saw the homes and the loved ones that they dreamed of as they were sinking to that *sleep that knows no waking.* I know not to which side they belonged. Probably to our side. The enemy would hardly have left their own wounded so long thus uncared for. Several

21. "Report of Col. Joseph O. Shelby, Missouri Cavalry (Confederate)," Jan. 31, 1863, *OR*, ser. 1, vol. 22, part 1, 201: "When all was quiet, [Confederate Lt. Richard A.] Collins, with his iron 6-pounder and a small support, made a promenade upon the principal streets of the city. . . . This little party, whenever a light appeared, fired at it, and it served not only to encourage our tired soldiers, but it told to the foe, with thunder tones, that we were still victors, proud and defiant." Col. Henry Sheppard, 72nd Enrolled Missouri Militia (Union), in Holcombe, *History of Greene County,* 449: "In the night I had the howitzer in the fort, a 12-pounder, pepper the rascals in the palisade college building, 250 yards away. The moon shown beautifully and the Dutch lieutenant (Lieut. Hoffman) made splendid practice. The secesh vacated it and at 1 a. m. I put a company in it."
22. Shelby's report, Jan. 31, 1863, *OR*, ser. 1, vol. 22, part 1, 201: "I drew my brigade off calmly and cautiously, formed them in and around the heavy stockade, and prepared to pass the night as best I could, although it was very cold, and the men had no fires, save the smoldering of consumed houses, burned by the terrified enemy at our first approach."

of our men did fall on that part of the field. The dying men were probably, some of them at least, my own dear friends and comrades. At any rate, several of these were found next morning upon that ground, their bloodless upturned faces covered with frost. I did not dare approach any of these wounded men, though I lay still among them for an hour or more waiting to learn the meaning of an extensive conversation a little beyond. The enemy seemed to be organizing some movement which they wished to execute as secretly as possible. There were no bugle calls, no loud commands. The officers were rousing the sleeping men as quietly as possible and getting them into line. Those nearest our lines were not yet being disturbed. For some time, I could not make out what it all meant.[23] At last, however, I discovered that the main body was moving out to the south-east, in the direction of Gov. John S. Phelp's farm which lay over a mile from town.[24]

I now wished to creep out and return to Col. Crabb with my information. I saw, however, an ambulance approaching me surrounded by a small party of men carrying lanterns. I must lie still a little longer. They were gathering up the wounded. As they approached, some of the wounded men near me called to them. These men were placed in the ambulance. Placing my big shot-gun under me, I lay flat upon the ground with my face in the dirt. "*Here's a dead man,*" was called out close upon my right. My heart flopped about violently. "*And here's another,*" was spoken right at me, as a lantern was lowered to the side of my head, and a boot was pushed gently against my side. I think my flopping heart ceased to move at all. I did not breathe. "*Well,*" said an officer, "*d—n it, don't fool away your time with dead men, find the wounded!*" They passed on. I was again alone in the darkness. I was growing

23. Shelby's report, Jan. 31, 1863, *OR*, ser. 1, vol. 22, part 1, 201: "The men lay on their arms until about 2 o'clock in the morning, when I deemed it best, as they were suffering greatly from cold and hunger, to withdraw, which was done quietly and in order, some of Colonel [Emmett] MacDonald's command and Major [Ben] Elliot's scouts picketing my flanks and front."

24. Edwards, *Shelby and His Men*, 139: "About midnight Shelby's brigade withdrew by regiments from the gloomy and fire-scarred town, and marched like silent specters across the cold gray prairie to their horses in the woods beyond, leaving behind a strong line of mounted skirmishers to remain until daylight. On their way back the hungry soldiers tarried long enough to visit the Hon. John S. Phelps' splendid mansion, now silent and deserted: but unlike their enemies on ten thousand other occasions, they simply took the necessary articles for food and raiment. The mellow and delicious apples, the rusty bottles hid away many feet down under the earth, the flour, bacon, beef, blankets, quilts, and shirts were all taken—but nothing more." Phelps was a Democrat and a Unionist. According to Michael B. Dougan, "Phelps, John Smith," *ANB*, "The Civil War crippled Phelps financially. His farm was looted first by Union troops, who thought the presence of slaves made him a secessionist, then the Confederates burned his buildings." See also "John S. Phelps Papers," http://www.ozarkscivilwar.org/archives/3549.

a little nervous and determined to depart. By too long a stay among the dead, I might become a dead man sure enough.

Turning around, I cautiously crept back on the same route by which I had come. I felt an irresistible impulse, however, to hurry. Creeping seemed soon to become an intolerably slow and laborious mode of locomotion. I concluded to risk rising up and walking. I thought the darkness would hide me. I did arise and look around. I was about thirty yards from the blacksmith shop, directly opposite the further corner. I was seen. "*Halt!*" came from the door, and three men stepped outside. I was already halted. I stood motionless. "*Who goes there?,*" was added. "*A friend, I reckon, who are you?,*" I replied. "*You come up!*" they answered, cocking their guns and bringing them to bear upon me. "*Well, I will come up,*" replied I, "*but I wish to know whether you are Federals or southern soldiers.*" By using the terms *Federals* and *southern soldiers,* I made them believe that I was a rebel, these terms being in common use among the rebels, but being rarely used among loyal men. They answered, "*We are southern soldiers.*" "*Oh! then,*" said I, "*you are all right. I am a southern soldier myself and got lost from my command in the last hard struggle as it was getting dark.*" "*Well,*" said they, "*you are all right now. Come up!*" By this time I had selected my course and had partially thrown them off their guard. I replied, "*Boys, if I was sure you were southern soldiers I would not care, but—*" At the word *but,* I darted past the end of the shop, thus placing a corner of the building between the guards and myself. A moment later, I was streaking it along the other side of a heavy boisdarc hedge. Not a shot was fired. I had escaped. But my night experiences on that battleground can never fade from my memory.

Having reached Col. Crabb's office, I made my report. He complimented me very highly, and, at my request, gave me permission to do any "*devilment*" to the rebels that I might find it in my power to do them. I hoped that I might find it in my power to do them a good deal of this same "*devilment.*" I hoped to capture the guards in that blacksmith shop, without alarming any body else. Could I succeed in doing this, I could then lead a body of men secretly through the shop and into the enemy's camp, and there could surprise his rear guard still sleeping around the beds of coals. In order to capture the guards without creating any alarm, I would dress myself and half a dozen men in citizen's clothing, and approach the guards. When they challenged us, we would claim to be southern men coming in to join the army under Marmaduke. Since squads of such men were constantly coming in, we would be believed. The guards would call us in to keep us till they could turn us over to an officer. When thus called in, some of us would seize hold of the guns of the guards, while the rest of us would place cocked revolvers to their heads, threatening instant death if they made the slightest noise. Having thus captured the guards,—if I should succeed in this—, I could easily accomplish the balance of the undertaking. I still think the plan was a good one. It took us some time, however, to get ready. The result of the delay was that, when we reached the shop, the guards and all their living comrades were gone. The dead alone of both sides held possession of the battleground.

Having failed in this undertaking, I took half a dozen mounted men and went on a reconnoitering expedition. I found the enemy feeding upon Gov. Phelps' farm. The men and the horses together were making a great deal of uproar. Leaving my men at a distance of 200 yards, I dismounted and crept on my hands and knees through the thicket of brush that lay on that side. I could hear horses making a noise not far from me on the other side of the thicket. I wanted a few of these horses. I also wanted a few men, especially officers. I was not destined, however, to obtain either horses or men. Morning was now dawning. What I was to do, I must do quickly. I crept on looking and listening. "*Halt!*" rang out some 30 yards to my right. Could I have been seen or heard? I kept perfectly still. "*Who goes there?,*" was added. "*Officer of the day,*" was replied. Then came, "*Advance, Officer of the Day, and give the countersign!*" "*All right,*" thought I, "*Mr. Officer of the Day, I will try to compliment you with the contents of my big shot-gun.*" Having relieved the guard, the officer, with about 30 mounted men, approached me, the men scattered out so, as they picked their way through the bush, that some would run right over me and others came between me and my men, thus cutting off my retreat. I was in a comparatively open space. I could not lie concealed. There was now too much light. I must now run for my life. I would let the Officer of the Day and his men alone, if they would only let me alone. I arose and fled. "*Halt! halt!*" resounded after me. I did not halt. Every time the word was repeated, I ran just a little faster. Again I had failed to distinguish myself by any remarkable feat of personal prowess.

Reaching my men, I sent two of them in to report to Col. Crabb the present status of the enemy's affairs. With the balance, I remained to make further observations. The uproar increased. Every body seemed to be out of humor. "*Some d——d thief has stolen my over-coat,*" yelled one. "*G-d d——n you, you never had any over-coat,*" yelled another. "*Fall in! G-d d——n you, fall in!"* roared an officer. *"Ho-ah! ho-ah! ho-ah!,"* roared a mule. *"Where's that feller that claims this sorrel mare? I'll be d——d if I'm going to take care of my own horse and every body else's too,"* yelled another. *"Close order! forward! march!"* roared another officer. *"Ho-ah! ho-ah—ho-ah!"* roared another mule. And so on in a thousand other cases. Fifteen minutes later, I sent back another report. It was now full day light. The rebel army was moving around to the east,—to our weakest point, the point at which they should have made their attack the day before. I dreaded this movement. We could not long resist an attack on this side if made in a charge. I sent my last man to warn Col. Crabb of the new danger that threatened us. I was glad that the Col. had command. He would hold out to the last. Gen. Brown, in my opinion, would have surrendered at discretion.

All alone now, I took a position on an eminence from which I could watch every movement of the enemy. I never saw a finer body of cavalry. The light of the morning sun, gleaming from their polished weapons, added to the brilliance of their appearance.[25] Presently they halted, just where I feared and expected that they would, due east of the town.[26] Here they formed in order of battle. Expecting them soon to come in on a charge, I now hastened back to town. Col. Crabbe had not been idle. Already he had the streets on that side strongly barricaded with steam boilers, heavy machinery, &c. He had perforated the brick buildings with port holes, and, at each port hole, had placed a sick man or a wounded man, propped up with a pile of flour sacks. He had done every thing that could be done to prepare for a desperate defence. *"Victory or death"* was the motto.[27]

25. Perhaps if Kelso had been closer, the sight would have appeared less impressive. General Marmaduke, in his report of Feb. 1, 1863, *OR*, ser. 1, vol. 22, part 1, 197–98, commented on his men being "indifferently armed and equipped, thinly clad, many without shoes and horses . . . without baggage wagons or cooking utensils." Colonel Shelby's report, *OR*, ser. 1, vol. 22, part 1, 204, remarked on their "unshod and miserable horses." Major Edwards, in *Shelby and His Men*, 134, remembered that for the shivering Confederate soldiers on that expedition, overcoats were "an article more desirable than purple and fine linen."

26. Col. Henry Sheppard, 72nd Enrolled Missouri Militia (Union), in Holcombe, *History of Greene County*, 449: "An hour later [after daybreak], with Gen. Brown's field-glass, I sat in the bastion [of Fort No. 4] and saw the long lines of the enemy working their way eastward from the 'goose pond,' where they had withdrawn during the night. To only one idea did it seem reasonable to attribute this movement—that the attack was to be renewed from the east and north."

27. Colonel Crabb's report, Jan. 10, 1863, *OR*, ser. 1, vol. 22, part 1, 186: "On the morning of the 9th, they appeared in full force to the east, and about 1 mile from town. Preparations were made to receive them. A cavalry force was sent forward to engage them and check their advance; but they declined another engagement and retired in haste." General Marmaduke's report, Feb. 1, 1863, *OR*, ser. 1, vol. 22, part 1, 197: "A little after sunrise the column moved eastward on the Rolla road." Colonel Shelby's

We feared the attack. We prepared for it. We waited for it. We ceased to fear it. We grew eager for it to begin. What was the enemy doing? Presently a flag of truce arrived with an order for us to surrender. Again Marmaduke had committed a serious error. He should have charged at once. We returned a message with the flag of truce, asking Marmaduke what he meant by the word, "*surrender*." We informed him that the word was not to be found in our books, and that until we knew the meaning of the word, we could not say whether we would or would not surrender. Our ignorance of the meaning of the word so disgusted him that, without any further ceremony, he marched away in a south-easterly direction.[28] We could hardly believe our eyes when we saw him leaving. We did not expect so easy a victory over such a force.

When he had been gone some two or three hours, we discovered through our field glasses, from the top of the Court House, a body of men on a hill several miles to the north of the town. Who could these be? With a party of 50 men, I went out to ascertain. Coming upon them by surprise, I bawled out:—"*Fire one gun and you all die! Down with your arms!*" The poor fellows were frightened out of their wits. They had no arms to "*down with.*" They were the sorriest lot of men I ever saw. Not one of them could have borne arms. Some were very old, some were blind, some were deaf, some had an arm gone, some a leg,—something was wrong with every one of them, and there were about forty in all. Through curiosity, they had assembled on that hill to ascertain, if possible, which army held the town.

On my return, I found the men still waiting ready for battle, and growing braver every moment as the prospect of a battle became more doubtful. Presently an old man came in with four fine horses and asked for Marmaduke. He said he wanted to sell these horses for fear the Federals

---

report, Jan. 31, 1863, *OR*, ser. 1, vol. 22, part 1, 203: "After the men had breakfasted the next morning, after ammunition had been distributed, and a leisurely forming of the brigade had been effected, we started from the scene of a hard fought battle . . . and we, after making a circuit of the town with floating banners and waving pennons, left it alone in its glory, because all had been done that could be done. Friday, the ninth, moved east with my brigade on the Rolla road." Confederate 2nd Lt. Salem Holland Ford (1835–1915), Co. F, 12th Regt., Missouri Cavalry, thought, like his commanders, that the battle was a success, if not quite a victory, especially considering, as he remembered it years later, "the enemy had more than five to our one and had twenty pieces of artillery." The Confederates, he wrote in 1909, "piled [the Union] dead very deep all about the outer defense" (Salem Holland Ford, Civil War reminiscence [photocopy], March 8, 1909, B 194, 20, Missouri Historical Society, St. Louis).

28. General Marmaduke's report, Feb. 1, 1863, *OR*, ser. 1, vol. 22, part 1, 197: "I addressed a letter, under a flag of truce, to General Brown, commanding at Springfield, stating that my wounded were left in charge of competent surgeons and attendants, and asking from him a proper treatment of all."

might take them. He said that he had taken the oath of loyalty to the United States, but that the oath was only from the teeth out. Seeing the mistake under which he was laboring, I told him that Marmaduke was too busy to see him, but that I could attend to his business as well as Marmaduke could. I told him that he had brought me exactly the number of horses I was wanting. I had a Sergt. take charge of the horses. *"Of course, you will give me a receipt for them?,"* said the old sinner, beginning to look a little uneasy. *"Oh! no,"* said I, *"You will not need any receipt." "But how will I get my **pay**?*["] queried he. *"You will not get it at all,"* said I, *"can you not **give** that much for the good of the cause?" "I expected pay,"* said he. *"I have expected many a thing that I did not get,"* said I. *"You will get no pay, and besides this, you will have to help us fight."* He looked frightened,—looked as if his zeal for the rebel cause had about oozed out. *"I do not want to fight,"* said he, *"and I have no gun." "Of course you **do** want to fight,"* said I, *"it is only your modesty that makes you say that you do not; and, as for a gun, I will furnish you one; and will also place a man behind you to shoot you dead, if you do not perform your full duty in battle. In violation of your oath, you came in here to help our enemies. Now you shall help us or die. You do not deserve the treatment of a prisoner of war, and you will not receive it. We are Federals; I am Kelso; now you know what to expect."*

Soon after the occurrence of this little episode, a long train of wagons of every description, about a hundred in all, came driving in from the south. These were driven by rebels, most of them old men, women, and boys, who came, they said, to haul off the sugar, the Lincoln coffee, the flour, and the other provisions that Marmaduke had assured them would be taken in quantities far greater than his army could use or carry away. We thanked them kindly for bringing us just the number of wagons and teams that we wanted.[29] Putting the few able-bodied men to work on our fortifications, we sent the other poor would-be plunderers back on foot, without any of the good things for which they had come.

Toward evening, finding that Marmaduke was really gone, our courageousness became truly wonderful. We felt that we could whip the devil himself, if he would only venture to show himself. We would pursue Marmaduke. Three hundred of us would chase six thousand rebels. Just think

29. Col. Crabb's report, Jan. 10, 1863, *OR*, ser. 1, vol. 22, part 1, 187: The enemy "came with the full expectation of easy conquest. They had invited their friends in the country to come and bring their wagons, promising all the booty they could carry; but, thanks to a kind Providence, brave hearts, and strong arms, they were most signally defeated in their designs of plunder."

of it.[30] We did thus chase them. We kept a long way off, of course, so that they should not know that we were after them. But we were chasing them all the same. Lieut. Col. Pound went in command; Capt. Flagg was second, and I was third.[31]

After a march of two or three hours, Col. Pound and Capt. Flagg became disgustingly drunk;—too drunk to keep their saddles. They were rolled into an ambulance and hauled along like a couple of dead hogs. I had charge of the look-outs and the advance guard. Presently I found that the command had halted and were in confusion. I stopped and waited. After awhile, I heard some one calling my name. I answered, and a subaltern officer rode up and informed me that the men were in a state of mutiny, refusing to advance nearer the enemy under the command of a couple of officers, gibbering, slobbering, and idiotic from beastly drunkenness. I ordered him back to inform the men that I had charge of the look-outs, and that just so soon as any real danger threatened us, I would put Col. Pound and Capt. Flagg under arrest and take full command myself. When the men heard this, they cheered loudly, and were willing to follow wherever I would lead. About midnight, Col. Pound ordered a halt at a farm house, and, without instructing the men what to do, he and Flagg and a subaltern or two went in and slept the sweet sleep of the drunkard. We could see the light of Marmaduke's camp-fires. Every thing depended upon me. I kept wide awake on the look-out. Most of the men managed to sleep with their bridle reins in their arms. The weary horses were glad to stand still and sleep. Next morning, weary and disgusted, we returned to Springfield.

For four days and four nights, I had no sleep and no rest. I had almost reached that point where it becomes a physical impossibility to endure more. But I was not still to rest. I do not now remember how it came about,—my mind was becoming so sadly confused—but I was ordered, or, more likely, I volunteered to go out in command of a party of 25 men to meet and to guard

30. "The Battle of Springfield, Mo.": "On Friday morning, the current of feeling in our midst had changed. Our troops were confident and exultant. They awaited the renewal of the attack, not only with equanimity, but with eagerness. We were, however, disappointed. The battle was not renewed, although a small party of the rebel cavalry made a feint at the eastern side of town, to amuse us and cover the retreat of the main body."

31. Holcombe, *History of Greene County*, 447: "Col. Crabb decided to let well enough alone, and not attempt to follow Marmaduke and Shelby, who were moving out on the wire road toward Marshfield. A renewal of the attack was feared by some, as the prisoners had learned and reported the presence of Porter's column, somewhere to the eastward. The cavalry was ready to advance if the order should be given, but no orders came, and only a reconnaissance a mile or so eastward and south was made."

a train that was on its way to Springfield from Cassville. We marched out some twenty miles or more. The sun shone out clear and warmed the air. The men slept soundly in their saddles. I could not trust one of them to stay awake and keep a look-out. I must keep awake myself. The horses, reeling and stumbling, slept as they walked. Hot water from my burning eyes constantly streamed down my cheeks. My sight was failing. My mind was failing. I tried to think what we had been doing for the last hundred hours or more. I had to give up the attempt. All things were in confusion. I could not unravel them. I tried to think where we were. I could not even make this out. Finally I thought that, maybe, I was simply dreaming a distressful dream. I pinched myself to wake myself. My flesh felt numb. I did not awake. At last I gave up all thoughts but two: "*look out for the enemy; look out for the train!*" To these thoughts, I would still cling. I constantly changed my position from side to side in my saddle. Still an irresistible sleepiness would come over me. I would then spring to the ground and lead my horse. Oh! how weary my legs were! How weary my whole body,—my whole being was! I would go to sleep while walking. I would dream that I heard the firing of guns. I would start to fall, and this start would rouse me. I would clamber back into my saddle, and go through the same routine. Of the intensity of my suffering, I need not speak. Language could not express it. Those who have ever suffered as I then did, know what I mean. Those who have never thus suffered could not possibly be made to understand my meaning.

About sun-set, we met a small party of Federal soldiers who informed us that the train we were seeking had returned to Cassville, and was already safe. For a few moments, the excitement of meeting these soldiers aroused us from the almost death-like lethargy that was upon us. But what should we now do? Without rest, neither horses nor men were able to return to Springfield, and not a man of the party was able to stand guard. I did not hesitate. I led my men a mile from the road and concealed them, one in a place, fifty yards apart, in a dense and extensive hazel thicket. Scattered thus, the enemy could not, in the darkness of night, find them while they slept. Going about fifty yards beyond my last man, I hitched my horse and, tumbling down, was soon fast asleep on the frozen ground. I did not wake till day-light. When I opened my eyes, all around me was white with frost. Never had sleep been sweeter or more refreshing. I hunted up my men. They were all still asleep. I found them by means of the noise made by their horses breaking and eating brush. Some of my men were beardless boys and, as they lay there still before me in the frost on the frozen ground, their faces looked so blue that I almost feared they were dead. When roused, they all declared that they had never slept better. By two o'clock P.M., we were in Springfield.[32] On the next day, with a small party of men, I visited Ozark. I found that my family had been pretty well robbed of blankets and such things, but that, otherwise, they had not been ill treated.

For some weeks, we lay at Springfield, making frequent scouts of three or four days each into the counties south and east of that place. On all these scouts, there was more or less of excitement. A few prisoners, horses, guns, &c. were captured. No fighting, however, was done on any of them. If I remember correctly, I was present on all of them. On one occasion, when I was third in command, the weather was very severe. Every night, all the other officers slept in houses. As usual, I remained out with my men, bearing all their hardships and privations, and cheering them with my words of praise and encouragement. Because I would thus remain out, I was made officer of the guard every night. On the last night out, a heavy snowstorm was upon us. We stopped at the farm of a wealthy old rebel. The men were hungry and were out of rations. The horses were in almost a starving condition. Here was an abundance of everything needful for both men and horses. I congratulated the men on our good fortune. As usual on such occasions, the officers were all invited in to enjoy a blazing fire, a bountiful repast, and warm, soft beds. All but myself accepted the invitation. Soon I received the usual order appointing me officer of the guard. In addition to this usual order, I was also ordered to forbid the men to take any corn, oats, or hay for their horses, or

32. Sunday, Jan. 11, at 2:00 p.m., was also the start of Springfield's funeral for the Union dead. The band and two companies of infantry marching as an escort, the bodies of the Union soldiers in wagons, their horses with their empty saddles, then the rest of the infantry, cavalry, officers, and citizens, moved slowly from Fort No. 4 back to the town square and then out North Street. Meanwhile, Marmaduke's forces, marching east, finally met up with and joined Porter's brigade. As Springfield buried its dead, fifty miles away the combined Confederate command battled a force of 880 Union men under the command of Col. Samuel Merrill at Hartville. Merrill's troops, with their sharp-shooting artillery, inflicted heavy damage on Marmaduke's much larger force until the Federals ran low on ammunition and had to retreat. The Confederates then marched through mountainous terrain in a snowstorm back to Arkansas. General Curtis praised his Union troops as heroes and reported to Missouri governor Hamilton Gamble on Jan. 12, 1863, that from Marmaduke's expedition, "the enemy got nothing but a good thrashing and one gun" (*OR*, ser. 1, vol. 22, part 1, 179). The Confederates, however, pronounced the expedition a success. They had destroyed forts and captured provisions, and they wrongly believed that they had forced federal troops planning an attack on Arkansas to fall back to Missouri. Marmaduke reported, too, that the raid had revived the spirits of Confederate sympathizers in Missouri (*OR*, ser. 1, vol. 22, part 1, 198).

to kill any pigs, sheep, turkeys, chickens, &c. for themselves. I was indignant. What were the men and horses to do? We were also forbidden to burn any rails, and we had nothing else for fuel. Without food or fire, the men would suffer severely. I called them together. I read them the order. Their faces grew dark, and deep, low curses were muttered among them. They asked me what they should do. I told them to make fires of *split timber,* to feed their horses on *dried vegetables* of any kind, and to eat such pigs, turkeys, chickens, &c. as happened to fall and break their own d——d necks or happened to be kicked and killed by the horses. Of course I was evading the villainous order I had received. The men took the hint. The horses soon had an abundance of good feed, great fires were soon blazing, and the air was freighted with the *"sweet smelling savor"* of roasting turkeys, chickens, &c. Besides all this, I found the men well supplied with apples and honey. They were in high good humor, and I had to eat a little with every mess in the entire encampment.

About the close of January, I think it was, we marched to Forsythe.[33] Here we remained a couple of weeks, seeing our horses die of starvation. We then marched to Linden, 15 miles south east of Springfield. Here we remained till the breaking up of winter. Our horses continued to die for want of forage. We then returned to Springfield where we remained, I think till the early part of May. While lying here, our regiment was broken up and incorporated with the 8 Reg. M. S. M. Cavalry, commanded then by Col. J. W. McClurg, but soon afterward by Col. J. J. Gravelly. My company became Co. M. of this regiment. Soon after this consolidation, my company and Capt. Breeden's— soon afterwards commanded by Capt Ozias Ruark—were ordered to Neosho

---

33. On Jan. 21 or 22, Kelso and other members of the 14th were back at Ozark. Capt. Samuel Flagg ordered Kelso to march Co. H to Forsyth, thirty miles to the south. The subsequent exchange between the two men prompted Flagg to file charges against the lieutenant, and seven weeks later, on March 11, 1863, Kelso found himself facing a court martial at Springfield. Kelso was charged with "conduct to the prejudice of good order and military discipline." Flagg's complaint held that Kelso, in front of the men, absolutely refused to obey the captain's order to march the troops to Forsyth. The lieutenant then said, according to Flagg, that he would not "move his company on any wild goose chase" and would not march until he saw the written orders that Flagg had received. Witnesses confirmed that Kelso had asked to see Flagg's orders, complained of a wild goose chase, and also that he said "he had been obeying drunken officers as long as he was willing." Kelso argued that improper orders and intoxicated officers had been a problem, and that he had also been provoked by Flagg's abusive language. The court found Kelso not guilty. John R. Kelso Court Martial Case File, Springfield, Mo., Jan. 21, 1863, NN-2499, Record Group 153, Records of the Office of the Judge Advocate General (Army), National Archives.

to operate against the various bands of bush-whackers that infested that part of the country.[34]

While at Springfield, I bought a pretty little house for a residence, and moved my family into it. They would now be among friends and be comfortable. My only trouble was Dr. Hovey. Leaving his family in Buffalo, he was soon in Springfield, pretending that he could do better in his profession there than he could in Buffalo. His real object, however, I then feared and as I now almost know, was to be near his too willing victim, my beautiful and beloved wife. I could hear of his being a great deal at my house, some scandal being created by the frequency and the time of his visits. My children, too, were loud in his praise because he sometimes gave them money of evenings to attends shows and concerts in the town. Thus he had all to himself the idol of my heart, the angel of my dreams. This he had with her own connivance. She was only too willing. While I was braving death for my country in a thousand forms, while I lay upon the cold ground thinking or dreaming of her, while the rain poured down upon me in the dreary night, my darling Susie, according to her own voluntary confessions afterwards made, was suffering this smooth-tongued serpent to pour into her charmed ear the tale of his illicit love, to fold her to his bosom, and to cover her lips with his hot amorous kisses. Will those who have loved, who have trusted, and who have been betrayed, blame me for writing bitterly about these things?[35]

34. On the reorganization of the MSM, see U.S. Pension and Record Office, *Organization and Status of Missouri Troops,* 21–47; however, the (incomplete) reproduction of General Orders No. 5 of Feb. 2, 1863 (see pp. 30–31), excludes the part about the reorganization of the 14th—instead, see *OR,* ser. 1, vol. 22, part 2, 97–98, and *Annual Report of the Adjutant General of Missouri,* 195. Flagg transferred to the 4th Regt., MSM, Feb. 4, 1863, and resigned from the military on Aug. 4, 1863 ("Soldiers' Records," MDH). Capt. Ozias Ruark had first served as a sergeant in the Cass County Home Guard and then as a private and second sergeant in the 14th MSM Cavalry. Col. Joseph W. McClurg had previously held the same rank in the Osage County Regiment of the Missouri Home Guard. In the 8th Regt., MSM Calvary, Colonel Gravelly had been promoted from second lieutenant (NPS Soldiers' Database).

35. John and Susie Kelso had two more children together: Augustus (1865–70) and John (1867–1935). They separated in 1871, and John, Sr., moved to California. Their final divorce decree was rendered on Jan. 30, 1874 ("Abstract of Divorce Records").

Appendix 1

Speech Delivered at Mt. Vernon, Missouri, April 23, 1864

My Countrymen,

Since I promised to address you on this occasion, my official duties have so occupied my attention, that I have had no leisure to prepare anything like a connected subject. Besides this, I have practiced public speaking very little, and never before attempted a political discourse. I shall, however, in my plain way, endeavor to communicate plain truths to plain people.

We are in the midst of a revolution, the most fearful, the most gigantic that the world ever knew. A revolution, the effects and influences of which, are destined to extend to all future ages, and to be felt by every individual, by every nation, and by every race. A revolution, which is either to purify the political atmosphere of the country, to bring freedom and joy to the millions of down trodden and oppressed, to demolish the strong holds of despotism, to give the zenith of glory to our republican institutions, to usher in the great political millennium; or, a revolution which is to roll back the gloom of the dark ages, to sweep with the besom of destruction our once happy land, to crush every effort of human liberty and advancement, to extinguish the star of hope that has so long cheered the nations of the world, to make this life what has been styled, *"a wilderness of woe."*[1] This, my fellow countrymen, is the revolution now in progress—the grand drama in which we are all actors, and it depends upon us,

Source: Kelso, "Speech Delivered at Mt. Vernon Mo.," in "John R. Kelso's Complete Works," 1–9.
1. The line "a wilderness of woe" is a common phrase in Christian literature. For example, see *The Pilgrimage of Man Wandering in a Wilderness of Woe; Wherein Is Shewed the Calamities of the New World, and How All the Principall Estates Thereof Are Crossed with Miserie* (London: [W. White], 1606); the poem "The Hindu's Song, and the Missionary's Response," *Evangelical Magazine and Missionary Chronicle* 29, supplement (1851): 771: "The world is a wilderness, / A wilderness of woe, / Where not a lovely flower appears, / But only rank weeds grow"; and the African American hymn "Is There Anybody Here Who Loves My Jesus": "This world's a wilderness of woe, / So let us all to glory go" (http://www.hymnary.org).

upon the loyal people of our nation, to decide which of these pictures shall represent the future condition of our country and of the world.

When we view the subject in this light, when we consider that we are helping to decide the destiny, not only of ourselves, of our children, of our nation, in the present contest, but of *all nations* and of *all ages,* how weighty the responsibilities that rest upon us! How unceasingly should we strive to discharge faithfully every duty devolving upon us, and how carefully should we guard against every false man and every false measure: Dearly has experience taught us, how dangerous a thing it is to trust the highest interests of our great nation in the hands of pampered aristocrats and corrupt politicians. Our motto now should be "*Try every man before you trust him.*" When we compare the constitution of our country, as it was only four years ago, with its condition at the present time, how great is the contrast. Then, all was peace and plenty. Beautiful villages dotted our fertile plains, churches and school houses were to be seen on every hand, happy congregations sang praises to God, and the merry laugh of the school boy cheered the traveler as he journeyed on our public highways. Rich harvests covered our fields, and numerous herds gamboled on our extensive pastures. Our loved ones were all around us, every family circle was complete, and all were happy. Now how changed! All is desolation. The breath of flame has swept away our happy dwellings, or, they remain the silent abodes of bats and owls. The thunders of battle reverberate among our hills and over our plains, and wolves and vultures feast upon the unburied bodies of our slain. You and I, my fellow countrymen, have had to flee far from those we loved, or hide, like wild beasts, among the rocks and the hills. Our wives and our little ones, robbed and abused, have had to flee, without money, without food, and without clothing sufficient to protect them from the pelting storms, through which they have had to travel. Some of them have sunk under the weight of their sufferings, and the wild flowers are now blooming over the lonely beds where they rest. Our gray-haired fathers have been murdered at their own firesides, and our aged mothers, in their wild grief, have called for help, when no help was near. The wailings of despair, have been heard in every valley, and the gloom of the wilderness has again settled upon many portions of our beautiful land. Serpents hiss and wolves howl among the desolated scenes of our departed joys. But why attempt to describe these things? Language can convey but a faint picture of the terrible scenes through which we have passed; but, the record of those scenes is graven upon our hearts, and, by the deeds of our arms, we will stamp that record in flaming characters, upon the deathless pages of coming years.

And whence, I ask, comes all this wretchedness? What has *caused* the desolation of our once happy country? Why are the unburied bones of our murdered countrymen bleaching in the sun? The answer is plain. In the midst of our prosperity, the demon *Treason* was at work. As did Lucifer, of old, plot the destruction of the government of heaven itself, so did the leaders of this rebellion plot the destruction of the best government of earth. Deeply corrupted by the fell influences of African Slavery, the wealthy classes of the South came to regard *honest labor as disgraceful, wealth as the only necessary virtue, and their own selfish interests as the principal object for which a government should exist.*

Their master spirits having long occupied the highest positions in the government, and having luxuriated long in the spoils of office, seeing their rivals, the true sons of freedom, coming into power, resolved to *ruin* what they could no longer *rule.*[2] They organized secret societies to secure concert of action, appealed to the low passions of bad men, blinded by misrepresentations the great masses of the poor and the ignorant, united every evil element, blackened the clouds of rebellion, and burst upon us in war's most terrific storms.[3] You all know the result. We were unprepared. We were driven before the storm, and the ruin we have described came upon us. Buoyed up, however, by a consciousness of the justness of our cause, we have struggled through the darkest hours. We have succeeded in turning back the tide of the rebellion, and again we are in possession of our desolated homes. And now, my fellow countrymen, after all these things, what is our duty? Half a million of our bravest and best comrades have already gone down amid the smoke and the thunders of battle. Shall their blood have been spilled in vain? Shall we now retire from the contest and leave the final great victory to the enemy? Shall we, after all we have suffered, submit to be spurned, with contempt, by the very men who have ruined us? Shall we not rather fall, as our comrades have fallen, on the field of glorious conflict? I believe that I speak to men who feel as I feel. We have all suffered too much; and, though some of you are Democrats, while I am a Republican, I am sure we shall not differ in regard to the first great duty that claims our attention—*the vigorous prosecution of the war.* For three years, you, like myself, have borne the toils, faced the

2. On Dec. 17, 1860, on the floor of the U.S. Senate, Sen. Benjamin Wade (1800–1878) of Ohio had charged that southerners "intend either to rule or ruin this Government" (*Congressional Globe,* 36th Cong., 2nd sess., Dec. 17, 1860, 30, part 1, 102).

3. On fears of a slave power conspiracy, see David Brion Davis, *The Slave Power Conspiracy and the Paranoid Style* (Baton Rouge: Louisiana State University Press, 1969); Leonard L. Richards, *The Slave Power: The Free North and Southern Domination, 1780–1860* (Baton Rouge: Louisiana State University Press, 2000); and Michael William Pfau, *The Political Style of Conspiracy: Chase, Sumner, and Lincoln* (East Lansing: Michigan State University Press, 2005).

dangers of this the most terrible of all wars. You have marched through the heats of summer, the bitter storms of winter; have endured hunger and thirst without a murmur, and have won victor's laurels on many a hard fought battlefield. Let our motto still be "*Onward to victory!*" Let us ever be at our post, and let us do all we can to rouse to the struggle every energy of our great nation.[4]

The duty next in importance to the vigorous prosecution of the war, is the *entire, the immediate, the unconditional wiping out of slavery, not only in Missouri, but in the entire nation.* I am aware that in touching upon this subject, I am treading upon dangerous ground, and I expect many of you to differ from me in regard to this matter. The time has come, however, when men should express their real sentiments, and as I am not ashamed of mine and am not seeking public favor, I boldly declare them. Time, I believe, will prove them right.[5]

Though raised among slaves and by ultra proslavery parents, I never was a proslavery man. Alone of all my people, I have advocated the cause of freedom—entire freedom. For this, I have been cast off by my kindred, banished from the great family circle, and, today, because of my principles, I have not the sympathy of a relative on earth of the name. Alone I have stood by the Union, and from my veins has flowed, and must flow, all the Kelso blood that is shed for the glorious old "*Star-Spangled Banner.*"

Admitting, however, that I had regarded slavery as a good thing before the war, I would now favor its abolition as a military—as an absolute necessity. I will, therefore, on this occasion, consider slavery only in regard to its political influence. Whatever may be said to the contrary, all reasonable men, both of the north and of the south, now admit that slavery was the cause, and is now the support of this great rebellion.[6] Can the effect cease, while the cause remains? If

4. By the spring of 1864, hopes in the North were rising somewhat. Gen. Ulysses S. Grant's victory at Vicksburg, Miss., in July 1863 extended "federal control throughout the lower Mississippi valley" and his victories at Chattanooga, Tenn., "opened an invasion route to Atlanta." Grant was put in overall command of federal forces on March 12, 1864. By April 9 he had an ambitious plan to march simultaneously against all of the Confederacy's major armies. One component of Grant's offensive, Gen. Nathaniel Bank's effort to drive up the Red River in Louisiana to take Mobile, failed by May, "leaving a substantial rebel presence threatening Missouri from the South" (Gerteis, *Civil War in Missouri*, 179 [quotations]; E. B. Long with Barbara Long, *The Civil War Day by Day: An Almanac 1861–1865* [New York: Da Capo, 1971], 451–511).

5. The Emancipation Proclamation of Jan. 1, 1863, though politically important, went no further than previous congressional action and applied only to slaves held in areas over which the federal government had no control. On April 8, 1864, the U.S. Senate passed a joint resolution thirty-eight to six abolishing slavery and approving the 13th Amendment; the House did not pass it with the required two-thirds vote until Jan. 31, 1865. After approval by twenty-seven states, the amendment went into effect on Dec. 18, 1865. Citizens of Missouri ratified the new state constitution, which abolished slavery, on June 6, 1865.

6. Former Confederates after 1865 tried to minimize slavery as the cause of the war, recasting it as a conflict of cultures or over constitutional rights—a revisionism known as the myth of the Lost Cause, a

an arrow has pierced the body and caused a corrupt and running sore, would you try to heal that wound without extracting the arrow? Remove the cause, and the effect will cease. Let us, then, labor for the removal of slavery. Let us insist upon such an amendment to the Constitution of our own state, and to that of the United States, as shall render slavery a legal, as it always has been, a moral crime.

Some one may ask what is to become of the negroes after they have been freed. I candidly confess that I cannot answer this question. I do not know, indeed, what is to become of ourselves. The great Ruler of nations will provide for them, as he always has for us. What I, for one, am in favor of doing with them, is, first to free them, make them help us through the present war, then colonize them[7] in Mexico, from which I am in favor of driving Maximillian and his frog eaters just as soon as possible.[8]

---

view that also distorted the national memory of the conflict. See Gary W. Gallagher and Alan T. Nolan, eds., *The Myth of the Lost Cause and Civil War History* (Bloomington: Indiana University Press, 2000). It is instructive to compare the statements of Jefferson Davis and Alexander Stephens when they were president and vice president of the CSA, which proclaimed that slavery was the "cornerstone" of the Confederacy (in Stephens's words), with their postbellum apologia (15, 20).

7. The colonization of freed slaves outside the United States had long been discussed and a few times attempted by (mostly white) opponents of slavery. Lincoln proposed it again in 1862. "In 1863 the U.S. Government sponsored the settlement of 453 colonists on an island near Haiti, but this enterprise also foundered when starvation and smallpox decimated the colony. The administration finally sent a naval vessel to return the 368 survivors to the United States in 1864. This ended official efforts to colonize blacks" (McPherson, *Battle Cry of Freedom*, 509).

8. Mexicans had been fighting their own civil war. The liberal republicans, led by President Benito Juárez, had been temporarily in control in 1861 when the Mexican Congress suspended payments of foreign debts incurred by the previous (conservative) government. Britain, Spain, and France signed a joint agreement to send troops to extract payment by force. France under Napoleon III had more ambitious plans, and French troops joined with the conservatives to battle the republicans. Although they suffered a humiliating defeat at Puebla on May 5, 1862 (Cinco de Mayo), French troops took Mexico City in June and pushed the republicans north. In Oct. 1863, Napoleon III began the process of installing Archduke Ferdinand Maximilian, younger brother of Franz Joseph I of Austria, as emperor of Mexico. On April 4, 1864, the U.S. House of Representatives passed a resolution sponsored by Maryland congressman Henry Winter Davis opposing the establishment of a monarchy in Mexico (for a report in the Missouri press, see "The Mexican Monarchy. The Vote on the Recent Declarations of the House—The Diplomatic Correspondence," St. Louis *Daily Missouri Republican*, April 12, 1864). Radical Republicans vigorously condemned the assault on North American republicanism and both the Republican and Democratic Party platforms in the campaign of 1864 had planks to that effect, but the Lincoln administration struggled to remain neutral to keep France from recognizing and supporting the Confederacy. After the Union victory in 1865, France began withdrawing troops, and when they did so, republican forces moving back down from the North overwhelmed Maximilian's troops and the conservatives. Some Union Army veterans helped the republican effort. Maximilian was captured and executed in 1867. See Robert Royal Mille, "Arms across the Border: United States Aid to Juárez during the French Intervention in Mexico," *Transactions of the American Philosophical Society*, new ser., 63 (Dec. 1973): 1–68; Jasper Ridley, *Maximilian and Juárez* (New York: Ticknor and Fields, 1992); and Robert H. Duncan, "Political Legitimation and Maximilian's Second Empire in Mexico, 1864–1867," *Mexican Studies* 12 (Winter 1996): 27–66.

Many make a great out cry against using negroes as soldiers.[9] They consider it very disgraceful to receive the aid of negroes in war, yet these same persons are not ashamed to depend upon the unrequited labor of negroes, for the very food they eat and the clothes they wear. These objections, so far as I have observed, are made only by persons in sympathy with the rebels, or who are, at best, of doubtful loyalty. For my part, if we had negroes enough, I should be willing for them to do all the fighting. They are good enough to fight rebels, and their lives are no more precious, in my estimation, than are the lives of loyal white men. I have, indeed, more than once, seen the time when I would gladly have received the aid not only of a negro, but even of a dog.

At this point, some one would, perhaps, like to ask whether or not I am a believer in "*negro equality.*" Far from it. I no more believe that the negro is, in all respects, equal to the white man, than I believe that the least boy on the ground, is equal to me in stature. Individuals are unequal in most respects, and so are nations and races. There is but *one respect* in which all men are born equal, and that is in respect to their *rights.* In the sublime language of the Declaration of American Independence, "*all men have certain unalienable rights, among which are life, liberty, and the pursuit of happiness.*["] So far, then, as these *rights* are concerned, I am a believer in "*negro equality,*" but no farther. In most other respects, the races are unequal and unlike. God seems to have adapted the one race to one climate and to one mode of life, the other race to another climate and to another mode of life. Besides this, there seems to be a natural law of repulsion between the two races, which makes them incline to separate, when both are left free to act. Miscegenation, then, or the mixing of the two races, must always involve a violation of this natural law of repulsion by which they are put asunder; that is, by the stronger race enslaving the weaker. When both races are free to act, they as naturally tend to separation as do oil and water when at rest. The presence of the negroes among us is the result of the violation, not only of this law of repulsion, but also of the eternal laws of justice. To detain them among us, will be to continue the violation of the same great laws, less we grant to them all the rights enjoyed by other freemen. With this view of the subject, I shall labor earnestly, not only for the emancipation of the slaves, but also of the entire removal of the African race from among us. Should the colonization of the negroes, however, be found impracticable, or should the majority of the loyal

9. The July 17, 1862, Militia Act permitted the use of blacks as soldiers in the Union Army. Regiments began to be formed in August, and the Emancipation Proclamation of Jan. 1, 1863, sanctioned the practice (McPherson, *Battle Cry of Freedom,* 500, 564–65).

voters of the nation oppose it, *then I shall contend for the removal of all legal distinctions on account of color.*

I am aware that the bare idea of negro suffrage is terrifying to all persons in the least tinctured with rebel sympathies, and it is regarded with suspicion, even by many whose loyalty can not be questioned.[10] For my own part, however, I would rather the loyal negroes be allowed the right of suffrage, than that the same right be allowed to rebels and their sympathizers. I think it safer to trust ignorant friends than intelligent enemies. Those who most loudly object to negroes voting usually object also to Federal soldiers voting; and, almost unanimously, favor granting the right of suffrage to returned rebels. It is well known that the negroes are intensely loyal, and that their votes would be unanimously cast in favor [of] the government, and against the cause of treason and rebellion. No wonder, then, that the friends of the rebellion are so bitterly opposed to negro suffrage. There are also many persons who greatly fear lest their daughters may marry free negroes, and lest, in a few years, certain devilish little mulattoes may be calling them *"grand pap."* I freely admit that the fears of these gentlemen are well founded. They know from *experience* how dreadful a thing miscegenation is, and knowing their *own* proneness to mix with the kinky heads, they may well tremble for their *posterity.* You who have travelled in the south, and have observed how pale many of the negroes are becoming, will not be surprised at the fears of these gentlemen. For the comfort of these unhappy chivalry, however, I will say that their virtue would be greatly protected by freeing the negroes who would then be far less likely to submit to the unholy desires of said chivalry. If, however, after all, they succeed in gratifying their inclination to mix with the kinky heads, the only difference will be, that in the case of freedom, they will be more likely to *know* their own posterity than they now are. But enough of this. No truly loyal man has any fears that either himself or his children will ever miscegenate with negroes under any circumstances.

---

10. On black suffrage in Missouri, see Parrish, *Missouri under Radical Rule,* and Margaret Leola Dwight, "Black Suffrage in Missouri, 1865–1877" (Ph.D. diss., University of Missouri, 1978). German Radicals generally supported giving blacks the vote, though many other Radicals had deep reservations, and conservatives (including most Democrats) were strongly opposed. In Oct. 1865, the Missouri Equal Rights League was organized in a St. Louis black church and began petition drives in support of black suffrage. In early 1868, the Republican Party leadership officially endorsed the idea, but in the fall 1868 elections, otherwise a landslide for the Radicals, a public referendum on black suffrage was defeated by nearly 19,000 votes (out of almost 130,000 cast). Congress, however, passed the 15th Amendment in Feb. 1869. Both houses of Missouri's Radical Republican–dominated legislature quickly endorsed it. The requisite number of states had ratified it by March 30, 1870. But on the limitations of the amendment, see, for example, Foner, *Reconstruction,* 422–23, 446–49.

The next great duty, and the last to which I shall call your attention, is the *disfranchisement* of *rebels* and the *confiscation* of their *property*. As I have already remarked, there are men who profess loyalty to the government, yet who are willing to deprive Union soldiers of their votes—willing to disfranchise those patriotic braves whose homes have been desolated, and who have, for more than three years, borne the toils of war in defense of our country. These same men, however, are loud against disfranchising *southern men;*—those who have plundered, burned, and devastated our country, and who are now returning among us, their hands still reeking with the innocent blood of our murdered friends and relatives. What can we expect of such men? Will they not vote for men of their own principles? If they succeed in again placing their party in power, will they not repeat upon us those scenes of carnage, which, for more than three years, have dyed our streams with blood?

Under the clemency of our great and good President, these thieves and murderers are daily returning among us.[11] No way humbled by a consciousness of their crimes, they seem to expect, and in many instances, actually receive more respect and protection than are extended to Union men. If they be allowed to vote, they, with their conservative friends will carry the elections in many parts of our own state. But shall they vote? They claim, as a *"southern right,"* the privilege of murdering union men, and of plundering and driving off union families; and they will again elevate to office and power such men as are known to favor said *southern rights*. Where, my beloved countrymen, where is our hope, if these men be allowed the means of our destruction?

When these men took up arms against the government of the United States, they declared themselves *aliens* and *enemies* to said government and thus, by their own act, voluntarily forfeited all the rights which they once enjoyed as *citizens* of the same. Can there, then, be any injustice in regarding them, as they regard themselves, as aliens to our government, and in requiring them to wait, before voting, as long at least as we require the loyal Germans to wait, who come to us because they love our government.[12]

11. Lincoln's Proclamation of Amnesty and Reconstruction, issued on Dec. 8, 1863, offered a full pardon and the restoration of all rights to those who took a loyalty oath and accepted the abolition of slavery. The proclamation, however, was aimed at and was an initial plan of reconstruction for southern states that had left the Union. In Missouri, a slave state that had remained in the Union, the political rights of former rebels were fiercely debated by conservative and radical Unionists. See Foner, *Reconstruction*, 35–43.

12. Missouri's wartime state (Unionist) government in Oct. 1861 required voters to take a loyalty oath, and in June 1862 debated its wording. "Some of the members wanted to prohibit from voting all persons who had ever taken up arms against the state and national government or had supported [the rebellion] in any way. Others . . . argued that it was unfair to exclude those who had forsaken the cause of the

Is it not also right to confiscate their property.[13] The Constitution of the United States not only gives us the power, but also makes it our duty to do this. The rebels knew this, when they resorted to arms, and they were willing to risk their chances. With their eyes open, they began an unjust suit against us, and now having lost it, *let them pay the costs.*

All these thieves and murderers, as soon as they return among us, become flaming *conservatives.* I remark this, merely as a notorious fact, without wishing to offend any of the loyal and brave men who still cling to the *name* of conservatism. I have no objection to the name, but I must say, in all candor, that I tremble for the fate of our cause, when I see many of the bravest and best men of our nation still bearing the same name with these returned thieves and cut throats, endorsing the same principles, and voting the same ticket. The crisis is too terrible. The loyal should unite with the loyal. Will any true friend of the union still cling to a name, or a party, after he has discovered that all the disloyal elements are united under that name and in that party? There are, there can but be two parties, the loyal, and the disloyal. In which should every union man be found? Division among ourselves is defeat, and defeat, at such a time, is ruin. Let us, then, my countrymen, in our coming elections, resolve to support those men for office upon whom the loyal—the Republican party—can most unanimously unite, whether those men be our individual choice or not. To enable us to do this, we should call conventions and nominate our most thoroughly

---

Southern Confederacy and were again loyal citizens. . . . Instead, the majority decided to allow the vote only to those who had set aside their weapons before December 17, 1861" (Boman, *Lincoln and Citizen's Rights,* 139–40). In Oct. 1863, Maj. Gen. John M. Schofield admitted to Lincoln that a large number of "returned Missouri rebels" had claimed that they had repented, taken their oath, and enlisted in the militia; Schofield thought that such allegedly "repentant rebel[s]" were useful in preventing more property damage. The Radicals triumphed in the fall elections of 1864 and controlled the state constitutional convention in the spring of 1865, passing a more stringent "Iron-Clad Oath" in which an applicant had to deny a list of eighty-six specific acts before being registered to vote. See Parrish, *Turbulent Partnership,* 169–70 (quotations), 202.

13. The Confiscation Act of Aug. 1861 authorized the seizure of property that was being directly used to aid the rebellion. The Second Confiscation Act of July 1862 allowed the confiscation of property (including slaves) to punish "traitors," but the law was confusing and virtually unenforced (McPherson, *Battle Cry of Freedom,* 353, 500 [quotation]; Foner, *Reconstruction,* 158). Some Radical Republicans in Congress pushed during the war and afterward for a much broader confiscation of rebel property. Thaddeus Stevens, for example, offered a plan in Sept. 1865 that would seize 400 million acres from the wealthiest 10% of southerners. He would distribute some of it to black freedmen (forty acres and a mule), and the rest would be sold to pay veterans' pensions, compensate for loyalists' wartime losses, and reduce the national debt (Foner, *Reconstruction,* 68, 235). In Missouri, Radical Republicans, especially from the western part of the state that had suffered the most from guerrilla warfare, "called for the confiscation of 'rebel' property and expressed regret that every disloyal person could not be hanged" (Parrish, *Missouri under Radical Rule,* 29).

tried men;—men who have, from the beginning, stood by our cause;—men, too, of untiring energy, and who are always sober and always at their post. Better select plain, honest farmers and mechanics, with only good common sense, to fill our high places, than trust wire-working politicians, tricky lawyers, or dram-drinking gamesters, however great may be their talents. For my own part, I have always been a laboring man, and my interests and sympathies are with that class. I regard the laboring class as the true nobility of America, and I am proud to belong to that nobility. I am not before you, however, as a candidate for any office. Though often solicited to become a candidate for Congress in your district, I have declined doing so, for the reason that there is already a republican candidate before you. Hon. S. H. Boyd, our present member of Congress, is before us for reelection. Should he and I both run, we would both be defeated. He can not be induced to withdraw from the race. He is determined to rule the party, in this district, or to ruin it. Two years ago I was the first man before the people, and my chances for election amounted to a certainty, until Mr. Boyd, suddenly leaving the Democratic party, announced himself as a candidate for Congress, on the Republican ticket. This forced upon me the disagreeable alternative of either withdrawing from the race and supporting him, or of seeing our party defeated. I withdrew as you all know, and secured his election. Unmindful of this magnanimity on the part of myself and my friends, he is now attempting to force the same necessity upon us, by declaring that he will run the race through. The people should, in convention, decide who shall be their standard bearer in the coming contest. I shall cheerfully support the man of their choice. Should I be that man, I shall gratefully accept the nomination and strive to merit the confidence thus reposed in me. In so dreadful a crisis as is now upon us, I do not think that any man should *seek* office, nor do I think that any true man should refuse to serve in any position to which his fellow citizens may see fit to call him. I thank you for your attention.[14]

14. Kelso decided to run anyway as an "Independent Republican." He defeated Boyd in a very close race (a difference of 113 votes, according to one count, out of a total 8,225)—the Democrat, M. J. Hubble, received only 400 votes. Boyd challenged the result; evidence collected and put before the House amounted to over 170 printed pages. Kelso kept his seat. See www.ourcampaigns.com, drawing data from Michael J. Dubin, *United States Congressional Elections, 1788–1997: The Official Results* (Jefferson, N.C.: McFarland, 1998), but compare John L. Moore et al., eds., *Congressional Quarterly's Guide to U.S. Elections*, 4th ed., vol. 2 (Washington, D.C.: CQ Press, 2001), 890, which has Kelso and Boyd 293 votes apart. On the election challenge, see "Evidence in the Contested Case of Boyd vs. Kelso," 39th Cong., 1st sess., Misc. Doc. No. 92, in *The Miscellaneous Documents of the House of Representatives, Printed during the Thirty-Ninth Congress, 1865–'66*, vol. 3 (Washington, D.C.: Government Printing Office. 1866). On Boyd, see chap. 2, note 16, above.

Appendix 2
Speech Delivered at Walnut Grove, Missouri,
September 19, 1865 (Excerpts)

Fellow Citizens,

The storm of war has ceased. The thunders that so lately shook our land to its very center, have died away in distant murmurings, and we are again cheered by the dawning of peace and prosperity. We may now pause and contemplate the results of the mightiest struggle ever recorded in the annals of the world; of the bloodiest, the most stupendous tragedy ever enacted on the stage of time. . . . Our first duty is to return our heart-felt thanks to Almighty God, and to our brave soldiers, for the salvation of our country, and then we should carefully consider the *origin and the nature of the war.*

Nearly all the wars in which the nations of earth have engaged, have originated from trivial or accidental causes, or from the caprice or the ambition of their rulers. Unlike those, our war has been one of *principles*—of antagonistic principles which, from the beginning, have underlain the whole fabric of our government.

The spirit of Slavery, that foulest monster of the dark ages, if not *invoked* at the formation of our Constitution, *was certainly permitted to enter it* together with the spirit of Liberty. Hence, from the beginning, our Constitution has contained, within itself, the elements of discord—of an *"irrepressible conflict."*[1] Hence, from the beginning, have been heard those deep mutterings that betoken the coming storm. Hence, when the storm came, it burst forth with the

---

Source: Kelso, "Speech Delivered at Walnut Grove Mo.," in "John R. Kelso's Complete Works," 10–27.
1. In a speech delivered at Rochester, N.Y., on Oct. 25, 1858, New York senator William Henry Seward (1801–72) had described the sectional conflict as "an irrepressible conflict between opposing and enduring forces, and it means that the United States must and will, sooner or later, become either entirely a slaveholding nation, or entirely a free-labor nation." For a discussion in the Missouri press, see, for example, "The 'Irrepressible Conflict': Wm. H. Seward's Brutal and Bloody Manifesto," St. Louis *Daily Missouri Republican*, Oct. 22, 1859.

accumulated thunders of seventy years. As roll the vast billows of ocean upon the rocks, so rushed the mighty hosts of Slavery upon the invincible ranks of the sons of Freedom. The nations of earth beheld and trembled. As the fallen angels contended for supremacy in heaven, so did the revolted minions of Slavery contend for supremacy on earth. The contending powers felt that this struggle was the mightiest and the last. Every nerve was strung, every energy aroused to the conflict, every other desire swallowed up in the all-absorbing desire for victory. Strong manhood, tender youth, and old age all rushed headlong into the conflict. Mountains of treasure and rivers of blood were poured into the fearful vortex of ruin in order to determine whether Liberty or Slavery should die. *"Long time in even scale the battle hung;"*[2] until, bursting forth from the chains of their oppressors, a vast host of the downtrodden sons of Africa, rushed, like a dark and mighty billow, upon the rebel foe. The great arch fiend of Slavery was troubled. His exhausted legions faltered—broke—and

"Rout, ruin, panic scattered all."[3]

And now, my fellow countrymen, we have but to follow up our glorious successes in arms, by wise legislation, and the victory, the full and complete victory, will be ours. Our country will be saved, slavery extinguished, and liberty forever established.

Terrible as the war has been, it came as a thing of course—as the natural result of a well known cause. Our earliest and greatest statesmen all saw it looming up distinctly in the dim vista of coming years. . . . You and I, my fellow countrymen, have also seen it as a present, a dreadful reality. We have been actors in the whole tremendous tragedy, and we are still upon the stage with the grand drama but half performed.

We will next consider the *progress of the war*, which now, assumes the form of political contest. Armies are no longer hurled upon armies, the thunders of battle no longer reverberate among our hills, and the lurid glare of our burning cities no longer frightens darkness from his home in night; yet the *real struggle, the irrepressible conflict* of antagonistic principles, is still going on. *Slavery*, though dead in name, still exists in *reality*. The *rebellion*, though overthrown in *arms*, is

2. John Milton, *Paradise Lost* (1674), book 6, lines 245–46: "Long time in even scale / The battle hung."
3. James Montgomery, "The Patriot's Pass-Word," in *The Select Poetical Writings of James Montgomery* (Boston: Phillips, Sampson, 1857), 125–28, a poem about the Swiss struggle for independence and the Battle of Sempach against the Austrians (1386), frequently anthologized in school textbooks as "Arnold Winkelried" or "Make Way for Liberty" (see William B. Lacey, *An Illustration of the Principles of Elocution* [Albany, N.Y.: Webster's and Skinner's, 1828], 242–44, and William H. McGuffey, *The Eclectic Fourth Reader* [Cincinnati: Truman and Smith, 1838], 79–81).

by no means subdued in *spirit;* nor has treason yet been made odious. Unpunished traitors, emboldened by the lenity of our government, are still plotting its destruction. Like Milton's Satan, overthrown in arms, cast down from the high positions they once occupied, maddened by disappointment, and burning with revenge, they are now endeavoring to accomplish by *guile* those dark designs which they long attempted to accomplish by *force.* As did the serpent of old in Paradise, so do they now glide among us *professing* an interest in our welfare, which it is impossible for them *to feel,* and which, if we suffer ourselves to be deceived by it, will prove the most dangerous form of enmity. With hands still reeking in the blood of our murdered brothers, and still clothed in garments torn from the cold forms of our heroic dead, they have the effrontery to claim equal rights and privileges with the patriotic defenders of our beloved country. Unhumbled by a consciousness of their crimes, they are endeavoring to convince us that they are more eminently qualified than ourselves to guide the wheels of state; and, I am sorry to know that they have so far succeeded as to be regarded by many as the very impersonation of *frankness* and *honor.* Even our great and good Executive now so regards them, though he once declared that he "*would hang traitors and make treason odious.*"[4]

So far from admitting that the war was *wrong* which they waged against the United States, they still cling to the same doctrine of secession, and show by their actions that they have, by no means, relinquished the hope of ultimate success. They demand that their debt shall be assumed and their disabled soldiers provided for the same as are our own. They profess to have relinquished *slavery,* yet they are maturing a system of *serfdom* which is *worse* than *slavery.* In order to creep into power, and to secure the removal of the Federal troops from among them, they profess great loyalty to our government, yet, they laud as heroes those who have committed the greatest number of murders upon our Union men, and praise the conduct of those who helped drive out Union families. They take the oath of allegiance as readily as they take bad whiskey, but how many of them consider that oath binding? Have they not long since become oath proof?

4. Andrew Johnson, speech of Sept. 11, 1865, in John Savage, *The Life and Public Services of Andrew Johnson . . . Including His State Papers, Speeches and Addresses* (New York: Derby and Miller, 1866), 405, previously published in the Missouri press and elsewhere as "The President's Speech. How the States Are to Be Restored," St. Louis *Daily Missouri Republican,* Sept. 17, 1865: "The South, true to her ancient instincts of frankness and manly honor, comes forth and expresses her willingness to abide the result of the decision [on the battlefield] in good faith"; Andrew Johnson, speech of April 3, 1865, in Frank More, ed., *Speeches of Andrew Johnson* (Boston: Little, Brown, 1865), xlv: "I would say death is too easy a punishment. My notion is that treason must be made odious and traitors must be punished and impoverished, their social power broken, though they must be made to feel the penalty of their crime."

Have not most of them, in the castles of the K. G. C. taken an awful oath to do everything in their power for the overthrow of the United States government, and for the extension of slavery, and were they not then and there instructed to regard as null and void all oaths, conflicting therewith, which they ever had taken, or which they might ever find it necessary to take?[5] If I am incorrect in my statements, I would thank some member of that order to correct me. Have we not seen enough to convince us that their oaths are not to be trusted?

Why are they so eager to have the Federal troops withdrawn, unless they wish to do what they dare not attempt while those troops are present? Why are they so eager to get the power into their own hands, unless they intend to wield it for their own purposes? Will their sworn enmity to our country lead them to labor for her good? Has *treason* rendered them more *loyal?* Has *war* rendered them more *friendly?* Has *murder* rendered them more *humane?* Has *theft* rendered them more *honest?* Has *perjury* rendered them more *truthful?* In a word, have *all the horrible crimes* of which they have been guilty, rendered them *better men and more worthy of our confidence?* Will the wolves that *tore* your lambs *yesterday, protect* them *today?* Will you take to your bosom the enraged viper that has already *stung* you? There may be an *"instinctive frankness and honor"* about the traitors of the south, but I fail to see it. If they had the power over us, that we have over them, how would *they* treat *us?* How do Union men fare even now, in

5. The KGC—the Knights of the Golden Circle—was a secret society that promoted the extension of the southern slaveocracy into Mexico, Central America, and the Caribbean. Probably founded in 1858, it began drawing press attention in June 1859. It then became a decentralized paramilitary organization supporting secession, but shortly after the beginning of the war, it seems to have become dormant in the South. Cells organizing southern sympathizers were said to have formed in Ohio, Illinois, Iowa, and Indiana by early 1862. Federal authorities began making arrests, and in July 1863 imprisoned the organization's main promoter, George Washington Lafayette Bickley. Scholars disagree about the power of the KGC. Frank Clement, in *Dark Lanterns: Secret Political Societies, Conspiracies, and Treason Trials* (Baton Rouge: Louisiana State University Press, 1984), thinks it was conjured almost entirely out of Bickley's fictions and Unionist paranoid conspiracy theories. David C. Keehn, in *Knights of the Golden Circle: Secret Empire, Southern Secession, Civil War* (Baton Rouge: Louisiana State University Press, 2013), argues that in "early 1861, the Knights formed a powerful militant force that helped wrest a number of key southern states, like Texas and Virginia, from the Union" (189–90). He also argues that although it remains unclear whether a cell continued to be active in Washington, D.C., during the war, "a number of the conspirators and allies who assisted [Lincoln assassin John Wilkes] Booth had ties to the KGC during its heyday of 1859–61," and that Booth himself was a member. Mark A. Lause, in *A Secret Society History of the Civil War* (Urbana: University of Illinois Press, 2011), takes something of a middle position: secessionists and Unionists alike greatly exaggerated the numbers of people actually involved in the KGC, but these exaggerations served their interests. Secessionists used the threat of the shadowy organization "to coerce that part of the population unwilling to accept" its agenda. "In fear of it, Unionists clustered in a common coalition, determined to keep Lincoln and his supporters in power by any means necessary" (152).

those rebel communities where there are no Federal troops? Do not violence and murder still reign?

"*Let us not deceive ourselves! Gentlemen may cry peace! peace! but there is no peace.*"[6] The struggle has only changed its *form*, not its *nature*. We still have to contend with a foe that is powerful, vigilant, and treacherous. Those who were *traitors a year ago* are the *same today*,—and, those who gloated over the blood of our *brothers*, would gloat over *our own*. All they want is the *power*, and that they will soon have, if we neglect our duty. *There can be no permanent peace in this nation, until the rebels are rendered totally powerless to do harm, and until every vestige is eradicated of that accursed institution whose degrading influence made them rebels.* What, then, shall be done with the rebels?

This question would be easily answered, if we had a *Hell* to put them in, as the Almighty had for *His* rebels; but, since we lack that one little convenience, we should take that course which shall best secure *justice to them and safety to ourselves*. Strict justice would require that they all suffer an ignominious death. By the laws of nations, as well as by the constitution and laws of our own country, *treason* is justly regarded as the highest crime that man can commit, and is visited by the most terrible punishments that man is capable of suffering;—that is, *death* and the *confiscation of property*. This law seems to be founded on that first great law of nature,—*self defense,*—without which neither individuals nor communities could exist. If an individual's life be assailed, it is not only his *privilege*, but also his *imperative duty* to defend himself, even if, in so doing, he be obliged to kill the assailant. The same is true of a nation, which is only a grand embodiment of individuals for mutual protection. If the life of a nation be assailed, the lives of all its individuals are endangered, and it becomes the solemn duty of that nation, as their common protector, to destroy those assailants, or at least, *to render them totally powerless to do further harm.* Every loyal person has a right to demand this of his government, and in our case, nothing less would be consistent with our present and our future safety, to say nothing of the wisdom of punishment in general, for the prevention of crimes. The rebels themselves admit the justice of this principle, and when they had the power, they executed it to the letter, upon those who dared resist their pretended government, although the persons so resisting, had never owed any allegiance to their so called government. When the

---

6. From Patrick Henry's "Liberty or Death" speech of March 23, 1775, which had become a staple in textbooks and collections such as Jonathan Barber, *The Elocutionist, Consisting of Declamations and Readings*, 2nd ed. (New Haven, Conn.: A. H. Malty, 1836), 47–50, and *American Oratory; or, Selections from Eminent Americans* (Philadelphia: Edward C. Biddle, 1840), 13–15.

rebels raised arms against the government to which they owed allegiance, they knew what they were doing, and what they were risking; and, with their eyes open, they staked their lives, their fortunes, and their vacant honor upon the result. They expected to *gain all, or lose all—to conquer or to die.* It is doubtful whether, in the beginning, any of them ever thought of such a thing as either asking or receiving pardon from our government. Whatever, therefore, is granted them short of the extreme penalty of the law, is an unexpected boon to them for which they would be grateful, if they were capable of gratitude. I, for one, am willing that they should *live;* but, I am not willing that they should be put in a condition to *endanger* the *lives, liberties,* and *interests* of *loyal men.*[7] Our President has granted them their pitiful lives and the liberty of their persons, but he can do no more than this without manifest injury and danger to *loyal* people of the nation, who surely have the first claim upon his protection. He can not restore them to full citizenship, without giving them a power totally inconsistent with the safety of the loyal people of the South, if not of the entire nation. He can not give back to them their forfeited property for the same reason, and because it is not *his* to give. Every man, woman and child of this nation has a just and legal interest in that property, and the President has no more right to take it from them and give it to traitors, than he has to take away any of their other property for the same purpose.

By the law relating to *treason,* the rebels have forfeited every vestige of right and title to their property. Besides this, in July 1862, Congress passed a law seizing the property of the rebels as *"enemies' property."*[8] Whether, then, we regard the rebels as *traitors,* or as *alien enemies,* they have lost their property which is now, to all intents and purposes, vested in the United States, and, once so vested, it can not be divested except by the people themselves, or by their representatives in Congress. . . .

I am aware that many oppose touching a dollar of rebel property; *some,* because they *sympathize* with the rebels and do not wish them punished; *others,* because they *fear* the rebels who would be likely to make a *"fuss,"* if their property should be confiscated. For my part, however, I shall favor the measure, whether any one else does so or not. I think it *just,* and *necessary,* and so far as the displeasure of

7. Foner, *Reconstruction,* 230: "While some constituents . . . demanded the execution of Southern leaders as punishment for treason, only a handful of Radical leaders echoed these calls. Rather than vengeance, the driving force of Radical ideology was the utopian vision of a nation whose citizens enjoyed equality of civil and political rights, secured by a powerful and beneficent national state."
8. The Second Confiscation Act of July 17, 1862.

the rebels is concerned, I have only to say that I have met their displeasure on more than *sixty battlefields*, and I can venture to meet it once more.

Besides confiscating the property of rebels, I would, as a security for the future, *totally disfranchise them until, by at least five years of good conduct, they have proved that they can be safely trusted.*[9] Let them be protected in their persons and in the fruits of their labor, but let them not intermeddle in the affairs of our government, until they are called upon to do so by the loyal people of the nation. The country is safe only in the hands of its friends.

We are entitled to full indemnity for the past, but, of this, alas! how little we shall ever receive! Can the rebels ever restore the untold millions of property which they wantonly destroyed? Can they ever restore to innocence and happiness the tens of thousands whom their unholy war has lured or driven to paths of vice? Can they ever restore gladness to the desolate hearts of the millions of widows and orphans whose loved ones they have slain? Can they ever restore to health and vigor the six-hundred thousand mutilated forms that have returned, mere wrecks, from the field of battle? Can they ever restore to reason the poor maniacs whom they drove to insanity by their unheard of cruelties? Can they ever reanimate the four hundred thousand cold forms of our heroic dead? Can they ever re-clothe in living flesh the sixty thousand ghastly skeletons—the victims of *tortures*, of *cold*, of *starvation*—in Libby, and at Salisbury, Andersonville and Belle Isle?[10]

9. When Kelso's 39th Congress debated the Reconstruction Act early in 1867, Radical leader Thaddeus Stevens introduced a bill that would have deprived former Confederates of citizenship for five years, but it failed to pass. The First Reconstruction Act of March 2, 1867, required southern states to call new constitutional conventions. Anyone disqualified from voting or holding office under the 14th Amendment would not be allowed to vote for or serve as delegates to these conventions, or vote and serve in the temporary military governments being established. (The 14th Amendment disqualified from voting or office-holding anyone who had previously held office at any level, had sworn an oath to uphold the U.S. Constitution, and had subsequently engaged in insurrection or rebellion or had given aid and comfort to the enemy.) Thus the law did not touch the vast majority of Confederate soldiers or those Confederate leaders who had not been officeholders before secession. In former Confederate states reconstructed by those conventions, "there was no simple pattern": "Five states disenfranchised few or no Confederates: Georgia, Florida, and Texas, where moderates committed to luring white Conservatives into the party controlled the proceedings; South Carolina, with its overwhelming black majority; and North Carolina, where the party's white base appeared firm. . . . Alabama and Arkansas barred from voting men under the Fourteenth Amendment as well as those who had 'violated the rules of civilized warfare' during the Civil War, and required all voters to take an oath acknowledging black civil and political equality. . . . Louisiana, where the likelihood of white support appeared bleak, disenfranchised Confederates . . . but exempted men willing to swear an oath favoring Radical Reconstruction. Mississippi and Virginia . . . also barred considerable numbers of 'rebels' from voting" (Foner, *Reconstruction*, 273–76, 324 [quotation]).

10. Confederate prisoner-of-war camps, Andersonville being the most notorious: "13,000 of the 45,000 men imprisoned there died of disease, exposure, or malnutrition" (McPherson, *Battle Cry of Freedom*, 796).

We are willing to forgive them for all these things, but we are not willing to forgive them for any further attempts to do us *harm*. We can *forgive*, but can we *forget?* There are some things which I, for one, can *never forget*. I can not forget the winter of 1861 when our wives and our little ones were driven from their pleasant homes and forced to travel through the piercing blasts and drifting snows. I can not forget the despairing looks of the poor women and children as they struggled, with frosted limbs, through the deep snow drifts. I can not forget the heartless refusal I met when I plead, at rebel houses, for them to take in, over night, those who were *actually perishing*. I can not forget how we huddled around our camp fires, and, in our bosoms sheltered our babes, while we were almost buried in the snows that came drifting and whirling, like vast billows, upon us. I can not forget those who sunk under the weight of their sufferings, and over whose lonely graves the wild winds of autumn are now wailing. I can not forget the fearful *vow* I made to *avenge* these wrongs. I can not forget—no! no! *I can not forget these things.*[11] I have thought of them while walking my lonely beat in the dark and silent night. I have thought of them while pouring the lead into that formidable old shot gun of mine. I have thought of them while creeping upon the traitor foe. I have thought of them while cheering my men in the deadly conflict. I have thought of them while taking aim and pulling trigger, and have felt a strange, wild pleasure while beholding my foes fall, before my own fatal shots. Yes! I have thought of these things; and, so help me God! I expect to think of them, whenever I see rebels intermeddling in the affairs of our government. But I am wandering from my subject. We will next consider *the present status of the rebel states.* . . .

[The rebel states] having failed to sustain themselves either as independent states, or as members of an independent confederacy of states, they have, as a matter of course, *ceased to be states at all,* and the country they occupied has relapsed to its original *territorial* condition. . . .

Before determining *who shall rule in the rebel states,* we should take time for reflection and consultation. . . . We have prejudices to overcome, old almost as our lives, and strong as our innate passions. If, laying aside all these prejudices, we decide in the sublime language of the Declaration of Independence, that in respect to their rights, *"All men are born equal, and are endowed by their Creator with certain inalienable rights, among which are life, liberty, and the pursuit of*

11. On Kelso's vow of vengeance, see chap. 4.

happiness"—if we incorporate this principle into our Constitution and thus make it equally applicable to all parts of the nation, we shall humble the haughty power of the aristocratic traitors of the South, lift to liberty and joy the millions of down-trodden and oppressed, and make our country glorious among the nations as indeed,

"The land of the free and the home of the brave."

If, on the contrary, we yield to our old prejudices, and decide, with the secession-ists, "that all men are *not* born equal,["] with respect to their rights, and that *one class only* are endowed by their Creator with certain inalienable rights, among which are the privilege of trampling down their fellow men, of luxuriating upon the fruits of their unrequited labors, of depriving them of the means of gaining knowledge, of prohibiting legal marriages among them, of sundering the fondest and holiest ties of which the human heart is susceptible, of violating helpless innocence without rebuke, of crushing from the souls of their victims all that is noble and God-like, of making this world to them, indeed, *"a vale of tears"*—if *this* be our decision if we reorganize the rebel states on the unjust basis of *color,* if the brave and loyal blacks, because they are such, be turned over help-less into the merciless hands of their former masters—*then will the victory be lost. Treason will have triumphed.* Slavery's clanking chains will again be heard. Liberty will hide her face and weep. Death will flap his horrid wings. The mighty army of our patriotic dead will give forth, from their graves, one last deep groan of anguish. The grim ghost of our murdered country will appear, in the near future, dark with despair and terrible with blood, while the deepest caverns of hell will reëcho the thundering applause of delighted devils. Who, then, shall rule in the rebel states? My answer is, *the whole loyal people of these states.* I never will, by my vote or otherwise, aid in organizing or in *re*organizing any state government upon a principle that would deny the dearest rights of man to a portion of its citizens on account of their color. This leads us to consider *The Elective Franchise.*

If it be true that in respect to their rights, "All men are born equal," then whatever is the inalienable right of *one man or of one race of men,* is undeniably the inalienable right of *all men and of all races.* If it be true that we should *do unto others as we would that they should do unto us,* and if we would not that others should enslave us on account of our color, or deprive us of the elective franchise, how dare we, a Christian people, do these things unto them? Can we hope for God's blessing if we continue to violate this His solemn commandment? Have not the judgments of the last five years been sufficient to teach us wisdom? Have not these judgments come upon us as the direct consequence of the crime of slavery? Shall we, then, defiantly commit the same crime under another name, and thus call upon ourselves still more fearful judgments? For my part, I think we have been punished enough, and I, for one, am willing to do justice to *all men*, even to the despised *African*. It is, I admit, only a solemn conviction of duty that enables me to do this, for in so doing, I have to overcome many of my oldest and strongest prejudices. Though I never was a proslavery man, yet reared up in a slave state and by ultra proslavery parents, I unconsciously imbibed many of their prejudices.

On account of the dissimilarity between the white race and the black, and, for some other reasons, I have long advocated their separation by the removal of the blacks. Having lately, however, fully investigated this subject, I am now convinced that to do so under existing circumstances would be *unwise, unjust* and *impracticable*. I therefore relinquish this doctrine, and join issue upon the grand practical question, now before the American people, of *universal suffrage,* or *the reëstablishment of slavery upon the new and dangerous basis of serfdom.*

Some of my colonization friends may blame me for abandoning a position which I held so long in common with them. I hope, however, that they will forgive me since I have made this change from *honest convictions,* and since this is the only political change I have made. Most of my friends have made greater changes than this within the last five years; and, imbued, as they are, with the spirit of progress and of patriotism, they will soon be with me in this.

I have already stated that I would have the rebels disfranchised for a time, because I do not think it would be safe, at present, to trust so great a power as the elective franchise in their hands. Their *ballots* would undoubtedly be cast for our destruction, as their *bullets* have been; and it might be with more fatal effect. They could make this disfranchisement quite temporary, if they so desired, by becoming really loyal and thus proving that they could be trusted. Should they fail to do this, how could they expect to enjoy the elective franchise?

There are many who are opposed to rebel suffrage, but who are equally opposed to negro suffrage. They favor placing the government of the rebel states in the hands of the loyal whites of those states. One serious objection to this plan is the fact that in many parts of the South, *there are no loyal whites,* and that in all parts, their number is *very small*. Besides this, they are usually of the poor and ignorant classes who are very little better qualified for governmental affairs than are the negroes themselves. A government placed in such weak hands would quickly be swamped amid the breakers that would incessantly roll between the exasperated millions of haughty *rebels* on the one side, and equally formidable hosts of discontented *freedmen*—as the *slaves* are now facetiously called—on the other. I might mention many other objections to this plan, the principle one, however, being the injustice and the danger involved in disfranchising five millions of brave and loyal people, just because their Creator saw fit to make them black. The loyal whites, all over the south, admit that they will be totally unable to protect themselves, after our armies are withdrawn, unless they can have the support of the loyal blacks. The loyal *whites* and the loyal *blacks* must share the same fate. If the *blacks* be oppressed on account of their *color*, the *whites* will be oppressed on account of their principles. If, therefore, we would have any loyal element survive at the south, we must protect that element by giving them at least as good a chance as we give the disloyal element;—that is, we must give the elective franchise to *all* the loyal people of the south without regard to *color*.

"But this is the *white* man's country," says one. My answer is, prove that to be a *fact*. I contend that it is the *people's* country. "How would you like a negro to step up by your side and *vote*," says another. Very well if he voted for the preservation of my life, my liberty and my country. I would much rather have a *negro* vote *for* these things, than to have a *rebel* vote *against* them. "If the negroes were allowed to *vote* they would soon be *marrying* among the *whites*," says another. Not unless the *whites* were *willing;* besides, the right of *suffrage* does not effect the right of *marriage*. The blacks are as free to marry among the whites now, as they would be if allowed to vote. Do not be alarmed! No Union man has any fears that either himself or his family will ever marry negroes; and, the rebels and copperheads who are so uneasy lest they may mix with the kinky heads, will find their greatest safety in the full freedom of the negroes. Make the negroes fully free, and they will immediately consider themselves too respectable to marry or in any way to mix with rebels or copperheads, who will thus be saved from the terrible evil of amalgamation, to which they have so long been subject. "But the negroes have not sufficient *intelligence* to vote judiciously," says another. To some extent this is *true*, and it is a reasonable objection. The same, however, is equally true of many white men, and I am heartily in favor of requiring a certain amount of education and of general intelligence in all men before allowing them to vote. Let the standard be one easily attainable by ordinary industry, and it will serve as a spur in urging them to acquire knowledge. Those who make the want of intelligence, on the part of the negroes, the only objection to their voting, would surely not refuse that right to those negroes who possess intelligence equal or superior to their own. Let them, then, fix the standard high as they can without excluding themselves, and I will never ask the right of suffrage for a negro who does not come up to that standard.

As a mass, the negroes had intelligence enough to be loyal, while their masters were rebels. They had intelligence enough to cast *bullets* with judgment, and they would soon learn to cast *ballots* with equal judgment. Of course they must learn; and in order to learn, they must be allowed the means of learning; that is, they must *exercise* the elective franchise before they can learn to vote judiciously. If a child be denied the use of his legs, can he learn to walk? If a boy be denied the use of water, can he learn to swim? If he be denied the use of books, can he learn to read? We can acquire skill in an art, only by practicing that art. So it is only by *practice in voting*, that men learn to vote judiciously. All American citizens, then, so soon as they possess sufficient general intelligence to know the nature and design of the elective franchise should be allowed to vote.

It is said that the slaves have been made *free*. In *name* they are free, but not in *fact*. Of right they have always been free, but what good has the *right* to freedom ever done them, while the *possession* of it has been withheld? So with the *name* of freedom, what good will that do them if freedom *itself* be withheld? They have been proclaimed free, but has that bettered their condition? Were I to see you naked and hungry, and were merely to *proclaim* that your wants were supplied, would that *proclamation* be real *food* and *clothing* to you? And what more has the mere *proclamation* of freedom to the slaves done for them? Does not slavery still exist in all its dread reality? Does not every southern breeze bring to our ears the sound of the lash, the baying of the blood-hounds, and the screams of agony? And are these poor victims *free?* How absurd the thought! What *one element* of liberty do they possess? What one element of liberty can they *ever* possess, if we leave them, as they now are, helpless in the hands of their enraged rebel masters?

When our poor starved prisoners escaped from the horrid pens in which rebel cruelty had confined them, they found no friends except these faithful blacks. By these, they were *never betrayed*. By these, they were fed, and, in the darkness of night, were led through swamps and over mountains, to the camps of their friends. In our gloomiest hours, we called upon them to aid us, and never was aid more promptly or more cheerfully given. By tens of thousands they poured into our ranks and soon a hundred thousand of them threw themselves upon the foe. Fort Pillow, Fort Wagner, Port Hudson, Petersburg—a score of battlefields the most bloody and the most glorious, all speak of their valor.[12] As

12. Famous battles where African American Union troops fought with distinction include the battle of Fort Wagner, S.C., July 18, 1863; the assault on Port Hudson, La., May 27, 1863; the battle at Petersburg, Va., on June 14, 1864; and the defense of Fort Pillow, a Union garrison in Tennessee, on April 12, 1864, after which the surrendering black troops were massacred by Confederate soldiers. See McPherson, *Battle Cry of Freedom*, 637–38, 686–87, 740, 748; see also Gaines M. Foster, "The Fort Pillow Massacre: An Essay Review," *Louisiana History* 48 (Spring 2007): 227–30.

rushes the mighty avalanche from Alpine heights, so rushed they, amid the hot smoke and the thunders of battle, upon the several ranks of the rebel hosts. On! on! through trenches, over ramparts, up to the very mouths of the cannons that mowed them down, they bore our flag, to victory and to glory. Unsurpassed in valor and patriotism, even by the invincible heroes of our own color, thousands of them, from whose bosoms the life blood was gushing, turned their glazing eyes upward to our "Brave old Flag," and poured out their last breath in cheers for victory and for freedom. Poor, brave, deluded men! They thought they were *free*. Our government had promised them freedom, and even in *dying* they were happy because they believed that promise would be faithfully performed to the loved ones they left behind. They did not know that the very people for whom they were thus dying, would have turned them over helpless into the hands of their enraged, rebel masters. It was better that they died. Death has made them *free* whom we would not. Alas! for those who did not fall! They came back, war worn and covered with scars, to find that their fond hope of liberty was only a delusive dream. They are reminded that they are *"niggers,"* are required to lay down their arms and go to work for their old masters, to whom they must look for all the liberty they are ever going to enjoy. This is enough. The stout hearts that bore up under the driver's lash, and amid the toils and dangers of war, are crushed by this heavy stroke of ingratitude and treachery.

There are, it is true, a small number who are willing to give them the sad alternative of expatriation. By these too they are informed that they are *"niggers"*; that this is the *white* man's country; that they are no longer needed and that they must leave. In vain they plead. Their services and our promises are alike forgotten. They must lay down their arms and bid adieu to their battle-torn banners. They must go. Go from the land of their birth. Go from the country they love so much, and for which they have fought so long and so well. Their wounded heroes must hobble away upon their crutches. We can not afford room in our soil, to bury the balance of their mutilated forms. Their tender infants, their aged parents—all must go. The fond mother must go from the sacred spot where her loved ones repose. Crushed and broken-hearted, all must go to toil and to perish in some foreign and inhospitable clime. O God! if it be so great a *crime* to be *black*, why hast thou made them thus?

These pictures are not overdrawn; and, I fully believe that when those of my friends who now differ with me in regard to these things, shall have carefully reflected upon them, they will do as I have done,—*boldly declare for the equal rights of all men.* The evils which I have depicted, and many others which I have not noticed, can be prevented, now and forever, only by granting the right of suffrage to all the loyal men of our nation. Let us do this, and all will be well. Upon our beloved country, now dark with storms and troubled with commotions, will soon dawn the sun-light of a grand and glorious future.

As to myself, my course is fixed. Let others do as they may, I mean to practice, in public as well as in private life, those principles of moral rectitude which were taught me long, long years ago as I sat by my mother's knee. You may differ from me in political opinions, but you never shall have reason to doubt my integrity as a man, nor my patriotism as an American. Unmoved by fear, favor or partiality, I shall stand by those great truths that underlie the whole fabric of civil liberty and of national prosperity; and I shall feel myself richly rewarded, if at the close to life, I can feel assured that I have contributed, be it ever so little, to the glory of our republic, and to the rights of man.[13]

13. Kelso recapitulated the main arguments in this address in "Reconstruction," a speech delivered in the House of Representatives, Feb. 7, 1866 (*Congressional Globe*, 39th Cong., 1st sess., Feb. 7, 1866, 36, part 1, 730–33). The remarks were also published separately as an eight-page pamphlet: John Russell Kelso, *Reconstruction: Speech of Hon. John R. Kelso of Missouri, Delivered in the House of Representatives, February 7, 1866* (Washington, D.C.: McGill and Witherow, 1866).

Appendix 3
Government Analyzed, 1892 (Excerpts)

When, however, men discovered the utterly mythical nature of all the gods—the assumed source of all governmental authority—and the consequently fraudulent nature of all the governments claiming to derive their powers from these mythical monsters, they unfortunately failed to discover, at the same time, the equally mythical nature of all governments, *per se,* and the consequently equally fraudulently nature of all the claims to rulership founded upon the authority of these mythical monsters. They unfortunately still regarded governments, as they had once regarded gods, as *per se,* actually existing and necessary powers to which all men, not themselves rulers, should be subject. They unfortunately still believed that the great mass of mankind should not be permitted to act severally, according to the dictates of their own judgment and their own conscience; that they should not be permitted freely to enjoy the bounties of nature and the full products severally of their own labor; that they should not be permitted to enjoy life, liberty, the pursuit of happiness, and other things now recognized by all advanced thinkers as natural and inalienable rights, except as prescribed by government—except according to the will of certain favored individuals of their own race, called rulers, the representatives of government, the mediums through which it operates. They unfortunately still believed that kings and other representatives of government had a *right* to rule over their fellow man to seize at pleasure—according to law, of course—upon their persons, their property, etc; and that they possessed the *power,* by their simple commands, to make it right for their subjects to slaughter their fellowmen, to burn their villages, towns, and cities, to carry away or destroy their goods, to make slaves of their women and children and to do any and all other acts which it would be horribly cruel and criminal to do without this authority. I once believed this very way myself; and

Source: Kelso, *Government Analyzed,* 47–50, 297–300.

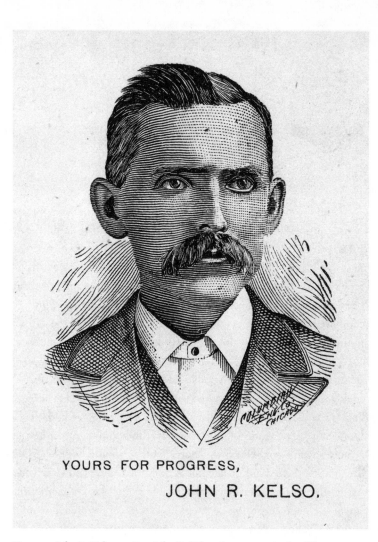

YOURS FOR PROGRESS,

JOHN R. KELSO.

Figure 5. John R. Kelso, c. 1890. John R. Kelso, *Government Analyzed* (Longmont, Col.: Privately printed, 1892), frontispiece. Photograph courtesy of the Huntington Rare Book and Manuscript Library, San Marino, California.

when our own government called upon its ignorant and superstitious devotees to go out and butcher our brothers of the South, I promptly responded to the call. I did not for a moment, think of questioning the righteousness of the required butchery. It was sanctified by the commandment of my *government;* and, to me, this was the commandment of my *god.* Believing that I was thereby fulfilling a sacred duty, and proving myself a good, brave and patriotic man, I cheerfully bore, for more than three years, every conceivable hardship and privation; took part in nearly a hundred bloody engagements; with my own hands, slew a goodly number of brave men, and after the fearful tragedy had been success-fully enacted; after five hundred thousands of brave men, on both sides, had fallen; after six hundred thousands had been made cripples or invalids for life, after millions had been made widows, orphans, beggars, tramps, lunatics[,] pros-titutes and criminals;[1] after vast areas of our country had been devastated with fire and the sword; after untold billions of dollars in property, produced by the toil of the poor, had been destroyed after a hideous burden of over six thou-sand millions of dollars, falsely called the national debt, had been fixed upon the labor of the country; after the poor and toiling *many* had been made the hopeless slaves of the rich and idle *few,* whose mere instrument the government had now become; after all these and many more great evils had been gloriously achieved, I looked back with exultation upon the part I had enacted in their achievement; and viewed with pride my own once well-formed and iron-like frame riddled and broken with many wounds. How blind I was, and yet how honest. How blindly, how piously, how patriotically inhuman even the best of us are capable of being made by superstition, whether with regard to those myth-ical monsters, called gods, or those equally mythical monsters called govern-ments. The people whom we were commanded to butcher and whom, at so fearful a cost to ourselves, to the country, to the whole world, we did butcher, had never done us any harm. They were our brother Christians, our brother Americans, our brother Masons, our brother Odd Fellows, our brother Good Templars, our brothers, many of them, in blood, the sons of our own mothers.

1. The estimated number of Civil War deaths had risen by the early twentieth century to 620,000, a figure that has remained the standard. However, a recent analysis of census data argues that the number was approximately 750,000, meaning that "1 in 10 white men of military age in 1860 died as a result of the war and 200,000 white women were widowed" (J. David Hacker, "A Census-Based Count of the Civil War Dead," *Civil War History* 57 [2011]: 307–48, 311 [quotation]). See also Drew Gilpin Faust, *This Republic of Suffering: Death and the American Civil War* (New York: Vintage Books, 2008), 250–65. Between 1862 and 1888, the U.S. government awarded over 400,000 pensions to its soldiers who had suffered disabilities as a result of their service. After a change in the law in 1890, the number of pensioners rose to 1 million by 1893. See Peter Blanck, "Civil War Pensions and Disability," *Ohio State Law Journal* 62 (2001): 1–107, data on 11–12.

Their only offense was that, in certain political opinions, they differed from those people of the north who were running the government. They simply wished to govern themselves—and to do this, they had a natural right—instead of being longer subject to a government which, in its tariff laws at least, did undeniably discriminate against them and rob them for the benefit of the great manufacturers and other capitalists of the north, by whom and for whom it was principally operated. . . .

"But," it may now be pertinently asked, "did we not, in our recent great civil war, preserve unbroken our great Union of States?" Yes, we did, but are we sure that in so doing, we did a *good thing?* The Union means simply the Government of the United States which, as I have already fully shown, is simply an immense band of robbers and murderers. This band we preserved unbroken, and thus gave it power to do more harm than it could have done us had it been weakened by being broken into two smaller bands. The result is that it has made a mockery of our liberties, robbed us almost to utter want, and reduced us to the most galling condition of slavery. Had the people of the south, who were then nearly all in favor of free trade, succeeded in gaining their independence, to which they had a perfect right, natural and constitutional, they would, doubtless, have become a free trade nation. They would, at least, have reciprocated with England her free trade policy. This would have given them an advantage over us so great as to fully demonstrate to our people the utterly ruinous nature of our whole tariff system, and to compel our weakened government to abandon this system. In preserving the Union, we did ourselves an incalculable injury.

"But did we not, by means of this war, give freedom to the slaves of the south; and was not this one good result of the war?" No, we did not *free* the *slaves* of the *South*. We simply *changed* the *form* of their *slavery* from a *bad* to a *worse*. We deprived them of the protection of their individual masters who, from motives of pecuniary interest, if not from any higher motives, amply and carefully supplied all their physical wants just as they did those of their very valuable horses and cattle. In place of these protecting masters, we gave them, as masters, soulless corporations and monopolists of all kinds, who work them harder, and, in return from their labor, afford them a much poorer living than did their old individual masters, and who yield them no protection at all. As a rule, these slaves are far less comfortable, far less happy than they were before we cruelly mocked them with the utter empty shadow of liberty. Instead of a great good, we did them a great harm.[2]

2. African Americans in the later nineteenth century, especially after the collapse of Reconstruction in 1877, were certainly exploited and certainly suffered. But to assert that they were better off and happier

Had we made these people really free, our act might have been regarded as one redeeming feature of the war. Even then, however, it would have been, not the *object* of the war, but simply a non-intended *incident*. We assured the people of the south all the time that we did not intend to free their slaves. It was only after great numbers of bloody battles had been fought, a majority of which were disastrous to ourselves, only after hundreds of thousands of our bravest young men had fallen, only after we began to need the *aid* of the *slaves* to *free ourselves* from the deadly *grip* which the *Rebels held upon our own throats,* that *we* thought of *freeing* the *slaves.* Then we thought of it only as a "military necessity." Only as such, did we accomplish it. For this "military necessity," which we did not create, we deserve no credit. For us to claim credit for freeing the slaves, *under compulsion,* is like thieves claiming credit for *dropping* their *plunder,* when too hard pressed by their pursuers to escape with it. If anybody deserves any credit for the so-called freeing of the slaves, it is certainly the *Rebels* whose persistent valor created the "military necessity" which *alone led* to its *accomplishment.*

The war is known to have been a result of a vast conspiracy of the capitalists of Europe and of America. The object of this conspiracy was through the war, to create an immense national debt, through this debt, to obtain full control of our government, and, through this control, to reduce our *entire laboring population* to the *most helpless forms of slavery.* These capitalists were the *full managers* of the entire arena upon which the battle between *capital* and *liberty* was to be fought. It was *they* who *planned* and *carried out,* to *full success,* the whole *bloody,* the whole *hellish programme.* By them, the question of slavery was used simply as a *red flag* to excite the *powerful* but *silly bulls, North* and *South,* to *gore* and *lacerate each other* until they were *both so weakened* that they could be *easily brought under the yoke.* Here you have it all.[3]

---

under slavery is simply to echo the rhetoric of the South's myth of the Lost Cause. See Roger L. Ransom and Richard Sutch, *One Kind of Freedom: The Economic Consequences of Emancipation* (New York: Cambridge University Press, 1977); Eric Foner, *Nothing but Freedom: Emancipation and Its Legacy* (Baton Rouge: Louisiana State University Press, 1983); Foner, *Reconstruction;* Gallagher and Nolan, eds., *Myth of the Lost Cause;* Blight, *Race and Reunion;* and Egerton, *Wars of Reconstruction.*

3. Dyer D. Lum (1839–93), another Union veteran to become an anarchist intellectual, also looked back on his earlier "logic of patriotism" as a "delusion." Lum did not see the Civil War as a capitalist conspiracy. But in it and through it the greed animating the soul of the northern industrial system expanded and came to dominate American civilization. "In preserving the Union we created a new union—of capital," Lum wrote. "From God to man the scepter passed, but progress did not halt. The priestly amulet and the kingly crown no longer have mystic power in government. . . . The purse has succeeded the crown as the symbol of authority." See "The Labor Movement. An Examination of Its Fundamental Principles and Ultimate Ends. The Concluding Chapter in Dyer D. Lum's Work, 'Social Problems of Today,'" *The Alarm,* July 28, 1888, 1.

And even if we had waged the war for the *abolition* of *slavery,* we would still have been *criminals.* When we consider the relation in which we stood to the people of the South, in regard to the slaves, what *right* had we, by *force,* to *compel* them, without *remuneration,* to give up their *slaves?* We of the North, tore the negroes from their homes in Africa and sold them to the people of the South. In our pockets, *we* had the *price* of these *slaves.* The *people* of the *South* had the *slaves themselves.* And is not he who steals and *sells* horses, human beings or anything else just as guilty as he who *buys* them? What *right* then, I again ask, have *we,* the *thieves,* to turn upon the purchasers of our stolen property and force them to give it up to us again while we flaunted the retained price of it in their faces? We should have *bought* the slaves *back* and then made them *really free.*[4] This we could have done at less than ten percent of what the war has already cost us.[5] And thus we see that even this seemingly extenuating incident of the war, the pretended freeing of the slaves will not bear fair investigation. So of all the other seemingly fair incidents.

When we consider that the principles upon which all, but purely defensive, wars are waged are those of pure and unmitigated robbery and murder, (Here the author laid down his pen in early January 1891).[6]

4. The proslavery South utterly rejected any interference with what slaveholders considered their inalienable right to slave property, even if compensated. Lincoln's offer of compensated emancipation was rejected even by the border states in 1862. See McPherson, *Battle Cry of Freedom,* 498–99, 502–4.

5. Kelso grossly underestimated the value of slave property. Economic historians have estimated it in 1860 as worth $3–6 billion. Even with the lower figure, writes Stephen Deyle, "the value of the southern slave population was still enormous when placed in a comparative perspective. It was roughly three times greater than the total amount of all capital invested in manufacturing in the North and South combined, three times the amount invested in railroads, and seven times the total value of all currency in circulation in the country, three times the value of the entire livestock population, twelve times the value of all American farm implements and machinery, twelve times the value of the entire U.S. cotton crop, and forty-eight times the total expenditures of the federal government that year. The domestic slave trade had made human property one of the most prominent forms of investment in the country, second only to land. In fact, by 1860, in the slaveholding states alone, slave property had surpassed the assessed value of real estate" (Deyle, "The Domestic Slave Trade in America: The Lifeblood of the Southern Slave System," in *The Chattel Principle: Internal Slave Trades in the Americas,* ed. Walter Johnson [New Haven, Conn.: Yale University Press, 2004], 91–166, 95 [quotation]). Lincoln estimated the cost of the war at $2 million per day, which would add up to about $3.6 billion total (see Andrew Weintraub, "The Economics of Lincoln's Proposal for Compensated Emancipation," *American Journal of Economics and Sociology* 32 [April 1973]: 171–77, estimates on 175). See also Claudia D. Goldin and Frank D. Lewis, "The Economic Cost of the American Civil War: Estimates and Implications," *Journal of Economic History* 35 (June 1975): 299–326, and Geiger, *Financial Fraud,* 157–58.

6. Kelso was suffering from his final illness when he wrote this last passage (the sentence in parentheses is a notation added by his wife, Etta Dunbar Kelso). He died on Jan. 26, 1891.

Chronology

[Bold = events in John R. Kelso's (JRK's) life; *Italics = Missouri events;* Standard typeface = national events]

December 1860–February 1861

Dec. 20, 1860–Feb. 1, 1861: Believing that the election of Republican Abraham Lincoln signals a threat to the southern "right" to slave property, South Carolina, Mississippi, Florida, Alabama, Georgia, Louisiana, and Texas secede from the Union.

Jan. 1861: Democratic Governor Claiborne Fox Jackson, in his inaugural address, insists that Missouri will stand by its fellow slaveholding states. In St. Louis, paramilitary groups supporting both the seceding southern states and the Union begin organizing.

JRK is a schoolteacher in Buffalo, Dallas County, Missouri.

March–April 1861

March 1861: The Missouri state convention rejects secession.

April 12, 1861: The South Carolina militia begins the bombardment of the U.S. garrison at Fort Sumter, in Charleston Harbor.

April 17, 1861: Governor Jackson rejects President Lincoln's April 15 call for 75,000 volunteers to quell the rebellion, calling Lincoln's action illegal, unconstitutional, revolutionary, inhuman, and diabolical.

April 21–23, 1861: Pro-secessionists seize the small federal arsenal in Liberty, Mo.; Jackson orders the state militia to assemble in St. Louis; Confederate President Jefferson Davis sends Jackson four artillery guns.

May–June 1861

May 6, 1861: Nearly nine hundred state militia men set up "Camp Jackson" on the eastern edge of St. Louis.

May 6 or 7, 1861: JRK delivers a pro-Union speech from the Buffalo courthouse steps (chap. 1).

May 10, 1861: Nathaniel Lyon, commander of the St. Louis Arsenal, with about eight thousand Missouri Volunteers and U.S. Regulars, surrounds Camp Jackson and forces its surrender. During the march of the prisoners to the arsenal, secessionists on the streets of St. Louis begin pelting U.S. troops with rocks and debris, leading to gunfire. Twenty-eight people die and many others are wounded.

Mid-May 1861: JRK disrupts a secessionist rally at Buffalo (chap. 1).

June 11, 1861: Negotiations between Jackson and Lyon break down. The next day, Jackson calls for fifty thousand Missouri men to enlist in the State Guard to resist federal despotism.

June 13–15, 1861: Lyon leads 2,500 troops from St. Louis to Jefferson City, the state capital, but Jackson and State Guard forces nearly as large have already evacuated to the southwest.

June 24, 1861: JRK helps organize the Dallas County Home Guards and is elected a captain, and then a week later, major (chap. 1).

July–August 1861

July 21, 1861: The Battle of First Bull Run (or First Manassas), Virginia. Union loss.

July 22, 1861: The Missouri state constitutional convention reconvenes, declares that Jackson and the pro-southern legislature that had left the capital had vacated their offices, and appoints itself the new provisional state government, naming a new governor and other executive officers.

Early August 1861: JRK goes to Springfield for ammunition for his troops and meets General Lyon preparing for battle (chap. 2).

Aug. 6, 1861: First Confiscation Act, allowing the seizure of slaves working for the Confederate military.

Aug. 10, 1861: The Battle of Wilson's Creek, ten miles southwest of Springfield, Missouri. A Union Army of 5,400 led by Lyon is defeated by State Guard and Confederate forces of 12,000. Lyon is killed, and the Federals retreat to Rolla, leaving the State Guard in control of southwest Missouri.

Aug. 15, 1861: JRK's Home Guard regiment divides in the retreat from the southwest. He goes to Jefferson City (chap. 2).

Aug. 18, 1861: JRK enlists as a private in the 24th Regiment Infantry (chap. 2).

Late August 1861: Kelso goes on a solo spy mission to Springfield (chap. 2).

Aug. 30, 1861: Gen John C. Frémont proclaims martial law in Missouri. He announces that anyone found with arms within Union lines will be shot, and that those supporting the rebellion against the U.S. will forfeit all property and their slaves will be freed. Lincoln revokes these two provisions on Sept. 2.

September–November 1861

Sept. 20, 1861: Col. James A. Mulligan's Irish Brigade is forced to surrender at Lexington, Mo., to the State Guard after a siege begun Sept. 13.

Oct. 16–17, 1861: Pro-Confederate forces led by Col. Jeff Thompson probe within fifty miles of St. Louis, destroy the Iron Mountain Railroad bridge crossing the Big River, and attack the federal troops garrisoned at Fredericktown.

Oct. 17, 1861: JRK and his regiment are sent to the Big River Bridge (chap. 3).

Oct. 28, 1861: Gov. Claiborne Jackson and the pro-southern members of the Missouri legislature convene in Neosho and pass an ordinance of secession. On Nov. 28, the Confederate Congress declares Missouri to be the twelfth state in the CSA.

Late October 1861: JRK goes on another solo spy mission to the southwest, speaking at Confederate recruiting stations as "John Russell" (chap. 3).

Nov. 2, 1861: John C. Frémont, whose army of eighteen thousand men had been moving south from St. Louis for a month and who had occupied Springfield a few days earlier, is relieved of command by President Abraham Lincoln. Frémont's successor, Maj. Gen. David Hunter, pulls Union forces back to Rolla and Sedalia, 110–120 miles to the north and northeast.

Early November 1861: JRK is ordered to help evacuate loyal families from Buffalo. His and other families suffer in a snowstorm while secessionists refuse them shelter (chap. 4).

December 1861–March 1862

Mid-Winter 1861: JRK visits Buffalo and gets revenge; he is captured by Confederate troops and escapes (chap. 4).

Feb. 6, 1862: Gen. Samuel R. Curtis and twelve thousand U.S. troops in Lebanon prepare to march on Springfield, occupied by the State Guard.

Feb. 13, 1862: Curtis's Army of the Southwest enters Springfield, the State Guard under Gen. Sterling Price having evacuated the night before.

Feb. 14–23, 1862: Curtis's army pursues Price's into northern Arkansas.

Feb. 6–20: JRK marches with Curtis to Arkansas (chap. 5).

Feb. 15, 1862: Union troops capture Fort Donelson, Tenn., weakening Confederate defense in the western theater.

March 6–8, 1862: The Battle of Pea Ridge, or Elkhorn Tavern, Ark.: Curtis's army defeats Confederate and State Guard forces. The United States would thereafter dominate the trans-Mississippi, and Confederates would never again occupy any significant amount of Missouri territory.

March 14, 1862: New Madrid, Mo., held by Confederates, falls to Union forces.

March 1862: JRK recruits and then joins the Missouri State Militia Cavalry as a first lieutenant (chap. 6).

May–September 1862
Confederate raiders and recruiters, often in collaboration with local guerrilla leaders, intensify their operations in the Missouri countryside.

May 30, 1862: JRK's regiment is attacked at Neosho (chap. 7).

June 6–July 1, 1862: The Seven Days Battle in Virginia: Confederate forces led by Robert E. Lee attack Union armies commanded by George B. McClellan and drive the Federals away from Richmond, the capital of the Confederacy.

July 16, 1862: The Second Confiscation Act declares all slaves held by Confederates are free and authorizes the president to use those slaves in any capacity whatever.

Aug. 1, 1862: Battle of Ozark: Kelso's company draws Col. Robert Lawther's men into an ambush (chap. 7).

Aug. 4, 1862: Battle of Forsyth (chap. 8).

Aug. 11, 1862: Confederate partisans along with guerrillas led by William Quantrill defeat Union troops at Independence and Lone Jack, Missouri.

Aug. 29–30, 1862: Second Bull Run (Second Manassas): Lee's Confederates defeat John Pope's Union Army.

Mid-September 1862: JRK leads an attack on the Medlock brothers' outlaw hideout (chap. 8).

Sept. 17, 1862: The Battle of Antietam (Sharpsburg), Md.: on the war's bloodiest day, neither side is clearly victorious, but Lee's invasion of Maryland is repulsed.

Sept. 22, 1862: Preliminary Emancipation Proclamation: Lincoln declares that in a hundred days, all slaves in Confederate-controlled territory (and only there) would be free.

Sept. 30, 1862: Confederate troops and an Indian brigade take control of Newtonia, Missouri.

October–December 1862

Oct. 12, 1862: JRK begins a plundering expedition to Tolbert Barrens with a force under the command of Maj. John C. Wilber (chap. 9).

Nov. 8–13, 1862: JRK, disguised as a Confederate, "Lieutenant Russell," captures rebels then fights hand to hand with Capt. Joseph Hale Mooney (chap. 10).

Dec. 7, 1862: Battle of Prairie Grove, Ark.: ten thousand troops led by Gen. John M. Schofield, having marched from Springfield, defeat Confederate forces and push them south of the Arkansas River.

Dec. 9–15, 1862: JRK and company destroy a Confederate saltpeter mine in Arkansas (chap. 11).

Dec. 13, 1862: The Battle of Fredericksburg, the third failed Union invasion of Virginia.

January–May 1863

Jan. 1, 1863: The Emancipation Proclamation takes effect, codifying emancipation as a war aim and authorizing the use of black soldiers.

Jan. 8, 1863: The Battle of Springfield, Mo.: Confederate Gen. John S. Marmaduke, leading 2,300 troops up from Arkansas, fails to take the town. Marmaduke fights federal forces again at Marshfield and Hartville, Jan. 10–11, before retreating to Arkansas.

Jan. 8, 1863: JRK fights in the Battle of Springfield (chap. 12).

Feb. 2, 1863: The 14th Missouri State Militia is disbanded; JRK's Co. H becomes Co. M in the 8th Missouri State Militia (chap. 12).

March 11, 1863: JRK faces court martial for "conduct to the prejudice of good order and military discipline" but is acquitted (chap. 12, note 34).

April 18–May 1, 1863: Marmaduke's Second Raid into Missouri; this time with five thousand men, he fails to take Cape Girardeau (April 26).

April 19–20, 1863: JRK, in disguise, tricks rebel cattle thieves into thinking that he is a dispatch-bearer for Marmaduke.

May 1–4, 1863: Battle of Chancellorsville, Va.: Lee defeats a much larger Union force commanded by Joseph Hooker.

June–December 1863

July 1–3, 1863: Battle of Gettysburg, Penn.: the Union Army repulses the last major Confederate invasion of the North.

July 4, 1863: Union Gen. Ulysses S. Grant is victorious after a siege of Vicksburg, Miss. (begun May 18), cutting off Arkansas, Louisiana, and Texas from the rest of the Confederacy.

Aug. 7, 1863: JRK is hit by a shotgun blast and wounded in the chest and left hand.

Aug. 21, 1863: William Quantrill and 450 Confederate guerillas from Missouri attack Lawrence, Kans.; they drag 183 men and boys from their homes and execute them. Union Gen. Thomas Ewing, Jr., then orders the evacuation of more than three Missouri counties on the Kansas border.

Sept. 7, 1863: Pursuing the enemy, JRK is thrown by and crushed beneath his horse; he dislocates his right hip and sustains other injuries.

Oct. 4–19, 1863: Confederate Col. Jo Shelby's raid (with 1,000–1,800 men) into Missouri defeats 300 Federals at Neosho, burns Sarcoxie, and captures Warsaw, but is beaten by a larger force at Marshall and forced to retreat.

Nov. 29, 1863: JRK and Capt. Milton Burch attack rebel bushwhackers in Jasper County, Mo.

January–September 1864

Spring 1864: Small groups of Confederate raiders up from Arkansas and local guerrillas continue to menace the Missouri countryside.

March 17, 1864: JRK is promoted to captain.

April 23, 1864: JRK delivers a political speech at Mt. Vernon, Mo. (appendix 1).

May 10–13, 1864: JRK and Capt. Milton Burch attack a company from the Second Cherokee Indian Regiment in Spavinaw, Ark.

May 30–31, 1864: JRK leads a company against insurgents at Mill and Honey Creeks, Mo.

June 3, 1864: JRK and company fight a guerrilla band near Neosho, Mo.

Aug. 13, 1864: JRK kills notorious bushwhacker Lt. Baxter at Cowskin Creek, Mo.

Sept. 2, 1864: Union armies led by Gen. William T. Sherman occupy Atlanta, Ga., after a campaign across the state begun on May 7. With sixty thousand men,

Sherman marches three hundred miles to the sea (Nov. 14–Dec. 22), cutting a sixty-mile-wide swath of destruction.

Sept. 19, 1864: Confederate Gen. Sterling Price invades Missouri with twelve thousand troops, fighting a costly battle to take Fort Davidson at Pilot Knob (Sept. 27).

Sept. 27, 1864: Bloody Bill Anderson's guerrillas massacre twenty-four unarmed Union soldiers taken off a train at Centralia, Mo.

October–December 1864

Oct. 3, 1864: JRK provides intelligence on Confederate Gen. Sterling Price's advancing army, estimated at ten thousand men.

Oct. 10, 1864: Camped at Boonville, Price meets with and gives legitimacy to guerrilla leaders as Confederate partisan rangers.

Oct. 23, 1864: The Battle of Westport: in the largest battle fought west of the Mississippi River, with over thirty thousand men engaged, Price's army is routed and Gen. Samuel R. Curtis's army chases them back into Arkansas.

Nov. 8, 1864: Union elections: Abraham Lincoln wins reelection, and Republicans will control three-quarters of Congress.

Nov. 8, 1864: JRK is elected in Missouri's Fourth Congressional District.

Dec. 15–16, 1864: The Battle of Nashville ends the Confederate invasion of Union-held Tennessee with a decisive Union victory.

1865

Jan. 31, 1865: The House of Representatives passes the 13th Amendment (the Senate had passed it on April 8, 1864), which abolishes slavery. It is ratified by the states on Dec. 6, 1865.

March 4, 1865–March 3, 1867: The 39th U. S. Congress.

March 13, 1865: JRK is promoted to brevet colonel.

April 2, 1865: After many months of trench warfare with heavy casualties on both sides, Gen. Robert E. Lee evacuates Petersburg and Richmond, Va.

April 9, 1865: Lee surrenders to Gen. Ulysses S. Grant at Appomattox Courthouse, Va. In the next weeks, other Confederate armies surrender, with resistance ending on May 26.

April 14, 1865: Abraham Lincoln is shot; he dies the next day.

April 18, 1865: JRK is mustered out of the army.

Sept. 19, 1865: JRK delivers a speech on Reconstruction at Walnut Grove, Mo. (appendix 2).

1866

Feb. 7, 1866: JRK delivers the speech "Reconstruction" in Congress.

April 9, 1866: Congress overrides President Andrew Johnson's veto and passes the Civil Rights Act, declaring that blacks have the full rights of citizens, which is given explicit constitutional sanction with the ratification of the 14th Amendment (July 28, 1866).

1867

Jan. 7, 1867: JRK joins Missouri Rep. Benjamin F. Loan in offering resolutions to impeach President Andrew Johnson.

1868

JRK runs for Congress again against S. H. Boyd but loses badly (Nov. 3).

1870

Feb. 3, 1870: The 15th Amendment, intended to prevent the obstruction of black voting rights, is ratified.

1877

March 2, 1877: Rutherford B. Hayes is awarded the presidency after a disputed election and a compromise that includes his promise to withdraw federal troops from the South, making the 14th and 15th Amendments unenforceable and ending Reconstruction.

1891

Jan. 26, 1891: JRK dies while writing *Government Analyzed,* in which he reevaluates the Civil War and his own participation in it (appendix 3).

Index

Johnson, Rick, 102
Julian, Stephen H., 94, 102, 104–5, 109

Keitsville, Mo., 88, 90
Kelso, Ella (sister), 1n1
Kelso, Etta Dunbar (third wife), xxxiii, 208n6
Kelso, Florella (daughter), xiv, 1n1, 29–30
Kelso, Florellus (son), xiv, 1n1
Kelso, Iantha (daughter), xiv, 52
Kelso, Ianthus (son), 16, 97, 122
Kelso, John Russell (JRK): boyhood in
    Missouri, xiii; marriage to Mary Adelia
    Moore, xiv, 1n1; and Methodism, xiv, 3n5; as
    schoolteacher, xiii, xxx, xxxii, 1n1, 3–4;
    marriage to Martha S. ("Susie") Barnes, 1n1;
    on antebellum politics, 1–3; supports Union,
    4–10; and slavery, xv–xvi; denounces
    secession, xvii, 5–10; in Home Guard, xvii–
    xviii; 10–21; meets Gen. Lyon, 19–20; enlists
    in 24th Infantry, xviii, 23; as spy, xviii, 26–31,
    35–43, 58–62, 64–65; goes to Big River
    Bridge, 32–34; evacuates loyal citizens, xix,
    48–55; vow of vengeance, xix, xxviii, 45,
    52–53, 57, 196; captured and escapes, 59–62;
    on march to Pea Ridge, 67–82; joins
    Missouri State Militia Cavalry, xx, 91; letters
    to wife, 92–93, 94–97, 100–11, 121; at Battle
    of Neosho, xx, 100–12; and Battle of Ozark,
    113–16; as Provost Marshall, 113, 120–21;
    and Medlock brothers, xx, 123–29; and
    Tolbert Barrens expedition, 130–37; as
    "Lieut. Russell," 139–42; and raid on
    Dubuque, 142–44; and raid on Capt.
    Mooney, 145–48; and destruction of
    saltpeter mine, 149–55; and Battle of
    Springfield, xx, 156–78; court martial of, xxi,
    177n33; injuries of, xxii, xxxiii; military
    activities after Jan. 1863, xxiiin23, 213–15;
    back pay, 31n23, 91, 96; elected to Congress,
    xxiii, xxvii–xxviii; as scholar, xxiii, xxvii, 56;
    reputation in Mo., xxiv, xxvi, xxviii–xxix;
    speech at Mt. Vernon, Mo., 179–88; speech at
    Walnut Grove, Mo., xxix–xxx, 189–202; and
    Reconstruction, xxix–xxx, 179–202; as
    Independent Republican, xxx; in
    Congressional election of 1868, xxxi; second
    divorce, xxxii, 178n35; "Works of John R.
    Kelso," xxxii; marriage to Etta Dunbar,

xxxiii; on Civil War, xxxiii–xxxv, 179–90,
    205–8; publications of, xxxii, 202n13; death,
    xxxiii, 208
Kelso, Martha Susan ("Susie") Barnes (second
    wife): divorce of, xxxii, 178n35; marriage
    and children of, 1n1, 178n35; after house
    burned down, 45–46; in snowstorm, 52; and
    Dr. Hovey, 55–56, 178; JRK letters to, 92–93,
    94–97, 100–11, 121; sells JRK's shotgun, 120;
    in Ozark, Mo., 130, 139
Kelso, Mary Adelia Moore (first wife), xiv, 1n1
Kelton, J. C., 64n26
King's Prairie, Mo., 86–87
Knights of the Golden Circle (KGC), 192

Laclede County, Mo., 50n11
Landis, John A., 163n14
Langston, Merivale, 92–93
Langston, Walter W., 92–93, 95
Laurence Co., Mo., xxii
Lawther, Robert R., 114–20
Lebanon, Mo., 30, 49–50, 62–64, 68
Lexington, Mo., Battle of, 22
Lincoln, Abraham, xix, xxix, 4n7, 10n19, 47n8,
    186
Lindsay, Anthony, 92–93
Lindsey, D. A., 6
Linn Creek, Mo., 30, 92–94, 99
Livingston, Thomas R., 102n8, 107n16
Loan, Benjamin F., xxx
Longmont, Colo., xxxiii
Lost Cause, Myth of, xxxi, 182, 183n5
Lum, Dyer D., 207n3
Lyon, Nathaniel, xvii–xviii, 12n24, 14n25,
    17–20

Mabary, John, 11–15
MacDonald, Emmett, 158n5
Mann, Henry Perrin, 72
Marion, Francis, 16, 32n1
Marmaduke, John S.: and Battle of Springfield,
    xx; second raid of, into Mo., xxi; army of,
    156–57; tactics of, 159–61; reports of, 171n25,
    171, 172n27; letter of, 172; assurance of
    plunder, 172–73; army's movements after
    Battle of Springfield, 173–74, 176n32
Matthews, Robert Pinckney, xvii, 9n17, 65n27,
    71n9, 78n17, 164